CHARLES JOHNSON
Embracing the World

CHARLES JOHNSON
Embracing the World

Nibir K. Ghosh
E. Ethelbert Miller

AUTHORSPRESS
Publishers of Scholarly Books

Worldwide Circulation through Authorspress Global Network

First Published 2011

by

Authorspress

Editorial

Q-2A Hauz Khas Enclave,
New Delhi-110 016
e-mail: authorspress@yahoo.com

Marketing

E-35/103, Jawahar Park
Laxmi Nagar, Delhi-110 092
e-mail: authorspress@yahoo.com

Charles Johnson: Embracing the World

ISBN 978-81-7273-565-4

Printed in India at Tarun Offset, Delhi.

Preface

At the University of Minnesota, Givens Collection of African American Literature, Special Collections and Rare Books, one will find Ethelbert Miller's correspondence from Charles Johnson. The first letter is dated October 3, 1989. That seems like a long time ago. Johnson has written many books and articles during the last twenty-one years. There has been a number of books about him: *Understanding Charles Johnson* by Gary Storhoff, *Charles Johnson The Novelist as Philosopher* edited by Marc C. Conner and William R. Nash, *Charles Johnson in Context* by Linda Furgerson Selzer, *Charles Johnson's Novels, Writing The American Palimpsest* by Rudolph P. Byrd and *Passing The Three Gates, Interviews with Charles Johnson* edited by Jim McWilliams.

So why another book about Charles Johnson and his work? Johnson extends the African American literary tradition by pushing and pulling us beyond the work of Toomer, Wright and Ellison, three writers that provide him with a lineage. In many ways Charles Johnson is our Marco Polo. His books open the door to the East. To a new generation he is well known for his Buddhist writings in popular journals.

Even before the election of President Barack Obama, Johnson was asking serious questions about race. If anyone can talk about the future of America, he can. His work upholds a moral and philosophical worldview. In *The Middle Passage* the question is, where is home? In *Dreamer* the central discussion is, how do you end evil without engendering new evil? In these times of what I consider to be literary pork, it's refreshing to find someone willing to craft and tell a good story. The work of Charles Johnson requires heavy lifting by our minds. His novels, stories and essays are healthy for us.

Charles Johnson lives in Seattle. He has many friends. He is a good man. These three simple sentences are the foundation on which one could write a book. The complexity of the human spirit requires a genius to make sense of what we do. Johnson has given us a body of work as rich as the sounds of Monk and Thelonious was last century. It's quite possible that Charles Johnson makes W.E.B. Du Bois and those double-consciousness suits outdated. No more victimization ditties. Johnson is our laughing Buddha, a man with gray hair and a crown of wisdom. He is a man on "the path" teaching us to follow, if we take the time and wish to understand the way.

Any narration of *Charles Johnson: Embracing the World* would be incomplete without our putting on record the deep appreciation and gratitude we feel towards all those who have made it such a successful venture. It is gratifying indeed that academics, scholars, critics and friends of Charles Johnson from different parts of the globe could respond so effusively in so short a time to create this enduring document in honor of one who defies stereotypes to reaffirm that excellence is color-blind. To one and all we express our heartfelt thanks. Our special thanks go to Professor Amritjit Singh for his proactive association with this volume.

For the permission to reprint material that have appeared elsewhere earlier, we acknowledge our thanks to The Johns Hopkins University Press for John Whalen-Bridge's "Waking Cain: The Poetics of Integration in Charles Johnson's *Dreamer*" [*Callaloo* 26:2 (2003), 504-521] and Geffrey Davis's "The Threads that Connect Us: An Interview with Charles Johnson" [*Callaloo* 33:3 (2010), 807-819]; to *African American Review* for Linda Selzer's "Master-Slave Dialectics in Charles Johnson's 'The Education of Mingo'" [*African American Review* 37 (2003): 105-14] and Ashraf H.A. Rushdy's Untitled Review of Marc C. Conner and William R. Nash, eds., *Charles Johnson: The Novelist as Philosopher*. Jackson: University Press of Mississippi, 2007 [*African American Review* 43.1 (Spring, 2009): 184-86], and to *Humanities Washington* for Chris Thompson's

"National Book Award-Winner Charles Johnson on Cartoons, the Dharma, and Kung Fu" (2010).

We are highly indebted to Charles Johnson himself for allowing us to enrich the collection with his valuable offerings. We are no less grateful to Mr. Sudarshan Kcherry of Authorspress for granting us the precious space to celebrate the life and work of an enduring spirit.

E. Ethelbert Miller

Nibir K. Ghosh

Contents

1

Introduction

— Nibir K. Ghosh

Eight years ago, when the Public Affairs Section of U.S. Embassy, New Delhi informed me that Charles Johnson—author of *Middle Passage, Oxherding Tale, Dreamer* etc., a MacArthur Fellow and winner of the National Book Award—was visiting India on a lecture tour, I was thrilled by the prospect of interviewing him against the backdrop of the Taj Mahal. My enthusiasm did not last long as his visit did not ultimately materialise on account of the Iraq war. Perhaps Fate had ordained that we would meet not in Agra, the city of *Sulahakul*, but in Seattle from where Johnson proclaims to the world the imperatives of embracing a standpoint that calls for an amalgamation of multidisciplinary and multicultural perspectives.

The chance to meet this celebrity came when I was awarded the Senior Fulbright Fellowship to work at the University of Washington, Seattle during 2003-04 on a project that was concerned with Contemporary African American Writings with special reference to the works of Charles Johnson.

We (my wife, Sunita, and I) arrived in Seattle on September 5, 2003. Around 6.00 p.m. the next day, we were pleasantly surprised to see at our dwelling none but the famed Charles Johnson himself who, accompanied by his daughter Elizabeth, came to visit us. I warmly welcomed him by wrapping a shawl around him as we honor scholars in India. Guess how he reciprocated! He gave me a huge packet he had brought for us. When I untied the fancy ribbons and opened the packet I couldn't believe my eyes. There lay in front of me over two score books—novels, essays, interviews, photo-autobiography, and so much more—all of which he had authored. His endearing inscription on each one of them made them all the more valuable. I instantly realised the extent of his magnanimity and goodness that I had hitherto seen in his emails since I came to know him around May 2002 or so.

I accompanied Johnson to some of his lectures and story-reading sessions and was deeply impressed by the tremendous audience response he generated with his forceful ideas and mastery of lucid language and expression. The warmth with which people, whites and blacks alike, would swarm around him after his talks and readings made me wonder whether there really was any visible color line in the U.S. where Johnson was concerned. Unruffled by current statistics that showed there were more Black Americans in jails than in schools and that racial prejudice continued to be unusually strong in American society, Johnson would often cite the instance of his own rise to fame to support his innate belief that "In this country no individual or group, white or black, could tell me *not to dream*." Focusing on the essential richness of black humanity, Johnson is quick to refute conceptualisations that deny that richness. Hinting at the danger of living in a parochial cultural fishbowl, he lyrically resonates the spirit of *Sulahakul* and foregrounds the need for a completely new outlook that makes some narrow race-centered complaints irrelevant in an increasingly complex multicultural and global economy. He not only loves to address the symptoms of change in terms of acute identity crisis but also tries to prepare the aesthetic ground for such a change.

My frequent long conversations with him contributed significantly to my understanding of the nuances and complexities of certain basic issues confronting contemporary America and also inspired me to engage in fruitful conversations many other celebrities within and beyond Afro-America. The animated exchanges that I had with authors like August Wilson, David Guterson, Octavia Butler, Jonah Raskin, Ethelbert Miller, Kathleen Alcala and others, besides Charles

Johnson, flowered into a precious collection titled *Multicultural America: Conversations with Contemporary Authors* (2005).

The imprints that my constant association with Charles Johnson left on my heart and soul only increased with the passage of time and I often wondered, in gratitude, how I could recompense his graciousness and generosity as a friend, philosopher and guide besides bringing into bold relief the dynamics of his creativity and vision that have gone into the making of America's most articulate ambassador of meaningful multiculturalism. The blueprint for the current anthology literally emerged out of this sense of indebtedness. In the initial stages, while the idea of a tribute volume lay simmering in the inner recesses of my mind, I wasn't really sure what response the idea would elicit from potential prospective contributors. Keeping my fingers crossed, I darted off the following message to Ethelbert Miller:

> As a mark of tribute to the life and work of our dear friend, Charles Johnson, E. Ethelbert Miller and I plan to edit an anthology that would bring together articles, research papers, poems and stories from creative writers, academics and scholars from various parts of the world who would love to celebrate the enduring spirit of Charles Johnson through their writings.
>
> The anthology will target readers in South Asia, especially India where, ever since I was associated with Charles Johnson as a Senior Fulbright Fellow at the University of Washington, Seattle during 2003-04, the aura of Charles Johnson is gradually registering its imprint.

Ethelbert responded spontaneously by putting the above note on his blog. The invitation to write for the book generated tremendous enthusiasm with the magic of Charles Johnson's charismatic personality casting a virtual spell on contributors who seemed extremely eager to join this interesting enterprise. When the great Chuck heard of the project, he immediately responded, like an effectual angel, by stating, "When I learned what you and Ethelbert were up to, I almost had heart failure. Your proposed book simply humbles me right down to my heels.

Thank you, good sir!" Overwhelmed by his magnanimity, I confessed to him in all honesty, "Dear Chuck, it's something I wanted to do for a long time now. One fine evening I just thought I'll throw a pebble at the waters around Ethelbert and wait for the ripples. See what excellent music has emanated from my experiment. I am happy indeed!"

The erudite articles, insightful essays, vibrant poems and stories, glowing tributes and animate interviews in this memorable volume not only address multifarious dimensions of the Charles Johnson canon but also bring into bold relief the magnetic appeal of a veritable activist relentlessly engaged in making the world a better place to live in. Also included in this volume are essays and stories by Charles Johnson that illumine variant issues and concerns ranging from the ambivalence of the American Dilemma to delineating the meaning of Barack Obama besides displaying his innate ability to contend with conflicting forces by celebrating life in the manner of Buddha, Du Bois, Martin Luther King Jr. and Mahatma Gandhi.

Though Johnson's visit to India is yet to materialise, his fascination for India has not lost its magic appeal, as is evident from what he told me:

> I often dream, naturally, of India—its beauty, antiquity, breath-taking art and remarkable people, the peace I feel instantly when my mind drifts to the Buddhist Dharma or Hinduism, that great democracy of Being. I am amazed by its astounding diversity where so many cultures converge in a spirit of oneness and harmony.

I am sure some day, and soon, this cultural ambassador—who understands and practices the quintessence of oneness and harmony through his life and work and is in perpetual readiness to embrace the world in both flesh and spirit—will give me the privilege of offering him this beautiful bouquet in the lyrical precincts of Emperor Shahjahan's dream in marble.

2

Who Turns the Wheel?

for Charles Johnson

— E. Ethelbert Miller

We dreamers.
Men of night emails and exchanges.
Composers of narratives and American songs.
We believers and followers of the Buddhist path.
We understand the blackness that surrounds us.
We surround the blackness, we follow it
Embracing ourselves.

We are brothers because everything in life
Is related to love. We take refuge in the future
Knowing the past is always found in the present.
Your silver hair filled with the roots of wisdom.
Now the lotus flower blossoms—erasing pain
And suffering. Paradise is no longer fiction. So many
Waiting to hear from you. Speak. Write.

3

Tribute to Charles Johnson

—Gary Storhoff

My first contact with Charles Johnson was his telephone call to me late in the evening years ago, congratulating me on an article I had published on one of his short stories, "Moving Pictures." Needless to say, I was surprised that a famous, award-winning author would take the time to read my article, much less call me to compliment me on it. During our conversation—filled with his boundless enthusiasm for literature and critical readings—I never quite dared to tell him that I was actually writing a book about his work; it would have seemed, I thought, rather presumptuous, and would have (I feared) raised danger flags for him in what was a delightful, collegial conversation.

But I should not have feared. As the years have gone by since that call, I have seen that Chuck's profound humility and wonderful generosity in extending himself to other people are fundamental parts of his character. Chuck is inevitably eager to help young scholars just getting a start in academia—or older ones who may need even more of a helping hand. An ardent e-mailer himself, Chuck will also refer people who need assistance. When he feels he cannot help as much as he wishes he could, he will make every effort to find someone who can.

On a personal level, I am very proud to call Chuck my good friend. I often wished that we lived closer, since he is in Seattle while I live in Connecticut. It would be good to hear his conversation more often! He never fails to ask about my own family, and he is especially curious about my son's career:

Chuck was once a cartoonist, and Wesley is now the 21st century incarnation of a cartoonist: a film animator. But perhaps the most emotional moment for me in our relationship was when I wrote to Chuck that I had just been diagnosed with cancer. Chuck's beautiful response was filled with his hope and optimism, but he was not oblivious to the tragic nature of the disease. I am not embarrassed to say that his reply brought tears to my eyes. The greatness of Chuck's writing ability has been obvious to me for almost 30 years, when I was introduced to his work. But his writing power *as an attribute of his character* never came home to me as emphatically as when I read his e-mail. Thank you, Chuck.

4

The Role of the Black Intellectual in the Twenty-first Century

— **Charles Johnson**

Anyone interested in the direction black intellectuals should take in the dawning 21st century need look no farther for clues than the Modern Library's "100 Best Nonfiction Books of the 20th Century," published on April 29 of this year. In a way, this somewhat controversial brief on "the best that has been known and said in the world" (to borrow a phrase from Matthew Arnold) in English during the last 100 years encapsulates the essential dilemma of the black scholar working within a predominantly white society at century's end. The list was voted on by a panel of 13 authors that included A.S. Byatt, Caleb Carr, Christopher Cerf, Shelby Foote, Stephen Jay Gould, Vartan Gregorian, John Krakauer, Edmund Morris, Elaine Pagels, John Richardson, Arthur Schlesinger, Jr., Carolyn See and myself.

The Modern Library list is, of course, not the only compilation of "the best." At this eleventh hour of the 20th century it is difficult to resist the temptation to make new catalogues for almost every field and discipline. Thus, we also have *Sacred Fire: The QBR 100 Essential Black Books*, edited by Max Rodriquez, founder of *Quarterly Black Review of Books*, which contains my foreword; as well as the Modern Library's "100 Best English-Language Novels," which contains only three black works of fiction (*Native Son, Invisible Man,* and *Go Tell It on the Mountain*); and the American Film Institute's "100 Top American Films, "a much-publicised list that included not a single motion picture written, directed or produced by persons of color.

Of all these lists the Modern Library's nonfiction catalogue is the most instructive for black intellectuals. Out of 100 books only seven are by African-Americans. These are *Up from Slavery* by Booker T. Washington, *Black Boy* by Richard Wright, *Notes of a Native Son* by James Baldwin, *The Souls of Black Folks* by W.E.B. Du Bois, *The Autobiography of Malcolm X* by Alex Haley and Malcolm X, *Why We Can't Wait* by Martin Luther King Jr. and *Shadow and Act* by Ralph Ellison. To be sure, these texts are among the most influential, discussed, and debated books in black literature since 1901. No one can doubt that they have been foundational—indeed *seminal*—for any and all discussions of race for the last five generations.

But compare now these "black" titles to the ones by white authors on the Modern Library listing. William James explores *The Varieties of Religious Experience;* John Maynard Keynes offers *The General Theory of Employment, Interest and Money*; G.E. Moore gives us *Principia Ethica*; and Lewis Thomas explores *The Lives of a Cell.* Readers would have to be blind not to see that the intellectual commerce represented by white authors ranges over all possible subjects and phenomenon—from mathematics (*Principia Mathematic)* to literary criticism (*Aspects of the Novel*), history (*The Making of the Atomic Bomb)* to philosophy (*A Theory of Justice)* —including titles on race (*An American Dilemma* and *The Strange Career of Jim Crow*) while the work of black intellectuals is confined to race alone.

The *QBR 100 Essential Black Books* only reinforces this depressing revelation since it consists entirely of works devoted to some dimension of the race problem. We must ask: How can it be that African-American intellectuals have not produced watershed *non*-racial works in the last one hundred years?

If I'm not mistaken, the answer can be found in the peculiar, limiting role assigned to black "intellectuals" in the 20th century. From Booker T. Washington to Wright and Ellison and Baldwin, from Amiri Baraka to Toni Morrison, Henry Louis Gates Jr. and Cornel West, the *role* of the black "intellectual" has been, first and foremost, that of

(1) Interpreting as a spokesperson the "black experience" to white people during the Jim Crow and post-Civil Rights periods, and (2) Addressing his or her literary and intellectual efforts *not* to the mysterious, inexhaustible world at large, *not* to the vast universe of unvoiced subjects that await exploration but instead to that smaller province of meaning assigned to people of color. In a word, 20th century black "intellectuals" were granted authority by the white world on but one worldly subject: *themselves*.

How could it be otherwise? Since the 1960s whites dare not speak on black subjects, regardless of how much research they may have done, because they lack "the authority of experience" that comes from being born and raised black. Thus, our "intellectuals" have the field of race all to themselves in what looks dangerously to be the *re*-segregation of the black mind. Needless to say, this territorial claim has been profitable in the short term for many black American writers, leading to six-figure book contracts (always on racial subjects), prestigious awards, much publicity in the media, high-profile status on the nation's talk shows, and very comfortable careers. The black "public intellectual," as he or she has been recently called, enjoys in America in 1999 a celebrity hitherto unknown to predecessors like sociologists E. Franklin Frazier and Charles S. Johnson. He is called upon to comment, on television or radio or in the newspapers, on every new wrinkle in black life, whether that be the controversy over Ebonics, the death of Tupac Shakur, the O.J. Simpson trial, a recent comment by Nation of Islam leader Louis Farrakhan, the "black take" on President Clinton's affair with Monica Lewinsky, or some other event in the African Diaspora, though clearly their opinions outside their fields of specialisation carry no more weight than that of the proverbial man on the street—and seldom (if ever) are they asked to speak with professional authority on scientific, technological, religious or non-racial international affairs that affect the state of the Republic. *Those* are still the province of whites and, lately, Asians scholars.

As you may have noticed I've been placing sneer-quotes around the word "intellectual." This is not to denigrate our cultural workers today but to indicate that it is important to distinguish between *scholars* and *intellectuals*. When asked to define the latter, Bertrand Russell once replied, "I have never called myself an intellectual, and nobody has ever dared to call me one in my presence....I think an intellectual may be defined as a person who pretends to have more intellect than he has, and I hope that definition does not fit me." Before the 20th century the term "intellectual" most often carried a negative meaning, denoting someone who reduced all knowing to pure reason. According to historian Russell Kirk, such "intellectuals" were denounced as sophists who overrated the intellect by *scholars* as various as Bacon, Hume and Coleridge. The true scholar, we come to see, is a man or woman of genuine epistemological humility, someone who realises that what we know, as Russell pointed out, is always "vanishingly small." Today, however, the black "intellectual" is all too often an informed pundit who presents his judgments and opinions in a public, mass market forum, rather than to colleagues, and the result is often comic when the "intellectual-celebrity" steps out of the field where he or she has genuine authority (artists, for example, who talk about the fields of economics or politics when they are amateurs; or, if you like, Morrison's recent statement that William Jefferson Clinton is our first "black" president, which was probably news to everyone in Clinton's family).

Celebrity, in short, can be as poisonous for contemporary intellectual integrity as the century's-old ghettoising of the black intellect and imagination. When one's reputation is founded not so much on a ground-breaking work of scholarship but rather on being well-known it follows that one must strive mightily to stay newsworthy, no matter how shallow, hastily executed, or ephemeral one's work becomes. The painstaking, slow work of scholarship becomes replaced by media appearances, often shameless self-promotion, and even the dubious distinction of being "controversial" buys one a headline in the press and Andy Warhol's 15 minutes of fame on the Oprah Winfrey show. But consider the reaction of Jean Genet when a reporter asked him how he felt about his becoming famous so fast. Genet replied that he wanted not fame but glory—and *that* only came long after a writer was dead. In other words, we can only see an author's work having critical significance in intellectual history if it endures for at least 50 years, finding its audience among several generations, each of which discovers in his text something of value for their own time as well as an enduring disclosure of the subject the author had explored. The standard is—and has long been—simply this: a scholar breaks new ground, makes a discovery, *advances* the methodology or content of a particular discipline, solves a problem, or clarifies a question in his field, quite often a question that others in his area are laboring day and night, worldwide and competitively, to answer (as, for example, the way Watson discusses the progress of scientific discovery in *The Double Helix*). And these are *objective* contributions, ones that everyone in a given field can agree upon, black, white or otherwise.

Now, I would do wrong—and I would lie—if I were to suggest that race-related scholarship has no value. On the contrary, this research is profoundly important, particularly in America, where the evolution of this republic—from the moment twenty blacks arrived at Jamestown on a Dutch ship to the triumphs of the Civil Rights Movement—is indebted to countless economic, cultural and political contributions from people of African descent. Yet, tragically, so much of this marginalised history is, as the late, great Ralph Ellison might put it, still "invisible." Often, when speaking to audiences in America, I ask them to try this imaginative thought experiment: *remove* black people from America's past. Remove them *totally*. What remains? Suddenly, members of the audience realise, after performing this phenomenological variation, that the 244 years of our history that involved the institution of slavery (1619 to 1863), the American Revolution, the Civil War and U.S. history since Reconstruction, become not only hopelessly unintelligible but patently inconceivable.

As a student of (black) American history since the 1960s, I have, therefore, always felt indebted to our scholars who did the difficult, "shoes-in-the-dirt" intellectual labor on which our efforts today rest—outstanding figures like John Hope

Franklin, Zora Neal Hurston (to name but a few) and especially that towering genius, W.E.B. Du Bois who, if we pause for just a moment to appreciate the magnitude of his achievements, we discover in his life and legacy a prototypical model for the possibilities of men and women of letters in *any* century.

Writer John Oliver Killens did not exaggerate (or at least not by much) when he described Du Bois as "the greatest American intellectual of the twentieth century." His doctoral dissertation *The Suppression of the African Slave Trade to the United States of America, 1638-1870* (1896) remains a canonical study in its field. He followed with equally watershed works of history and sociology, *The Philadelphia Negro* (1899) and *Black Reconstruction in America* (1935)—accomplishments rich enough to constitute a career in themselves, but these publications were only the beginning for his prodigious and protean work in the 20th century, merely Act One for a mind so creatively fertile and expansive that its restlessness, rigor and most of all singular *vision* inevitably propelled Du Bois into the fields of poetry, fiction, philosophy, cultural criticism, autobiography and memoir as well as a lifetime of political activism for his people. "His influence as a writer and reformer, "said President Nnamdi Azikiwe of Nigeria, "will never diminish..." The reason, I believe, for the longevity of Du Bois' *oeuvre* can be found, not solely in the vast content of his contributions, but equally in the motivating spirit, the "fire in the belly" that gave rise to his breathtaking achievements. That spirit is brilliantly on display in his enduring classic *The Souls of Black Folks* (1903), where he writes:

> ...to make men, we must have ideals, broad, pure, and inspiring ends of living,—not sordid money-getting, not apples of gold. The worker must work for the glory of his handiwork, not simply for pay; the thinker must think for truth, not for fame. And all this is gained only by human strife and longing; by ceaseless training and education; by founding Right on righteousness and Truth on the unhampered search for Truth.

It is clear from these words that Du Bois, like many men of his era, believed that the work of the mind was, first and foremost, a *moral* work. And that art and scholarship were the fruit of one's *entire* being, which involved the life of the spirit, the Feeling Heart (as he phrased it in his 1923 speech "Criteria of Negro Art") and the intellect. Compare his words—this wisdom—to a passage by Orestes Brownson's address, "The Scholar's Mission," delivered in 1843 at Darmouth College:

> I understand by the scholar no mere pedant, dilettante, literary epicure or dandy; but a serious, robust, full-grown man; who feels that life is a serious affair, and that he has a serious part to act in its eventful drama; and must therefore do his best to act well his part, so as to leave behind him, in the good he has done, a grateful remembrance of his having been. He may be a theologian, a politician, a naturalist, a poet, a moralist, or a metaphysician; but whichever or whatever he is, he is it with all his heart and soul, with high, noble—in one word—religious aims and aspirations.

Scholars of the caliber of Du Bois, and our other intellectual predecessors, would be enormously discouraged, I believe, by the thinness of black letters today, by our most visible "public intellectuals" allowing themselves to become simply entertainers in an amusement society, and certainly by the sparse representation of black Americans in the most demanding fields of study. Yet we must acknowledge that in general, and on the whole, the American academic *Zeitgeist* is hardly constituted these days to produce a Du Bois or a William James. Look at the report, "The Dissolution of General Education 1914-1993," released in 1997 by the National Association of Scholars at Princeton, which found that in 1914 almost 90 per cent of American colleges made an introductory course in history mandatory—in 1993 only 2 per cent of colleges did so. Philosophy courses suffered as well, dropping from more than three-quarters of colleges in 1914 having them as requirements to just 4 per cent in 1993.

While I am no fan of author Denise D'Souza's book *The End of Racism* (1995), I am convinced we must pay attention to the startling research he presents on the distribution of blacks in fields that require an analytic and quantitative approach to phenomenon. His numbers are taken from National Academy Press's "Summary Report 1992: *Doctorate Recipients from United States Universities.*There, we discover that in the early 1990s only five black mathematicians were at America's twenty-five top-ranked universities, and that less than 2 per cent of this nation's scientists are black. D'Souza, being no friend of black people, pulls no punches. For doctorates earned by various groups in 1992, he provides the following breakdowns:

	Whites	*Asians*	*Hispanics*	*Blacks*	*Native Americans*
Mathematics	423	51	12	4	2
Computer Science	376	86	8	5	2
Physics and Astronomy	733	92	30	7	6
Chemistry	1,211	132	42	17	6
Engineering	1,874	447	72	48	11
Biological Sciences	3,043	262	101	61	13

D'Souza adds to the depressing numbers above the observation that, "Remarkably, nearly one-half of all black doctorates were in a single field, education, with most of the rest in fields like social work and sociology. In a long list of specialised areas, such as algebra, geometry, logic, atomic physics, geophysics, paleontology, oceanography, biomedical engineering, nuclear engineering, cell biology, endocrinology, genetics, microbiology, geography, statistics, classics, comparative literature, archeology, German language, Italian, Spanish, Russian, accounting and business economics, in 1992 there were no blacks who earned doctorates in the United States."

The fact of such weak black representation in the scientific and technological fields that will dominate the dawn of the 21st century tells us that, as a people, our greatest challenge is to create and sustain a new black culture that nurtures a passion for knowledge *for its own sake*. In America, in the past century, black culture has produced an overabundance of athletes and entertainers, indeed, even a surplus of lawyers and people with degrees in the "soft" sciences (ethnology, sociology, psychology); the objective of the *next* century should be, if we are wise, the development of a generation of black scholars capable of speaking with authority and enthusiasm on *any* and *all* subjects that define the human condition. In other words, the responsibility for the intellectual vigor of our lives in the next 100 years will not rest with a handful of public pundits and spokespersons, but with ourselves. We must establish, culturally, a passion for learning in our children from the moment they are able to speak. In our schools—and in our social lives—we must reward and hold up as role models the eggheads and nerds, the overachievers and driven, type-A personalities. Personally, I don't think it would be a bad idea for our churches to create something equivalent to the Jewish bar mitzvah, that coming-of-age ceremony in which a thirteen-year-old boy or girl is publicly embraced as a member of the community, but only after he or she has spent a year in preparation, studying a lengthy section of the Torah that they will be called upon to recite before their congregations, selecting poetry or literature for this event that marks their transition from childhood—in short, doing intellectual and cultural work to earn their respected place among others.

Think about it.

For if we do not rise to this challenge, I fear the world will leave us behind, locked claustrophobically in a parochial study of ourselves, producing book after book with titles prefixed by the world "black"—books that, at the end of the 21st century, will be as absent from lists of "the best" as African-American titles are from the Modern Library's recent, revealing inventory.

5

The Threads That Connect Us: An Interview with Charles Johnson

— Geffrey Michael Davis

In Spring 2009, Charles R. Johnson, holder of the S. Wilson and Grace M. Pollock Professorship for Excellence in English and former director of Creative Writing at the University of Washington, taught his last course as a full professor of English. His retirement is the appropriate moment for a retrospective look at the life and career of one of the most prominent black writers of our time. Johnson's work continually pushes against the limits and boundaries of our understanding of identity, asking us to rethink logics we have come to take as given.

Davis: I guess my first question will be the most obvious one: how did it feel to make the decision to retire from the University of Washington?

Johnson: This is my thirty-third year of teaching at the University of Washington. I started here as a 28-year-old assistant professor in 1976, and I feel these last three decades at UW have been rewarding. But I've also been thinking about retirement and becoming a professor emeritus for several years now, devoting all my time to creative work and study.

Davis: It's interesting to hear you say that you're looking to devoting some time to study. What subjects in particular are you looking forward to spending more time with?

Johnson: I'm presently in my tenth year of studying Sanskrit, a language I love. I try to devote at least one hour a day to study, review and translation, but given my schedule of teaching, writing, speaking engagements, and public appearances, it's often hard to find that hour every day. I look forward to having more time to think in Sanskrit. Also, I'm very passionate about the remarkable breakthroughs I see happening in all the sciences and have subscriptions to five science journals for lay people, which pile up in a corner of my study during the school year—I can usually only read a stack of them when I'm in an airport, on a plane, or in my hotel room when I'm out of town for some engagement. But all of it thrills me, from new work in cosmology to cloning, from nanotech to DNA sequencing. One day I plan to write a very philosophical science-fiction novel, perhaps soon after I retire.

Davis: Have you made any plans to travel more frequently after you finish teaching?

Johnson: I don't have any travel plans. But if I do travel, my preference is to visit Theravada Buddhist countries in the Far East, such as Thailand, a country I knew was my spiritual home the moment I arrived there in 1997 to do two weeks of research on "The Asian Sense of Beauty" for an article Microsoft hired me to write for their on-line travel magazine "Mungo Park" which, unfortunately, was cancelled before I could get back to the States and write that particular piece.

Davis: You were living in Stony Brook, NY, before accepting the assistant professor position in creative writing at UW; you had recently published *Faith and the Good Thing* (1974). Was publishing that novel key to your decision to accept the position in Seattle?

Johnson: Yes, I think it was. The English department at UW wrote to me in early 1975 after I published the novel, asking if I would be interested in a position here. At the time, I was a Ph.D. student in philosophy, had taken my qualifying exams, and proposed my dissertation project (this later became the book *Being and Race: Black Writing Since 1970*). I was naturally thinking about applying for positions in philosophy departments, although these were few and far between, especially for someone who was ABD (All But Dissertation). So I sat down in New York City at a restaurant with critic Roger

Sale (now retired from UW) for an interview; he was traveling through the east and also interviewed writer Clarence Major. To my surprise, UW's English Department hired us both. This was a blessing for me at the time because in 1975 our first child was born, we were living on my $4,000-a-year TA salary, and I had hanging over my head not only the dissertation to write but a second novel, *Oxherding Tale*, to compose. That first year at UW gave me the financial stability and creative space to work on that second novel, teach furiously, and begin in the winter of 1977 what became twenty years of writing screen-and-teleplays for first PBS, then Hollywood in the 1990s.

Davis: Buddhism has been a major influence in your writing, especially since the publication of *Oxherding Tale*, and in your life in general. Has it also influenced your teaching?

Johnson: Everything I do is informed by the Buddhadharma, including teaching. It has always been my practice when I enter the classroom to leave my ego, desires, and miscellaneous list of personal "likes and dislikes" outside the door. Students aren't paying their good money for any of that—only for what I can teach them about craft and aesthetics. So, yes, teaching for me is (like everything else) an opportunity for spiritual practice, selflessness, and a chance to serve others.

Davis: What do you feel (or hope) students have gained most from this style of teaching?

Johnson: I describe my approach to teaching—I call it "applied aesthetics"—in a 2003 article, "A Boot Camp for Creative Writing," which was published in *The Chronicle of Higher Education* and will soon be reprinted in *Writer's Digest*. That approach places almost as much work on my students as it does on me, not just in terms of their producing a great deal of their own writing in ten weeks but also in respect to students helping each other. I let them know on the first day this is their workshop, not mine, that my goal is for it to feel like a kind of institutionalised Paris café where we meet weekly, share our creations, and constructively critique each other's efforts. They must perform as both creative writers and critics, as class leaders and editors for the work of others. So the class does sharpen their creative, critical, pedagogical and even social skills.

Davis: Now that you have taught creative writing at UW for over thirty years, are there relationships that you have developed or maintained with former students of yours that are particularly significant to you?

Johnson: Obviously, yes. I first taught David Guterson (*Snow Falling on Cedars, The Other*) in the late '70s or early '80s and we remain friends to this day. Last Friday, on October 24th, I read my tenth Bed-time Story, "Night Hawks," at the tenth anniversary of Humanities Washington's yearly fund-raiser (five of my previous stories for this are in the collection *Dr. King's Refrigerator and Other Bed-time Stories*), and one of the other readers was Daniel Orozco, who was one of my graduate students in UW's MFA program 15 years ago and is now a successful writer and teacher in Idaho. It was a delight to read with him. A few years ago at this event I also read fiction with writer Kathleen Alcala, whose MFA thesis committee I served on in the 1980s. I have many, many former students spread all over the world, and many have done very well, among them Richard Gelfond, co-owner of IMAX.

Davis: In your autobiographical essay "I Call Myself an Artist" (1994), you describe your arrival in Seattle, Washington: "From the moment we arrived...I felt I'd found the region, the landscape, and the lifestyle I'd been looking for since I left Evanston." In a recent article titled "Northwest Passage" (2008), which appeared in the *Smithsonian*, you describe the atmosphere of Seattle. Being a native of that area (I was born in Seattle and raised in Tacoma), your descriptions of the city and the surrounding area rung true and made me ache for that green-gray beauty of the Puget Sound. I think you accurately identify its cosmopolitan feeling and its influence on creativity and the imagination. I wonder if you could talk more about specific influences Seattle has had on your writing. Have other places had similar or opposite effects on you or your work?

Johnson: Over the last 33 years I've come to realise that the only place in America I want to live is Seattle or somewhere nearby in the gorgeous Northwest. Writer Jonathan Raban put it so well when he wrote that other places have their "school rules" that are "hard and explicit." You have to conform, shape yourself to fit in if you're in Chicago, New York City, Los Angeles, or even some rural town in South Carolina. You don't have to do that in Seattle. Here you can simply be yourself. A day hasn't passed in the last three decades when I haven't been aware of that rare freedom we have here, and the stunning beauty of Nature right outside our windows.

Davis: The piece you mentioned earlier, "Night Hawks," focuses on the important role that fellow Seattleite the late August Wilson played in your life—the ways in which he helped you to reflect on the cultural turmoil you have witnessed and to understand the significance of a life "devoted unselfishly day and night to art." Can you tell us more about this relationship?

Johnson: Writing is a solitary, lonely activity. What August and I enjoyed were long evenings (seven to ten hours) of just relaxing and talking and letting our hair down. This is rare for so-called "successful" writers, and even more rare for black male writers in America. My friend, writer John McCluskey (We co-authored *Black Men Speaking*), told me that he and a few other faculty members at Indiana University invited filmmaker Melvin van Pebbles to their campus. After van Pebbles' presentation, they all went to dinner. At some point in their conversation, McCluskey told me, van Pebbles got tears in his eyes. The others at the table were surprised, and asked him if anything was wrong. No, he replied. He said he simply never has the chance to sit down with other black artists and writers—the experience brought tears to his eyes. August and I experienced this joy as often as we could—whenever we both were in town. We couldn't have been farther apart in, say, our politics, but that didn't matter one bit. In August, I saw a man with the true spirit of an artist, someone who loved the creative process as much as I did, who had devoted himself to it since the 1960s as I had done, and who shared my deep respect for the generation of our parents, the hard-working, moral men and women who raised us at the very end of the era of segregation. Here in Seattle we did many literary events together; we were, naturally, at the same literary events for the 15 years he lived in Seattle.

Davis: I'm struck by this rarity you mention for "successful" black male authors to meet informally and talk. Could we hear more on this, especially any thoughts you might share about what it means to you to be a black male author?

Johnson: I described my 15 years of good, long dinner conversations with August Wilson. My best friend, Art Washington (he did the *Showtime* dramas on Jimi Hendrix and Adam Clayton Powell, and has spent more than 30 years in the industry), and I have been like brothers since we worked at KQED. We talk or email each other almost every day. But notice the difference in our disciplines of choice. Wilson was a playwright; Washington is a full-time screenwriter. I'm primarily a novelist, short story writer, essayist and cartoonist. There is little overlap in terms of our primary creative focus, and therefore no professional competition. When you have two black males writers (or any two writers in general, regardless of race or gender)—Richard Wright and Ralph Ellison, say, or Wright and James Baldwin (who told Wright he was the "father," and therefore he, Baldwin, had to "kill" him) —there is the possibility for a kind of Cain/Abel jealousy and professional competition to arise. I find it remarkable and refreshing that this did not seem to arise between Ellison and Albert Murray. With August and Art, I always deferred (graciously and gratefully) to their greater experience in theater and Hollywood, and they deferred to my greater experience as a literary and visual artist, and as a philosopher. Mutual respect was always present, and even the desire to collaborate on new projects. (Art and I have worked on things together for decades, and pitched stories together to Barbara Streisand, Denzel Washington, and Wesley Snipes, and conference called together with *Marvel*'s Stan Lee.)

Davis: In writing, you have described your wife, Joan, as "educated, extremely independent and, though kind toward everyone, [with] one of Hemingway's 'built-in shit detectors,'" and you have compared her values to those of your father: frugality, lack of pretense, and unshakable morality ("I Call"). I wonder if you can talk more about Joan's influence on your work or on your life in general? Can you talk some about the impact of Joan's own commitment to social work in Seattle?

Johnson: We were born exactly seven days apart in April, 1948, and really only a matter of miles from each other in

Evanston and South Chicago (I'm older by a week). I often joke that our fathers possibly impregnated our mothers at exactly the same moment. She is, I know, the only woman on this earth I could have spent my life with, the only woman I've ever met (we met when we were twenty-years-old in the summer of 1968) who I felt it was my personal duty to make happy. Our values are identical. What impressed me about her was how she and her three sisters and two brothers had grown up poor in a violent housing project, but her spirituality was so deep, so clear, so uncompromised that she emerged from that experience not only beautiful but also kind, generous, balanced, forgiving, and resourceful when times are hard. She has been a K-12 teacher (right after we married), has a master's degree in social work from UW and until recently worked with patients dying of cancer and AIDS, and with teenage girls in one of those facilities where they are one step away from being incarcerated. Since childhood she has loved the description of the perfect wife in the Book of Proverbs (which I published an essay about). I can testify that she *is* that mature and solid woman in the Book of Proverbs, the one whose "children arise up and call her blessed; her husband also, and praiseth her." I believe the late Paul Newman said when he was asked about other women that, "Why should I go out for hamburger when I have steak at home?" That's always been how I've felt about my wife Joan.

Davis: Toward the end of "I Call Myself an Artist," you list certain events you saw as "the finest moments of my life": your marriage to Joan New, the births of your children, and the tribute to Ralph Ellison during your acceptance of the National Book Award for your novel *Middle Passage* (1990). Do you see a common thread between these moments? What qualifies a moment as "fine" for you? Have there been any additional fine moments since your tribute to Ellison?

Johnson: I would include on that list the day SUNY Stony Brook lured me back to their campus under the pretense of giving me an honorary degree, which they did give me, but also my real Ph.D. in philosophy, back-dated to 1988 when I published *Being and Race*. One of my old Stony Brook colleagues said to me that, to his knowledge, this has only happened one other time in the history of philosophy—when

Wittgenstein (who was famous but had not finished his doctorate) wanted to teach, so his old profs got together and awarded him the degree. I add this moment because my doctorate in philosophy means as much (and in some cases more) to me as the literary prizes or awards I've received. The Ph.D. in philosophy was one of my dreams since I was 18-years-old. Philosophy, which literally means "the love of wisdom," is my passion, pre-dates my interest in writing literary fiction, and obviously informs my devotion to Buddhism.

Davis: Your drive as a writer has been devoted to writing "philosophical fiction," and you have recognised such writers as Richard Wright, Ralph Ellison, and Jean Toomer as influences. Now that you are retiring from university teaching, what does a retrospective glance reveal to you about your sense of accomplishment thus far with your life goal of filling the void of "genuine philosophical black literature"? Are there other writers or thinkers that you feel have influenced your writing and/or philosophy?

Johnson: Well, the great writers—and philosophers—who influenced me strongly are legion, and not just limited to Wright, Ellison, and Toomer. Sadly, my first philosophy professor, Dr. John Howie, whose course on the pre-Socratics I took in 1966, died a few weeks ago. I last saw him when I delivered the 16th Paul Tillich Lecture (on Tillich's critique of Buddhism, a version of which I published in the winter 2006 issue of *Tricycle*) at Harvard Divinity School a few years ago. He came to that lecture, and I dedicated it to him. He was a graduate of Boston University, where he was influenced (as Martin Luther King Jr. had been) by the school of Boston Personalists, who I mention in my novel *Dreamer*. I also owe much to phenomenologist Don Ihde (my dissertation advisor), and especially to John Gardner, who brought me into the book world in the first place, and provided me with a model for the wide range of things an inventive literary writer and scholar could do.

As for my goal of enriching black American (and American) fiction with 2,000 years of Western and Eastern philosophy—well, that's done. Although I've prolifically turned out books, essays, articles, stories and drawings and more since 1998, my "job" in regard to that specific project or literary program I started in the 1970s was over with *Dreamer.* I'm confident I did the work God put me here to do.

Davis: So let me make sure that I understand: are you saying that your job as a writer is complete, or is it that your writing project itself has changed, has assumed a new "job" other than creating philosophical writings?

Johnson: My creative work will continue until the last day of my life, until I take my last breath. But decades ago I made myself a promise that by the age of fifty, which is the year I published *Dreamer*, I planned to have all my duties and responsibilities to everyone in my life—parents, teachers, colleagues, editors and publishers, friends and family, and students—discharged or completed. For the last ten years, there hasn't been anything I "have" to do, only the things I want to do creatively that nourish me spiritually, intellectually and artistically. See this in terms of the Hindu "Four Stages of Life." In youth (spring), our job is to study and acquire skills. In adulthood (summer) we enter the work world with its various obligations and put those skills and that knowledge into play. In middle-age (fall) we serve our family and community as householders, creating wealth so that we can help others achieve happiness and avoid suffering. Then at the beginning of old age (winter) we retire from the worldliness of the world to devote ourselves exclusively to matters of the spirit, to knowledge (*vidya*) and preparation for death. In every "stage," I create, the intention and motivation behind the creative work matures, changes and evolves during one's passage through life.

Davis: I know at least one critic, Linda Selzer, who argues that your fiction is not only important because it incorporates philosophical ideas into literature, but also because it enriches the practice of philosophy itself by pushing beyond the analytical to imbue philosophical questions with phenomenological force. Can you speak a bit about why such an approach to philosophising might be valuable?

Johnson: People mistakenly believe that philosophy is all about abstractions, that it happens in an irrealised realm of ideas divorced from the messiness of the world. That is a mistake. A major misunderstanding. Philosophical ideas begin in the muck and mud of experience, of daily living, and we only abstract them—or lift them out of immediate experience—in order to discuss and analyse them. As a writer of philosophical fiction, I saw my job as being one where I returned those perennial philosophical questions back to the drama, the sweat and struggle of everyday life where they arose in the first place.

Davis: In your recent article "The Meaning of Barack Obama" (2008), you describe Obama's background as an "interpenetration of backgrounds that transcends dualism" and "seemingly exotic but in fact very common"—"a kind of blank slate on which Americans have projected their deepest and most visceral social and cultural longings"—and you quote David Brooks in the *New York Times*: "people on almost all sides of an issue can see parts of themselves reflected in Obama's eyes. But it does make him hard to place." In various ways, these descriptions, for me, echoed the fluidity or mobility of some of the characters in your fiction. I'm thinking here of characters such as Rutherford Calhoun and the god of the Allmuseri in *Middle Passage*; Andrew Hawkins and Horace Bannon in *Oxherding Tale*; and Dr. Martin Luther King Jr. and Chaym Smith in *Dreamer*. What do such figures tell us about your understanding of identity?

Johnson: They tell us that we are *process*, not product; that we are *verbs*, not nouns. That our "identity" is fluid (not fixed or static) and better described by Heraclitus than Parmenides, and put rather well by Alfred North Whitehead when in *Process and Reality* he talks about actual entities and subjective aims. This question of "identity," or what is the self (which is for me the deepest of philosophical questions from which all others arise), came to mind for me today when I read this passage by Joseph Goldstein on *Insight Meditation:* "When perception is stronger than mindfulness, we recognise various appearances and create concepts such as "body," "cat", "house," or "person".... On some clear night, go outside, look up at the sky, and see if you can find the Big Dipper. For most people that is a familiar constellation, easy to pick out from all the other stars. But is there really a Big Dipper up there in the sky?"

There is no Big Dipper up there. "Big Dipper" is a concept. Humans looked, saw a certain pattern, and then created a concept in our collective mind to describe it. That concept is useful because it helps us recognise the constellation. But it also has another, less useful effect. By creating the concept "Big Dipper" we separate out those stars from all the rest, and then, if we become attached to the idea of that separation, we lose the sense of the night sky's wholeness, its oneness. Does the separation actually exist in the sky? No. We created it through the use of a concept. Does anything change in the sky when we understand that there is no Big Dipper? No.

We are deceived often by concepts and the creations of our own minds. "Race" is one of those illusions, as is the idea of an enduring unchanging self, a notion David Hume beautifully exploded in *A Treatise of Human Nature.*

Davis: The same David Hume that, as you say, exploded the notion of race is also known for making vitriolic statements about the inferiority of the "Negro Race." Understanding that we all have contradictions (and I know your short story "Alethia" from *The Sorcerer's Apprentice* takes up the mixed record of philosophers on race), I wonder if we might hear more on how (or if) you reconcile these conflicting gestures made by Hume.

Johnson: The anti-black racism found historically for 2500 years in Western thinkers before 1970 is well documented. All these white men and women were (predictably) flawed products of their times, and they reflect the cultural/intellectual limitations of their times. (Just as we reflect the strengths and weaknesses of our present moment in human history.) However, just because Hume erred egregiously on the subject of black people, that does not mean he erred when discussing the question of our experience of the self. He didn't—Hume got it exactly right in a remarkable stroke of brilliance (the absence of any empirical evidence for the "self" or "soul") that recalls Buddhism's use of *vipassana* meditation to determine what is or is not in our thoughts, and also phenomenology's use of noetic analysis. There is really nothing here that needs to be reconciled if we understand that it isn't necessary to throw the baby out with the bath water. See it in light of the Yin/Yang symbol: a spot of darkness (ignorance) in the light; and a spot of light (wisdom) in the darkness. My story "Alethia" does address this question, as literary scholar Linda Selzer magnificently demonstrates in her new book. A black student or scholar encountering these flaws and mistakes in white writers (and any other writers, for that matter) will cringe, but they need to behave like grown-ups. He (or she) needs to respond to it analytically and critically, and not allow himself (or herself) to be overcome with anger or emotionalism, which serve nothing. It would be rather silly, don't you think, to dismiss the groundbreaking work of James Watson on DNA just because he's poorly informed and mistaken about black people? I admire him for the former and pity him for his ignorance about the latter (and that ignorance might well change if he takes the time to learn a few things about the African Diaspora).

Davis: Where does (or should) the physical body fit into our understanding of *self*? During a recent reading, poet Li-Young Lee talked briefly about what he saw as the danger of a Western tendency to champion the mind over (and, sometimes, at the consequence of) the body in our attempts to understand ourselves and our connections to those around us. Characters in your fiction have also pushed my understanding of how to live (well) inside a body. I'm thinking again about figures such as the god of the Allmuseri and Horace Bannon. I wonder if you could talk specifically about how you see the body in relation to knowledge and/or identity.

Johnson: The privileging of the mind (or spirit) over the body in modern philosophy begins with Descartes' division of human beings into mind-substance and body-substance. That ontological division is pre-figured in medieval Christianity (and that is probably what Li-Young Lee is referring to). However, we have learned from the phenomenologists, especially Maurice Merleau-Ponty, that consciousness is always embodied and cannot be experienced empirically any other way. Phenomenology dissolves the old error of mind/body dualism, because we understand that the body is the mediation between consciousness and the world (of which it is a part). Take a look at one of my most reprinted and anthologised stories, "China." There, an aging, black postman is very out of touch with his body and is dying, physically and spiritually. But through exposure to the martial arts, then meditation, he manages to restore his body and spirit, his health, and transcend by the story's end the false dualisms—or illusions—so many in the West fall into. Another often reprinted piece I wrote when I was still in graduate school at Stony Brook, "The Phenomenology of the Black Body," also speaks to this issue, as well as a new book by philosopher George Yancy, *Black Bodies, White Gazes* (2008).

Davis: Last year I heard Henry Louis Gates Jr. give a talk at the Pennsylvania State University about one of his current projects, which was concerned with tracking the ancestry of black Americans in order to identify the multiplicities of our biological roots. In your Obama piece, you also use DNA research to help undo socially constructed notions of racialised difference and to highlight the historical tenets and common ancestry we all share. Do you see your work in relation to that of Gates or other black intellectuals?

Johnson: Dr. Gates kindly included a link for my recent Obama essay on his website, The Root.com. We recently exchanged a few messages, and I praised him highly for his interview with James Watson, which he told me received over 3 million "hits" in a 24-hour period. I think he and I are very much in agreement about the importance DNA research has for clarifying the issue of racial identity.

Davis: A recent Forbes essay describes the potential for an Obama presidency to "sunder the connection between 'Western-ness' and whiteness." The essay goes on to discuss the cultural value of this deconstruction: a softening of non-Western resistance to the "better ideas" of the West. Do you see this evaluation in agreement with your own?

Johnson: That Forbes article was written by Tunku Varadarajan, formerly the op-ed page editor at *The Wall Street Journal*. It was Tunku who got me to write two op-eds for WSJ, one of which—"Shall We Overcome? The Black American Condition Today"—brought me a tremendous amount of positive replies and was featured in *Society* magazine (July/August 2006) with essays in response to it by seven other writers and thinkers. I hope Tunku's position is right, that Western-ness in the 21st century can be seen as not monopolised by whites, who only make up 17 per cent of the world's population. The other 83 per cent are people of color.

Davis: Your recent piece "The End of the Black American Narrative" (2008), seemed to be in strong conversation with earlier essays by Ralph Ellison. How do you see your article in relation to Ellison's work or the work of other black intellectual writers?

Johnson: I've always been an integrationist, as Ellison was. As a Buddhist who understands the experience of dependent origination (which states that nothing arises independently), also known in Sanskrit as *pratitya samutpada*, and which Thich Nhat Hahn calls "inter-being," I'm very sensitive to the inter-connectedness of all life, how all things are interwoven, and you might say my *oeuvre* is on one level simply about revealing those threads that connect us all.

Davis: This past election was a historical event that I believe many Americans will remember as they do other watershed moments in our nation's history. Would you mind sharing with us what it felt like to you to vote in this election?

Johnson: I felt for the very first time in my life that I was voting for a candidate I really cared for. For black Americans in the past, and since the founding of this nation, we only had a choice between two white candidates for president, and black people would wonder, "Which one of these two dislikes black people the least?" Obama is such a global candidate, in his biology and biography, that this was not a question black voters had to consider.

Davis: If Barack Obama's campaign will, as you say, take the temperature of racial attitudes in America, I see your article on the black American narrative as taking the temperature of (the potential for) de-racialised attitudes. Do you agree with this parallel? Given the strong response to this article, what do you think the results of the temperature-taking are so far?

Johnson: I agree with that parallel. I think Obama's campaign has been remarkable in the sense that people worldwide love this bi-racial, black man. Whether people like it or not, in the 21st century we will have to experience—and approach—others as individuals. To do otherwise, to approach them in terms of the illusion of race, is to insult them.

Davis: The end goal of "The End of the Black American Narrative" is to consider what we do next if the function of the black American narrative "has outlived its usefulness as a tool of interpretation." You provide a list of sites that would begin the interrogation you posit, including "new and better stories, new concepts, and new vocabularies and grammar based not on the past but on the dangerous, exciting, and unexplored present, with the understanding that each is, at best, a provisional reading of reality, a single phenomenological profile that one day is likely to be revised, if not completely overturned." Ultimately, you recognise that this change will and should produce narratives "of individuals, not groups." Are there current projects you are working on that will be the model for such narratives? What might this look like?

Johnson: I've been working on that project all my life. My story "Kwoon" has no racial identification for its central characters, also my story "Moving Pictures," and several other stories I've written recently and in *Dr. King's Refrigerator and Other Bedtime Stories*. "Race" does not figure into the drama of those stories

Davis: In an interview with Jonathan Little (1993), you said that "Every major character for me is a character of evolution and change. They are not the same at the end of the book as when we first saw them. The ideal novel would be one in which there are no minor characters, where there are no flat characters....What I want is the process novel where everybody mentioned is a main character in the process of evolution. That would be the ultimate moral fiction." Later in that same interview, you also stated, "I would like to believe that I could write book after book after book and someone could believe that they had been written by different people....Things could absolutely change in terms of the overall experience effect, from book to book. That's the kind of freedom I would like to see from novel to novel, from story to story." Although functioning on two different levels—the micro and the macro, freedom of the character(s) and freedom of the author—these two goals of fiction appear to be running parallel. I wonder if you could talk more about how you see this "process of evolution" functioning in everyday life.

Johnson: Well, just to throw this in, let me say that I did a radio interview when my second collection of stories, *Soulcatcher and Other Stories* appeared, and the woman who interviewed me said when she first read those twelve fictions, she thought they'd all been created by different people and that I had just compiled them. That's the effect I want to create with every story. As Whitman said, we contain within ourselves "multitudes," and can draw upon any of this richness when creating a story. *Dreamer* is, for example, informed by the philosophical and social and political vision of Martin Luther King Jr., not entirely by *my* vision. My story "Menagerie" is, for the most part, informed by the existentialist God-is-dead thesis, and "Exchange Value" by Marx's distinction between use value and exchange value. As I told writer Nicholas O'Connell (another of my former students) in an interview in Jim McWilliams' book *Passing the Three Gates*, "The great fight in life and in literature is to prevent some form of idea or situation from enslaving you. It's to keep your mind open and your eyes open and your life open, to find new ways of not being limited...." In other words, the goal in both life and literature (and certainly in Buddhism) is to realise our *freedom.*

Davis: As you look back at your career at the University of Washington, what do you believe will stay with you the most?

Johnson: The joy of working with talented students, and the benefit any artist experiences when he teaches: namely, you have to deeply understand both practice and theory if your goal is to help others in the classroom, and doing that critically sharpens an artist's own understanding of aesthetics and his craft.

Davis: What is next for Charles Johnson, professionally and personally?

Johnson: More of what I've been doing professionally since I was 17-years-old: writing and drawing and publishing, spiritual practice, and finding inexhaustible joy in this mysterious universe in which we find ourselves.

Davis: I would like to thank you for generously sharing your time on this project.

6

Waking Cain: The Poetics of Integration in Charles Johnson's *Dreamer*

— John Whalen-Bridge

In an essay on African Americans in relation to Buddhism, Charles Johnson interprets Martin Luther King, Jr., as a kind of Buddhist exemplar. Johnson writes of King that "His dream of the 'beloved community' is a Sangha by another name, for King believed that, 'It really boils down to this: that all of life is interrelated. We are caught in an inescapable network of mutuality, tied in a single garment of destiny.'"[1] Johnson's King is very much a bodhisattva dedicated to the idea of healing through integration, and Johnson's artistic ambition has been to develop a poetics of integration which cultivates political, aesthetic, philosophical and spiritual forms of integration.[2] To resist the ways in which racism has epidermalised Being,"[3] Johnson combines the ideal of racial integration with various philosophical and religious discourses that profess a redemptive vision of human inter-subjectivity, particularly Buddhism.[4] *Dreamer* presents the reader with five specific divisions, which I will discuss in five sections to follow, that obstruct the realisable world that King termed "beloved community": (1) essentialist claims about human identity, which are in the novel dialogically answered by Buddhist claims that no such inherent identity exists; (2) class divisions between middle-class and poor blacks, which Johnson links to the rise of Black Power and contemporary American identity politics; (3) the segregation of American literary history by focusing on ethnic sub-traditions exclusively; (4) religious mythic doctrine that, improperly understood, authorises divisive thinking; and (5) the "curse of canonisation" that has enshrined King's memory only to *contain* it so that it does not become the basis for social action. At the end of Johnson's most politically engaged novel to date, King is slain and America is ready to forget his deeper message, but the narrator of *Dreamer*, Matthew Bishop, has learned that the aforementioned obstacles are in reality doorways to "beloved community."

"... That Mysterious Dichotomy Inscribed at the Heart of Things"

In the opening pages of *Dreamer*, Martin Luther King is a frustrated man grappling with an intractably divided world, a world seemingly cursed by "that mysterious dichotomy inscribed at the heart of things"(18). Johnson has researched King's final years exhaustively and presents a version of King that is startlingly resonant with the King from Oates' *Let the Trumpet Sound,* to mention just one of the books Johnson lists in his acknowledgements.[5] However, Johnson's narrative abruptly parts ways with the historical narrative of King's life with the introduction of a character named Chaym Smith, a man who looks exactly like King but in many ways can be thought of as King's opposite. He has the same height, weight, and birthday as King, but he is a lower-class failure instead of the paragon of black middle-class aspirations. He regards himself as a Buddhist rather than a Christian, and he makes scathing comments about King's asserted ideals of universal equality.

Dreamer is a novel of many levels, and one could approach the primary split between the characters King and his exact look-alike Smith in several ways. This dichotomous character set can be interpreted as a psychoanalytic return of the repressed, or a magic realist or postmodern decentering of historical narrative, but I am mainly concerned with how the meeting of King and Smith allegorically figures a dialectical interplay between two worldviews, a typically Western one which we can call "dualistic,"[6] and one associated with Eastern philosophies which is commonly discussed as "nondualistic."[7] The two characters are both black men, so the primary integration in the novel is not between black and white Americans but rather between Eastern and Western standpoints from which to view political struggle. The drama of *Dreamer* centers on narrator Bishop's realisation that King and Smith are not opposites, and the breakdown of rigid binaries is implicit from the beginning of the novel, since King, the Western/Christian minister is the relatively selfless man, whereas Smith, the avowed Buddhist, is a latter-day Cain figure who is given to intense bouts of self-consciousness and envy.

Two early passages in *Dreamer*, both of which precede the meeting of King and his uncanny double Smith, set egolessness and divisiveness in opposition, and this set of alternatives represents the primary philosophical tension of the novel. Is the world best understood as a cauldron of warring selves, or is it an awful mistake to give division ontological priority over nondualistic unity, as Buddhist-oriented philosophies suggest? The first passage, from the italicised prologue to the novel,[8] invokes division in a way that links it to Christ:

> In the Upsouth cities he visited, violence followed him like a biblical curse, but one step ahead of his assassins. Despite his clerical vows, or perhaps because of them (I am come to send fire on the earth, Luke 12:49), he walked through a world aflame. Chicago in the hundred degree summer heat of 1966 was the site for the special form of crisis his wing of the Movement produced: families divided, fathers at the throats of their sons, brothers spilling each other's blood (13).

King (the "he" in this passage) not only struggles with the pain of division just as Christ on Earth had to, but, like Christ, he comes to symbolise painful division: the message of agapic love, however much it points toward a transcendent state beyond division, threatens real historical identities and so arouses tremendous resistance. King, like Christ as described in Luke, calls for a healing unity and yet foments division. The passage from Luke quoted in *Dreamer* links readers familiar with the New Testament to the invocation of division which follows it, wherein Christ says, in Luke 12:51–53: Do you think I came to bring peace on earth? No, I tell you, but division. From now on there will be five in one family divided against each other, three against two and two against three. They will be divided, father against son and son against father, mother against daughter and daughter against mother....[9] Despite his vows, or because of them? Bishop's ambivalent phrasing in the "upsouth cities" passage expresses perfectly the paradoxical relationship between religious tradition and political activism: if politics is, as Henry Adams defines it in a sentence quoted in *Dreamer*, "the organisation of hatreds," how can a religious minister dare to get involved in any kind of political activity? Representing King at just the moment when he chose to widen the movement's scope, including his widening call for economic justice and an uncompromising resistance to the war in Vietnam, *Dreamer* develops the paradox of what might be called "divisive transcendence." The effort to heal America in Johnson's novel even causes division among King's advisors, such as when they warn him to avoid the tricky north: "You can't win there. You don't know cities. Stay on your own turf"(15). King's advisors are no more successful at dissuading him than were Christ's advisors when they pleaded with him to stay away from Jerusalem.[10] The divisions of *Dreamer* are not just the obvious ones between black and white or between racist and nonracist: Johnson gives the reader an overview of developing tensions, divisions, and psychic fault lines *within* the Civil Rights Movement.

Just after presenting division as the overwhelming fact of life faced by the Movement workers, Bishop introduces a minor character who exemplifies "egolessness" in counterpoint to the strife-ridden atmosphere surrounding the King camp. This woman, the grandmother of one of King's staff volunteers, is called Mama Pearl: "The staff fell in love with her that day, her feathery wig that knocked twenty years off her total of seventy-eight, with the way she worked her toothless mouth like a fish while listening to King explain his plans in Chicago, bobbing her head and asking, 'Is you, really?' with her head pushed forward, wig askew, and feet planted apart in two shapeless black shoes. She was utterly unselfconscious. Egoless, and flitted round the flat as though she had feet spun from air"(29). The sentence beginning with the word "egoless" has no subject, which conveys with admirable precision and economy the Buddhist sense that the transcendence of "self" in no way means that the subject becomes a zombie without a personality. To be utterly unselfconscious in the way Mama Pearl is when she says 'Is you, really?' in no way implies the lack of human spirit. This uneducated woman is undistinguished in many ways but is highly distinguished in the way she carries herself in front of the famous civil rights leader. Egoless in the way she can meet the Minister I-to-I, she is the embodiment of grandmother wit. The opening pages of the novel contrast divisive self-consciousness and the "egolessness" of a Mama Pearl to prepare readers for the sudden, shocking meeting of King and his uncanny double Smith.

Bishop presents King and Smith as dialectical opposites when they first meet, though this relation undergoes key shifts through the course of the novel. Before Smith shows up at King's door, King's work (spanning, in *Dreamer*, from King's northern campaign in Chicago in 1966 to his return to Memphis in 1968) has faced mounting frustration. King is under great stress as journalists and other critics accuse him of having lost his focus and of having been left behind by successive developments within the Civil Rights Movement. King is a weary and confused man who must face grave doubts within unfamiliar territory:

> A decade after his Montgomery victory, and spiraling successes through the South, nigh Hegelian in the mysterious way the Movement kept changing as he chased it, and changing him, pushing him higher and higher, beyond anything he'd dreamed possible in college, from local bus boycotts to unqualified calls for integration, and finally to grander dreams of global peace and equality—a decade after his finest triumphs for nonviolence, the press, and even people who'd joined hands with him singing "We Shall Overcome," now saw his methods as outmoded,his insistence on loving one's enemies as lunacy, his opposition to Black Power as outright betrayal (16).

This cascading one-sentence summary of King's political career is punctuated by a much briefer one, summing up the sense of urgency within the King camp about the effort to extend the

Southern campaign for equal rights into Northern cities: "Oh, he needed a victory here." The dramatic, dialectical shifts of King's rise point to the painfully frustrating contradiction between insisting that one love one's enemies (and thus not surrender to a dualistic self-other distinction, however tempting) on the one hand and becoming identified in the minds of one's critics as a self-promoting politician on the other. Failure is manifold, but amid this frustration and failure there is a dialogic exchange of sorts between the language of division and that of wholeness. On the one hand, King's esoteric spiritual message is ignored: "Every social evil he could think of, and every 'ontological fear,' as he was fond of saying lately, arose from that mysterious dichotomy inscribed at the heart of things: self and other, I and Thou, inner and outer, perceiver and perceived"(18). The suffering of the world, according to these sentences, flows from our illusory sense of being divided from each other. King's concern (almost foreknowledge) about his own doom enmeshes him in this seemingly universal tendency toward painful divisiveness, but King consistently meets division by refusing to grant it inevitability: "Martyrdom held no appeal for him, but for every sorcerer named Jesus there was a Judas; for every bodhisattva called Gandhi, a Poona Brahmin named Nathuram Godse. The way to the crown was, now and forever, the cross. And it made no sense to carry the cross unless one was prepared to be crucified"(18). In Johnson's alignment, Jesus and Gandhi, and also Judas and Gandhi's assassin Nathuram Godse, are interchangeable figures. Furthermore, for every Abel whose gifts are received by God, there exists also a Cain who responds with violence when his gifts are rejected by God. ("Chaym," the reader is told, is an etymological variation of "Cain.") Mirroring and opposing Smith is the King we see in the prologue: he is a "bodhisattva" like Gandhi and Christ, a man of great gifts and almost inexhaustible stamina and idealism, but he is not a man without limitations.

Class Consciousness and the Racial Shadow

King, on a losing streak, needs a victory in Chicago. In the first chapter, he is, amid such worries, interrupted by the *aide-de-*

camp Bishop, who narrates *Dreamer*. A young philosophy major who has dropped out of school temporarily to work with King, Bishop insists that King must see a certain visitor, and when Bishop presents Smith to him, King, astonished, steps back as if he had been struck and whispers "Sweet Jesus...." Bishop registers the full shock in his description: "... he looked spellbound. Then shaken. He might have been peering into a mirror, one in which his history was turned upside down, beginning not in his father's commodious, two-story Queen Anne-style home in Atlanta but instead across the street in one of the wretched shotgun shacks crammed with the black poor" (32-33).

The otherness of Smith, in King's imagining, recalls to his mind the otherness of the urban poor, and thus the division between King and Smith figures the class division within the Civil Rights Movement: division at one level constantly resonates with division at another.

Even King's own language reverberates with psychic and social division in this passage, and yet in *Dreamer* divisions of this sort come to signify the illusory nature of division. When King says "Sweet Jesus" upon meeting Smith, is King taking the Lord's name in vain, or is his utterance an unwitting expression of the identity of Christ and this man who is apparently a bum? The interdependence of beings is a commonplace of Mahayana Buddhism, but there is precedent for seeing nonduality as the heart of Christian teachings as well in Matthew 25:40: "The King will reply, 'I tell you the truth, whatever you did for one of the least of these brothers of mine, you did for me.'" That is, to see the interdependence of all Creation with God's love and Being is to see in a Christian way, to see as Christ sees.[11] Despite the differences between Smith and King (or between "the least of these brothers" and Christ), King's stunned enunciation points toward the identity of the two men. And Smith, as an unsuccessful black man, is certainly "the least of these brothers": Bishop tells us that Smith "was the kind of Negro the Movement had for years kept away from the world's cameras: sullen, ill-kept, the very embodiment of the blues"(33). As the embodiment of the blues, Smith is the quintessential outsider; as "Sweet Jesus," he is, simultaneously, the theological center of King's world view—its quintessential insider. But King never really comes to understand Smith as an incarnation of Jesus in the novel, and *Dreamer* is *not* concerned with King's development. Bishop is the character who develops in this novel, largely as a result of his perception of King and Smith. Of these two, King is a kind of avatar of enlightened living, whereas Smith stumbles as often as not.

The pairing of King and Smith provocatively introduces, into King's attempted moment of rest, the "house and field" split that Malcolm X often invoked and which Johnson previously used as a structural device in the opening chapter of *Oxherding Tale* (1982). When Smith sees the middle-class black congregations that support King, he says with some disgust, "God loves these Negroes. What do I *say* to them?" (130). In this capacity Smith functions as King's "racial shadow": whereas King, who Bishop at one point thinks of as "always a credit to the race" (71), Smith represents those aspects of African-American manhood that are likely to bring shame upon an assimilated black intellectual such as Bishop.

In her overview of the problem of the literary double in Asian-American literature, Sau-ling Cynthia Wong focuses on the double's role as a kind of return of the repressed ethnic self: "The racial shadow draws out mixed feelings of revulsion and sympathy from the protagonist, usually compelling a painful reassessment of the behavioral code which has thus far appeared to augur full acceptance into American society" (92). Clearly differences exist between Asian-American and African-American relationships with the racial shadow, but Wong's concept helps us see exactly why Smith's appearance is so disturbing to the King headquarters, so much so that Bishop writes that the events of the evening, including the rioting and other divisiveness, "had torn space and time" (32).

While there would be no reason for King to be present in Chicago if African Americans were fully assimilated in American society, Smith insists that the Calvary AME church members who support King are, at least in comparison with ghetto blacks, *relatively* assimilated. When Smith insists that "God loves these Negroes," he forces Amy and Bishop to recognise that God loves some Negroes more than others: as the gifts of Abel are received more favorably than those of Cain, so the presence of middle-class, Bible-quoting black leaders is much more welcome to mainstream America than the angry indictment offered by a Malcolm X. Smith exemplifies some stereotyped notions of African-American manhood (sexual swagger and, especially, anger in response to white racism rather than Gandhian *satyagraha*), and so the King/Smith confrontation extends Wong's theory of how the literary double in ethnic American literature expresses the return of those aspects of the ethnic identity that have been disowned so that (relative) assimilation can occur.

Nonetheless, Smith does not appear in Johnson's novel only to force a recognition of disowned aspects of African-American selfhood, since, in Johnson's novel, this confrontation is very much a two way street: Smith will alter others' views of the world, especially Bishop's, and he certainly gives King pause in thinking about himself. Johnson's fictional technique works on one level to foreground the class specificity of King's Movement, and the doppelganger theme also allows a Brechtian "alienation effect" to shock King (and readers) out of our conditioned views of his life. After their meeting, King is upset, even "shaken in his certainty that all were equal in the eyes of the Lord" (44). As if notions of Christian and love had been offered to the Devil, Smith responds in words that "echoed in the deepest coils" of King's ears,

> [w]ords Smith had almost hissed, hurling them at him like stones and with such hurt that he, about to open his mouth in a parable, offering one of his standard apothems for suffering, stopped as if he'd been slapped. All his explanations were suspended, bracketed, and shimmering in their place was the ineluctable presence of this man who could have been his brother were it not for the fact that he appeared to be damned. Or fallen (44-45).

Smith is a figure of resentment and anger, just as King is one of grace even under the most challenging of circumstances. While Smith approaches the King camp because he wants to help, his reaction to meeting his double is full of anger, but what is King's response? It is tempting to suppose that King might become somehow deepened by this interaction. His deep concern for the man is noted, but phrasing such as "*could have been his brother* were it not for the fact that he appeared to be damned" suggests that King cannot imagine anyone from his own family turning out as Smith has. Or, perhaps, "the fact that he *appeared* to be damned" is telling, since it demonstrates that Johnson's King must linguistically disassociate himself from Smith, even as he works to make the man's life more comfortable.

Why, then, the "slap"? I would argue that the real slap is intended for the reader. Johnson uses the literary technology of the "uncanny" to achieve what has been called "the liberation of perception," and this liberation can also be quite shocking.[12] Johnson provides the theory behind this kind of shock in his phenomenological study of postwar black fiction *Being and Race,* in which he connects mental bracketing to meditation, art, and phenomenology. In a passage describing a studio drawing class, Johnson correlates the discipline of learning an art such as drawing to meditative disciplines. First the artist must unlearn habitual seeing in which one draws not an object but rather one's *idea* about an object. The "heavily conditioned seeing" that precedes such unlearning is, in Johnson's terminology, the calcification of perception... that figure-drawing classes seek to liberate—we might well call this retraining of the eye the artist's equivalent of the phenomenological *epoché,* or "bracketing" of all presuppositions in order to seize a fresh, original vision. (Johnson, *Being* 5).

Meditation, artistic practice, and philosophy in Johnson's discussion are all-of-apiece in the way that they can undermine delusory perceptions, and the shock produced by the artistic technique or the philosopher's insight counteracts the "calcification of perception," and this is just the sort of shock King receives when he meets Smith. As a down-and-out version of King himself, Smith's presence shocks King into the recognition that King's slogan of universal equality might not be universally satisfying. After Smith leaves, King turns to Bishop and says "Keep that man away from my wife, you hear?"(43). The scene hints at the sort of picaresque comedy

Johnson exploited to advantage in *Oxherding Tale*, but the irony is in King's perception of Smith's otherness. Sympathetic though he is to Smith's plight, King firmly draws a sharp line between himself and his Other. He remains an obverse reflection of King, offering Bishop (not King) a vision of how King's life might have unfolded if he had been born not in a Queen Anne-style house but instead into that owned by Malcolm X's father. Bishop, observing King's reaction to Smith, notes that Smith's scraggly beard is "as rubicund in tint as Malcolm Little's" (33).

The Black Dharma Bum

It is certain that Smith belongs to one sort of counter-culture or another, but which? By extension, how should readers think about Johnson's appropriations of Orientalist themes in his work?[13] While it may initially seem like he is a one-of-a-kind writer, his work fits well into a number of sub-traditions of American writing. Rudolph P. Byrd in his excellent article "*Oxherding Tale* and *Siddhartha*: Philosophy, Fiction, and the Emergence of a Hidden Tradition" recognises the achievement of Johnson's philosophical pluralism and aesthetic cross-fertilisation, but the broadly ecumenical value systems implicit in Johnson's work make it seem odd that the hidden tradition that Byrd delineates is almost entirely black. "Inaugurated and dominated by male authors," Byrd writes, "this tradition of adapting complex philosophical systems—Platonism, Eastern Philosophy, Continental Philosophy, Christianity, and psychoanalytic theory—to construct a coherent fictional universe seems to be, with the exception of selected novels by John Gardner and Rebecca Goldstein, the sole province of African American writers" (Byrd 316).[14] In following the lead of Johnson's essay "Black Philosophical Fiction" (which Johnson developed into his book length argument *Being and Race: Black Writing since 1970*), Byrd leaves us with the impression that African-American authors delve into comparative philosophy more than European-American authors do. While Johnson is an academically trained philosopher, many authors will come to mind who mix ideas from various disciplines and traditions.

Ursula Le Guin, who has recently translated the *Tao-te Ching* and who uses Buddhist and Taoist themes in her work, fits the category of "philosophical novelist" as well as Octavia Butler, whom Johnson discusses in "A Sangha by Another Name" for her use of Buddhist themes in her science fiction trilogy (45).

One could arrange Johnson (or any of the writers mentioned) into any number of possible traditions, and this sort of multi-valence is one criteria for arguing that one writer is more important than another, but to identify a racially organised subtradition bespeaks a wish to racially separate rather than integrate authors, and thus it could be argued that Johnson is not best read as a "black philosophical novelist," even though he has written several essays on this tradition. Rather, we might better consider that the *contribution* made by African-American authors such as Johnson to the American tradition of cross-cultural philosophical and religious exchange has not been sufficiently recognised. The tradition in which I wish to contextualise Johnson is anything but hidden. We slight Johnson's achievement as a literary integrationist if we fail to see that by reincarnating the dharma bum within the context of the Civil Rights Movement he has imaginatively integrated the largely white male Beat tradition in American literature.

The dharma bum as America's postwar trickster plays havoc with supposedly firm lines of identity at every opportunity. Cynical and street-smart, Smith insists to his face that King's "dream" of equality is a pipe dream. After serving and getting wounded in the Korean war, he spends time in Japan and Southeast Asia, including one year in a zendo, where he claims to have been an adept monk: "I stayed in the East, sorta like being an exile, till I healed" (35). He reports that his teacher found his meditation "correct" and that all the other monks were impressed with his ability, so much so that he was made the cook, a highly esteemed position within the ranks of Sôtô Zen.[15] He is also an artist who has produced highly accomplished paintings (though he remains dissatisfied with them). Like the dharma bums of Beat literature, he has traveled in Asia, studied Buddhist meditation, and is serious about art.

However, Smith's counter-cultural lifestyle is also a road to pain. Smith is occasionally capable of great selflessness, such as when he marries a woman named Juanita so that her sons will not grow up fatherless. When, suddenly, she and the children are murdered, the novel does not say by whom, but there is a strong suspicion that Smith killed them. The police find Smith in a semi-amnesiac state after Smith's family has been killed, but they lack sufficient evidence to prosecute (39). Smith is simultaneously a Zen hero, a rebellious artist, and a miserable wretch who may have killed his wife and her children. He is sometimes the sort of bohemian street-bodhisattva praised by Kerouac in his 1958 roman à clef *Dharma Bums*, although the connection between antinomian freedom and the painful side of drugs and criminality is explored more responsibly than in much Beat literature of this period.[16]

Like Alan Watts' Beat Zen, the dharma according to Smith has less to do with conventional morality than most Asian Buddhists would expect. Shortly after saving Bishop's life, as Smith does when Bishop, at a street demonstration, takes the rhetoric of "brotherhood" more seriously than he should, Smith torches his apartment to spite the landlord who evicts him. Smith's presence at one point inspires the usually timid Bishop to "go ballistic" in a diner. When the employee Arlene refers to King as "Dr. Coon"(71) and places change on the counter rather than make contact with Bishop's brown skin, the ordinarily docile young man trashes the room as if he were Christ among the money-changers. Smith, delighted to see Bishop show such manly anger, brings Bishop to question the habitual patterns of his life, but in the process he certainly subverts King's non-violence directives. Smith also angers other characters. Amy, the granddaughter of egoless Mama, says she would like to hit Smith because of his arrogance, except that that would be like hitting Rev. King. Smith provokes dualistic distinction quite regularly.

In the first half of the novel, Smith is always envious of King and hungry for the recognition that King receives, insisting he can do anything King can do, only better. When King, worn down by an exhausting schedule, suggests that

Smith go to a church to receive a reward for him, Smith is eager to play the role. It seems like Smith will put his talents to good use on this evening, but then, just before driving him to the church, Bishop catches Smith injecting himself with heroin. Even though he has injected himself with narcotics, he becomes sick with stage fright. Surprisingly, the actual performance is stunningly good, and Bishop is impressed with what Smith has pulled from within himself—but then Bishop learns that *King* arrived at the last minute to give his rousing sermon. Smith, like a frustrated Cain, is forced to acknowledge that his gifts are less valuable than those of King, who overflows with grace even when he is supposed to be too exhausted to speak. However much Smith may have valorised himself in his own estimation as a rebel or outsider, Smith's vanity is pierced by King's brilliantly unselfconscious self-presentation. King's electrifying speech has a humbling effect on Smith: "Smith watched with perfect, everyman impotence and awe the love and admiration showered on his famous twin, seeing the Good but powerless to be it, lost in his littleness, and to me it seemed King's double was undergoing a kind of living death in the great man's presence"(142).

Waking Cain

In Johnson's Buddhist revision of the Genesis story, Cain undergoes a symbolic death when he is confronted with his own difference from the beloved Abel. At just this point, midway through the novel, Johnson retells the story of Cain and Abel: Bishop, while taking a long train ride, reads an academic study of the Cain mythos.[17] In a world divided into predators and prey, the Abelites of this world are, in Bishop's summary, "dinner." Abel has God's blessing, but Cain, as the more dramatic figure, has garnered more attention, has evolved through the course of Western literature, and has received increasingly sympathetic treatment by Romantic and post-Romantic writers. Bishop begins to see "the tortured shadow of Cain everywhere" (161) and to understand Cain as a "metaphysical revolutionary": "His war was with God, the Father who spurned him. Of the two—him and Abel—only Cain possessed subjectivity. A complex inner life. It was said that Western man himself was Cain, cursed with the burden of restlessness and the endless quest for selfhood" (161).

In the second half of the novel, beginning after King's speech that was so humbling for Smith, something happens that changes the course of Smith's life. When Smith and Bishop prepare to sneak out through a back door, a man mistakes Smith for King and asks to speak with him. Bishop insists that time is short, but Smith (doing a wonderful imitation of King) offers the man a ride home and gives the man truly comforting counsel all the way. The problem: the man, who is himself an envious and jealous Cain-figure, believes a flashy minister *like* King (Johnson is careful never to allege that King himself ever had adulterous affairs) has become involved with his wife. The man has deviously gotten close to "King" in order to attempt revenge. When the jealous husband takes out a gun and shoots Smith, who survives the attack but is altered by it, Johnson poetically suggests that *all* Cainite division, hatred, and violence flow from cases of "mistaken identity"—if we saw our interdependence clearly, violence would never arise in the first place.

Having actually proved himself able to serve King, Smith begins to flourish as a human being. In an echo of Mark 10:45, Smith has finally had a chance to serve rather than be served, "to give his life as a ransom for many." Subsequently, he is less cynical and self-serving, he begins voluntarily to help those around him, and, as he learns to serve, he begins to physically resemble Martin Luther King *less*. After the shooting and recovery, Smith—who previously quipped to Bishop that blacks were outsiders who would *never* be able to fit into the larger community—settles into a small rundown church to help mend its communal spirit. Smith now influences Bishop in entirely positive ways. As Smith evolves spiritually, he lectures Bishop about Buddhist emptiness and even teaches him Tai Chi Chuan (183). The new Smith is much less an excluded "racial shadow" and instead becomes a teacher who helps Bishop develop self-understanding. This momentary happy period in Smith's life is the calm before the storm.

Confusion multiplies as King's assassination draws nearer. Just before King is assassinated, Smith is picked up by some F.B.I. agents who have knowledge of his prior crimes (such as the arson) and who want to use this information to press him into some sort of service that will damage King. Confusingly, Smith agrees to cooperate with the F.B.I. to betray King even though, readers have been led to think, he has undergone some kind of transmutation. Furthermore, despite the numerous links within the novel between Smith and Cain, Smith is *not* directly implicated in King's assassination. Leaving readers to wonder in this manner, *Dreamer* recapitulates the confusion and suspicion Americans have been left with since King's death. When someone at the funeral asks where Smith is, Bishop responds that he is "everywhere."

More confusing still: Bishop, who is writing an insider's history of the Civil Right's Movement, ponders whether Smith's biography will be a "gospel"(102). Bishop's sanctification of Smith is equivalent to writing the life story of Judas Iscariot and calling *that* a gospel, since "Christ betrayed" is inseparable from "Mankind redeemed"—but Christian "fortunate Fall" theology usually stops short of appreciating Judas in this way. Neither a strictly Christian nor a strictly Buddhist interpretation of the novel will work: Bishop presents Smith, within the novel's hybrid Christian-Buddhist framework, as a paradoxical savior. The simultaneity of his fallenness and his emptiness (of inherently fallen nature) gives Bishop hope. The theological dimension of the Cain mythos is investigated in chapter eight: understood as a Wholeness from which man separates himself through pride, the God of the Old Testament seems less capricious about accepting Abel's gifts while rejecting those of Cain. "Accepting the gifts" follows from Abel not seeing himself as separate from God, whereas Cain gives only to alter his relationship with a God from whom he suffers separation: the harder he tries, the wider the gulf between him and God becomes. This sounds like a Buddhist solution to a Judeo-Christian problem, but, working against the grain to achieve an integration of spiritual value systems, Johnson puts just this exegesis into the mouth of the Christian preacher Littleton:

> I can't believe our Lord is unfair. Remember, it is because He loves the brother who kills that He marks him so no man will do him harm, and it appears none did, for nowhere in the Bible are we told that he dies. And does not God say to the elder brother after rejecting his gift that if thou does well, shalt thou not be accepted? Long ago, in ancient times, the elder brother's name was interpreted to mean 'possession,' and I believe his sacrifice was intended not to honor the Creator but to glorify himself, to win the Lord's favor like a trophy, or an ornament he might wear (157).

Put in a Christian vocabulary, Cain is guilty of idolatry. Considered through a *Buddhist* vocabulary, Cain might be said to have karmic attachments which obscure his recognition of God (meaning, actually, his felt oneness with God).[18] Whichever vocabulary we choose, the Cain story is fable of the disastrous consequences of selfishness, but the retelling in *Dreamer* stresses that the judgment upon Cain is not immutable. Cain, if he can overcome his selfishness, can "doeth well" (236).

Only if we reinterpret the Cain and Abel myth as a story of Cain's story as a tragedy of self-misrecognition do Bishop's twin claims at King's funeral, that Smith is "everywhere" and that *we* killed King, make any sense at all. We metaphysical revolutionarics and celebrants of difference are responsible for the "death of Abel." This failure to honor unity more than division is the chief target of Johnson's nonfictional essay, "The King We Left Behind" (to which we will return).

Smith is also "everywhere" in a positive rather than a dreadful sense, since all beings, empty of any particular permanent nature, reflect the *struggle for* the good (which we associate with Smith) as well as the *achievement of* the good (which we associate with King). The opportunities to struggle for a less divisive world are "everywhere."[19] Smith is never just a simplified version of Cain. At the end of the novel, he is a Cain who has caught at least a glimpse of the goodness of Abel. As he goes off with the F.B.I. men, Smith does not ask whether he is his brother's keeper; he asks Bishop to pray for him, which Bishop does: "I wept for my counterfeit, fatherless status, gave myself over to it shamelessly, and by the end of my halting, stumbling appeal I felt emptied, no longer trying to bring a distant God's grace to my finite desires as His cast-aside son, but only wishing, *Thy will be done*" (214). The emptied self might at first appear to signify exhaustion or vanity, but the opposite is the case. Early in the novel Bishop reports feeling alienated from his Bible (54), but at the moment of Smith's non-violent acquiescence to his fate Bishop is reconciled: the Lord's Prayer, in Bishop's enunciation, functions as a Buddhist shrine offering. "Emptied" is honorific in the narrative's Buddhist manner, as Bishop at this moment is recognising the teacher (meaning Smith, not King) through the teacher's actions rather than through the teacher's faults. In Smith, Bishop recognises a reflection of the divine within the body of a decidedly non-saintly black man. This Abelite recognition does not come easily in our Cainite world of difference, as the author of Hebrews suggests when he acknowledges that many will overlook the virtues of Melchizedek: "Of whom we have many things to say, and hard to be uttered, seeing ye are dull of hearing" (5:11).

Lifting the "Curse of Canonisation"

Having undergone a transformation after the assassination attempt, Smith ceases to be a Cain-figure and is several times compared to Melchizedek, the exemplary priest who briefly appears in Genesis and Psalms but who is mainly remembered for eight references in Hebrews.[20] The author of Hebrews presents him as a type of Christ, and so the Melchizedek references in *Dreamer* link back to King's whispered "Sweet Jesus" upon first meeting Smith. Another of the few facts of his life is that he is "fatherless"—like Smith and Bishop. Bishop initially compares Smith to the Biblical priest in an expression of shock at the difference between this man and King, but, like King's whispered epithet, the reference turns out to be prophetic. Genesis glosses Melchizedek as "king of righteousness" and "king of peace." Johnson's punning echolocation finds the equality of King and Smith, since Smith (as Melchizedek) is a "king" (*Harper's* 625). As Chaym is a form of Cain, which in Hebrew leads to "metalworker," Chaym Smith is both a king and a smith—part royalty and part bluecollar everyman.[21] His transformation from doomed wanderer to a type of Melchizedek closes the distance between Bishop and the King who seems utterly beyond reach. Johnson shows, through a tangled web of names and allusions, that King, Smith, Melchizedek, and Christ all partake of one another. Bishop learns that Smith, short of "the Galilean mark" though he is, "might sometimes—and occasionally—doeth well"(236). In other words, Smith is not damned for all time, even if he is, currently, down-and-out. In *Dreamer* King is at all times a figure of inspiration for Bishop, but it is a sign of Bishop's deepening understanding of King's dream that *Smith* becomes a source of inspiration.

Bishop learns to overcome his "ontological fear" until otherness is understood as a temporary phase rather than an essential quality. Bishop strikingly compares Smith to Christ early in *Dreamer*, thinking "of that ancient Christian story of the couple who found a bedraggled old man at their door, invited him inside, fed and comforted him, and only after their guest left discovered he was the Nazarene" (41). Be nice to the stranger *just in case* the stranger is Christ in disguise? No: the way that Bishop learns is to love the stranger, the other, the guest, or "the embodiment of the blues" precisely because he *is* Christ. In whichever vocabulary Johnson expresses the idea, the emptiness of any particular self of inherent, unchanging meaning is the opening that engenders compassion.

Smith is also the bridge connecting the too-saintly King back to the fallen world of contemporary American identity politics, and this too is signaled by the Melchizedek reference. Hebrews is a letter by an early Christian to a group of "Jewish Christians," but the writer is especially concerned that the people he addresses are backsliding into Judaic practices and beliefs. The writer who exhorts these Jews to have faith in the New Covenant and to abandon the old ways is often impatient with his readers, even calling them slow learners (5:11). By analogy, Johnson is addressing Americans who have heard King's "gospel," but have subsequently fallen back from King's vision of selfless commonality into an erroneous practice of separatist race pride.[22] Johnson's sentiments in "The King We Left Behind" directly parallel those of Bishop at the end of *Dreamer*. As the author of Hebrews uses Melchizedek to chastise the transitional Jewish Christians he addresses, Bishop calls Americans to task for exploiting racial division for personal gain. Bishop is especially angered by the claim (attributed in *Dreamer* to Andrew Young) that, "when King fell on that balcony, Jesse Jackson covered his palms with the minister's blood, wiped them on his sweater; then the next day he flew to Chicago to appear bloodstained before the press, declaring he'd held a dying King in his arms"(233).[23] Johnson and Bishop both express disgust at the vanity of contemporary American politics. Still thinking of Jesse Jackson's bloody theatrics, Bishop notes the reference to Mark 10:35 during the playing of a taperecording of King's sermon "The Drum Major Instinct." In this sermon, "James and John, the sons of Zebedee, approach Jesus with their desire to sit beside him in Glory" (233), even though their rightful place is elsewhere. Jesse Jackson, this textual collage suggests, has shown himself as hungry for honor as the sons of Zebedee. The obscure Melchizedek reference becomes quite pointed when we realise that Johnson is calling Americans slow learners for failing to judge African-American political leadership rightly.

Johnson complains in "The King We Left Behind" that the authentic King has been replaced by a hollow fake: "Without our consciously rejecting him, he has been left behind. In a way, images of King have never been more ubiquitous, but his vision suffers from the curse of canonisation" (Byrd 194). The most superficial aspects of King's life have been valorised in public memory, such as when we hear replays of the "I Have a Dream" speech on the radio every January 15th, but King's more searching call for Americans to find ways to overcome iniquity and division have been ignored. Johnson also bristles at the way cultural nationalism has stepped into the void left by King's assassination: Eldridge Cleaver, Huey Newton, and Malcolm X are for Johnson "the true spiritual fathers of today's Crips and Bloods"(195). Citing the "scandal of Afrocentrists," Johnson reviles the anti-Semitism and spurious racial mythology of "ice people" and "sun people" (196). Like Bishop at the end of *Dreamer*, who claims to the annoyance of Amy that "we all" are responsible for King's death (234), Johnson blames America *en masse* for having lost sight of King's healing vision: "each and every one of us is an apostate. We are all responsible for this sea change in race relations, and the substitution of the 'beloved community' with 'identity politics'" (Byrd 196).

While the Melchizedek comparison is on the one hand a prophet's cry against apostates, it also insists on the continuing validity of King's "good news." The Smith who was a self-regarding egotist with a "drum major instinct" overcame himself, at least for a while, and this King-inspired self-overcoming is precisely what brings Bishop to think of Smith as "a priest in the order of Melchizedek." Though Bishop struggles to gather enough confidence to express this vision to others, his growth in the novel has been to learn how, figuratively speaking, King survives his own assassination. While King is alive Bishop never once doubts King. Speaking of himself in the first paragraph of the book, Bishop states to the reader that he has "the eloquence of neither Guido the Angelic nor Teresa of Avila, and so with each halting sentence I pray for words to demonstrate how this was the beginning of the northern crusade to undo the work of the Devil" (13).[24] Initially Bishop doubts his own capacity to write his insider's history of the Civil Rights Movement, but through a cross-fertilisation of Buddhist and Christian typological thinking Bishop learns to patch together the teachings of King *and* Smith in a way that makes sense. Only then can Bishop be expected to extend the ministry. If Smith (as a fatherless man outside of orthodox priesthoods) is a type of Melchizedek, and if Christ is a type of Melchizedek, then Smith is also a type of Christ.

Bishop's "gospel" concerning the Smith/King interaction becomes a compelling alternative to the "canonised King" of American civic religion. Bishop's testament—his gospel of the life of King-and-Smith—boldly reinterprets King's life in recognisably Buddhist terms, but in a way that actualises both Christian and Buddhist understanding, since its allusive and narrative strategies highlight the "inescapable network of mutuality" in ways that question the gap between Christian *agape* and Buddhist *shunyata*. Buddhist-Christian dialogue in the novel metaphorically represents other kinds of dialogue, as

Johnson's poetics of integration foregrounds the ways in which all identities *must* rely on other identities. Nor is this reliance a form of abject dependence: the absence of inherent selfhood engenders compassion and creates the possibility of "beloved community," since "each of us has a secret the other needs to learn." Paraphrasing Merleau-Ponty, Johnson writes that "You can see my social back as I cannot. I can see your social back, and we move together towards enlightenment and completion, because we all do have different perspectives. But they do complement and qualify each other" (Little 3).

Notes

1. Johnson quotes King from "A Christmas Sermon on Peace," delivered at the Ebenezer Baptist Church on Christmas Eve, 1967, published in King's *The Trumpet of Conscience* and republished in *A Testament of Hope: The Essential Writings and Speeches of Martin Luther King, Jr.* (254).
2. See Jonathan Little's excellent overview of the discipline-crossing nature of integration in Johnson's work "The Integrative Imagination" (3-8) in the first book-length study of this writer, *Charles Johnson's Spiritual Imagination.*
3. The full sentence from *Oxherding Tale* is spoken by the character Andrew Hawkins: "Although nearly anything you said about slavery could be denied in the same breath, this much struck me as true: the wretchedness of being colonised was not that slavery created feelings of guilt and indebtedness, though I did feel guilt and debt; nor that it created a long, lurid dream of multiplicity and separateness, which it did indeed create, but the fact that men had epidermalised Being" (52).
4. When we think of American authors who work seriously with Asian philosophy and religion, we usually consider Gary Snyder, Allen Ginsberg, Jack Kerouac, and other Beat writers. Charles Johnson is not widely known as a Buddhist writer, but he has written regularly for the Buddhist quarterly *Tricycle: the Buddhist Review* (vol. IX, no. 2; vol X, no. 1), and he has recently published a brief essay on meditation for the *Chronicle of Higher Education* entitled "The Elusive Art of Mindfulness."
5. The division between the novelist and the historian's King is an important one to all readers of *Dreamer*, particularly when we consider Johnson's biting critique of "the curse of canonisation" in his essay "The King We Left Behind." I will address this issue in another essay.
6. Johnson presents Christian dualism as a fact of the world with which his King must struggle. In non-fictional writings such as his

essay on African-American Buddhism "A Sangha by Another Name," Johnson acknowledges the significance of the black church in America but also, as a Buddhist writer, indicates the "otherness" of philosophical dualism, insofar as it is a quality of the West and not the East, of the Christian and not the Buddhist: Historically, no other institution's influence compares with that of the black church, and I believe it will continue to be the dominant spiritual orientation of black Americans. It provides a compelling and time-tested moral vision, a metaphysically dualistic one that partitions the world into good and evil, heaven and hell; posits an immortal soul that no worldly suffering can harm; and through the agapic love of a merciful Father promises in the afterlife rewards denied in this one. Christianity, in part, made black Americans a genuinely Western people, on the whole identical in their strivings and sense of how the world works with Northern Europeans in the Judeo-Christian tradition. ("A Sangha" 45)

7. The possibility of a fully integrated selflessness, usually discussed in relation to religious practices such as those of Buddhism or Christianity as presented by mystics such as Meister Eckhart, is indicated by the word "nonduality." The difficulty of defining philosophical nondualism is discussed fully in David Loy's *Nonduality: A Study in Comparative Philosophy*. Simply put, nonduality is the "nondifference of subject and object" (Loy 25), which is to say that it is the experience of a "self" that has shifted dramatically beyond our skin-bound sense of self. Loy quotes the following sentence from Dôgen: "I came to realise clearly that mind is not other than mountains, rivers, and the great wide earth, the sun and the moon and the stars"(25). The self Dôgen writes about (or from) does not exclude elements we would typically designate as "other," such as the earth and sky. It would appear that, from the nondual point of view, you are what you see.
8. The chapters in *Dreamer* which focus on King as opposed to Smith (prologue and chapters two, four, and twelve) are italicised.
9. While direct quotations from *Dreamer* follow Johnson in citing the King James' version, the apparatus in the *NIV Study Bible* has been quite useful in the writing of this essay. As I am primarily concerned with *Johnson's* King, I do not here enter into a full discussion of King's theology. See Leo Erskine's *King Among the Theologians*.
10. See Matthew 16:21ff.
11. Galatians 3:28: "There is neither Jew nor Greek, there is neither bond nor free, there is neither male nor female: for ye are all one in Christ Jesus." King echoes this passage in "A Christmas Sermon on Peace" when he says "One day somebody should remind us that, even though there may be political and ideological differences between us, the Vietnamese are our brothers, the Russians are our brothers, the Chinese are our brothers; and one day we've got to

sit down together at the table of brotherhood. But in Christ there is neither Jew nor Gentile" (King 255). We note that King does not say all people exist in brotherhood *if and only if* they convert to Christianity, and this non-exclusivity is the ground on which Buddhist-Christian dialogue may take place. To see as Christ sees—that is, to see in a way that does not reify differences—is to perceive nondually. To assert, however, that only *Christians* can see in this way is inherently dualistic. Buddhist-Christian dialogue tends to occur between those Buddhists who can find room in their vocabularies for "God" and between those Christians who do *not* insist that, as it were, only Christians can see "as Christ sees." The historical King, as Johnson points out in fiction and non-fictional statements, was committed to a non-exclusivist spirituality, even though he was also committed to the work of Christian conversion.

12. On Johnson and the liberation of perception, see William Gleason's "The Liberation of Perception: Charles Johnson's *Oxherding Tale.*"
13. Johnson gives a nice summary of his attempts to develop fiction from a Buddhist point of view: "according to the Buddhist philosophy of no-self, you recognise emptiness (*shunyata*) as the ultimate nature of reality. In my own fiction, I have worked to dramatise that insight in novels such as *Oxherding Tale* (1982), a slave narrative that serves as the vehicle for exploring Eastern philosophy; *Middle Passage* (1990), a sea adventure tale about the slave trade (and a rather Buddhist African tribe called the Allmuseri); and *Dreamer* (1998), a fictional account of the last two years of Martin Luther King's life that highlights his globally ecumenical spirituality" ("A Sangha" 111).
14. First published in the *African American Review* (Volume 30, Number 4), Byrd's essay is reprinted in *I Call Myself an Artist*.
15. At least since Dôgen's writings in the 13th century, the tenzo (cook), a supposedly lowly role, has been revered within the Zendo. See Dôgen's "Instructions for the Tenzo." In the Zen monastery, this position of honor reflects well on the sincerity of his practice, although he *is* later dismissed from the temple because he is a black man and a *gaijin*—which teaches Smith that even the supposedly enlightened Zen Master can still be a fully-flawed human being.
16. Chaym Smith recalls the romantic individualism of Japhy Ryder more than the inhibition of Ray Smith, though it can still be said that *Dharma Bums* and *Dreamer* both center on a dyad of characters: an ideal, quasi-enlightened character exists in counterpoint to a wayward person named "Smith."
17. Bishop's reading of a study about Cain in the mid-1960s might be Johnson's (anachronistic) homage to Ricardo J. Quinones's *The Changes of Cain: Violence and the Lost Brother in Cain and Abel Literature*. Johnson thanks Quinones on *Dreamer*'s acknowledgements page for calling his attention to the book.

18. Cain's error is in his understanding of his relationship with the divine. The *NIV Study Bible* glosses Genesis 4:3–4 as follows: "The contrast is not between an offering of plant life and an offering of animal life, but between a careless, thoughtless offering and a choice, generous offering.... Motivation and heart attitude are all-important, and God looked with favor on Abel and his offering because of Abel's faith (Heb 11:4)" (*NIV* 11).
19. To say in a Christian context that everyone killed Christ is another way of saying *because of our sin*, he died. When Bishop says everyone killed King, he interprets King's assassination as a voluntary offering of self meant to heal the painful sense of division afflicting "everyone." Self offering to benefit others is valued equally in Christianity and Buddhism.
20. Depending on the translation: *NIV* has eight, the *New King James* nine. Melchizedek is described as an exact likeness of Christ in the *New King James*: Melchizedek is called "A Picture of Christ" in the header to Hebrews 7.
21. Glossed in the *Harper's Bible Dictionary*, "Smith" directs readers to a reference in *Sirach* (also called *Ecclesiasticus*) 38:28: "The smith also sitting by the anvil, and considering the iron work, the vapour of the fire wasteth his flesh, and he fighteth with the heat of the furnace: the noise of the hammer and the anvil is ever in his ears, and his eyes look still upon the pattern of the thing that he maketh; he setteth his mind to finish his work, and watcheth to polish it perfectly...." A prototypical metal smith in this text is a careless person, but the passage praises the fastidious man who surpasses expectation.
22. For a study concluding 1) that the 1960s Race Pride Movement has made America more inclusive than ever but 2) that "[t]hose who hope for a more just society will have to look beyond Race Pride" (127), see Joseph Tilden Rhea's *Race Pride and the American Identity*.
23. In his text to *King: The Photobiography of Martin Luther King, Jr.*, Johnson speaks of the achievements of Jackson as King's loyal and hardworking lieutenant.
24. The reference to "Guido" is a printer's error and should read "Guigo." In a private communication to the author Johnson has written that There was a moment in this novel's creation when my models were texts like Guigo's *The Ladder of Monks* and the anonymous *The Cloud of Unknowing* (especially that), treatises written by men of the cloth or contemplatives for young spiritual aspirants. That reference on the first page, and the novel's last line, were intended to echo that obscure and almost unknown (today) tradition. E-mail from Charles Johnson to John Whalen-Bridge, 24 July 2000.

Works Cited

Byrd, Rudolph P. "*Oxherding Tale* and *Siddhartha*: Philosophy, Fiction, and the Emergence of a Hidden Tradition." *I Call Myself an Artist: Writings By and About Charles Johnson.* Ed. Charles Richard Johnson and Rudolph P. Byrd. Bloomington: Indiana University Press, 1999.

Dôgen. "Instructions for the Tenzo." *Moon in a Dewdrop*: *Writings of Zen Master Dôgen.* Ed. Kazuaki Tanahashi. Trans. Arnold Kotler and Kazuaki Tanahashi. San Francisco: North Point Press, 1985. 53-66.

Erskine, Leo. *King Among the Theologians*. Foreword by Bernice A. King. Cleveland, OH: The Pilgrim Press, 1994.

Gleason, William. "The Liberation of Perception: Charles Johnson's *Oxherding Tale*." *Black American Literature Forum* 25.4 (1991): 705-26.

The Harper's Bible Dictionary. Ed. Paul J. Achtemeier *et al.* San Francisco: Harper and Row, 1985.

Johnson, Charles. *Being and Race: Black Writing since 1970.* Bloomington: University of Indiana Press, 1988.

_______ *Dreamer.* New York: Scribners, 1998.

_______ "The Elusive Art of Mindfulness." *The Chronicle Review* (April 13, 2001): B10-12.

_______ *King: The Photobiography of Martin Luther King, Jr.* New York: Viking Press, 2000.

_______ *Oxherding Tale.* New York: Plume, 1995.

_______ "A Sangha by Another Name." *Tricycle: the Buddhist Review* 9 (Winter 1999): 43-47, 110-13.

Kerouac, Jack. *Dharma Bums*. New York: Penguin, 1991.

King, Martin Luther, Jr. *A Testament of Hope: The Essential Writings and Speeches of Martin Luther King, Jr.* Ed. James M. Washington. San Francisco: Harper Collins, 1986.

Little, Jonathan. *Charles Johnson's Spiritual Imagination.* Columbia: University of Missouri Press, 1997.

Loy, David. *Nonduality: A Study in Comparative Philosophy.* Amherst, New York: Humanity Books, 1998.

NIV Study Bible [*NIV*]. Ed. Kenneth Barker *et al.* Grand Rapids: Zondervan Publishing House, 1995.

Quinones, J. *The Changes of Cain: Violence and the Lost Brother in Cain and Abel Literature.* Princeton, NJ: Princeton University Press, 1991.

Rhea, Joseph Tilden. *Race Pride and the American Identity.* Cambridge: Harvard University Press, 1997.

Wong, Sau-ling Cynthia. *Reading Asian American Literature; From Necessity to Extravagance.* Princeton: Princeton University Press, 1993.

7

The End of the Black American Narrative

— *Charles Johnson*

> It is ambition enough to be employed as an under-labourer in clearing the ground a little, and removing some of the rubbish that lies in the way of knowledge.
>
> —John Locke, *An Essay Concerning Human Understanding*

> Back to the things themselves!
>
> —Edmund Husserl

As a writer, philosopher, artist, and black American, I've devoted more than 40 years of my life to trying to understand and express intellectually and artistically different aspects of the black American narrative. At times during my life, especially when I was young, it was a story that engaged me emotionally and consumed my imagination. I've produced novels, short stories, essays, critical articles, drawings and PBS dramas based on what we call the black American story. To a certain degree, teaching the literature of black America has been my bread and butter as a college professor. It is a very old narrative, one we all know quite well, and it is a tool we use, consciously or unconsciously, to interpret or to make sense of everything that has happened to black people in this country since the arrival of the first 20 Africans at the Jamestown colony in 1619. A good story always has a meaning (and sometimes layers of meaning); it also has an epistemological mission: namely, to show us something. It is an effort to make the best sense we can of the human experience, and I believe that we base our lives, actions and judgments as often on the stories we tell ourselves about ourselves (even when they are less than empirically sound or verifiable) as we do on the severe rigor of reason. This unique black American narrative, which emphasizes the experience of victimization, is quietly in the background of every conversation we have about black people, even when it is not fully articulated or expressed. It is our starting point, our agreed-upon premise, our most important presupposition for dialogues about black America. We teach it in our classes, and it is the foundation for both our scholarship and our popular entertainment as they relate to black Americans. Frequently it is the way we approach each other as individuals.

As a writer and a teacher of writing, I have to ask myself over and over again, just what *is* a story. How do we shape one? How many different forms can it take? What do stories tell us about our world? What details are necessary, and which ones are unimportant for telling it well? I constantly ask my creative writing students two questions: Does the story work, technically? And, if so, then, what does it *say*? I tell them that, like a work of philosophy (which is the sister discipline to storytelling among the interpretive arts), a narrative vision must have the qualities of coherence, consistency, and completeness. The plot of a modern story must be streamlined and efficient if it is to be easily understood. And, like Edgar Allan Poe in his 1842 essay "On the Aim and the Technique of the Short Story," I argue that a dramatic narrative should leave the listener with "a certain unique or single effect" that has emotional power. For the last 32 years, I've stressed to my students that a story must have a conflict that is clearly presented, one that we care about, a dilemma or disequilibrium for the protagonist that we, as readers, emotionally identify with. The black American story, as we tell it to ourselves, beautifully embodies all these narrative virtues.

The story begins with violence in the 17th-century slave forts sprinkled along the West coast of Africa, where debtors, thieves, war prisoners and those who would not convert to Islam were separated from their families, branded, and sold to Europeans who packed them into the pestilential ships that cargoed 20 million human beings (a conservative estimate) to the New World. Only 20 percent of those slaves survived the harrowing voyage at sea (and only 20 percent of the sailors, too), and if they were among the lucky few to set foot on American soil, new horrors and heartbreak awaited them.

As has been documented time and again, the life of a slave—our not-so-distant ancestors—was one of thinghood. Former languages, religions, and cultures were erased, replaced by the Peculiar Institution, in which the person of African descent was property, and systematically—legally, physically, and culturally—denied all sense of self-worth. A slave owns nothing, least of all himself. He desires and dreams at the risk of his life, which is best described as relative to (white) others, a reaction to their deeds, judgments, and definitions of the world. And these definitions, applied to blacks, were not kind. For 244 years (from 1619 to 1863), America was a slave state with a guilty conscience: two and a half centuries scarred by slave revolts, heroic black (and abolitionist) resistance to oppression, and, more than anything else, physical, spiritual, and psychological suffering so staggering it silences the mind when we study the classic slave narratives of Equiano or Frederick Douglass. Legal bondage, the peculiar antebellum world, ended during the Civil War, but the Emancipation Proclamation did not bring liberation.

Legal freedom instead gradually brought segregation, America's version of apartheid. But "separate" clearly was not "equal." Black Americans were not simply segregated; they were methodically disenfranchised, stripped of their rights as citizens. From the 1890s through the 1950s, the law of black life was experienced as second-class citizenship. In the century after the Emancipation Proclamation, members of each generation of black Americans saw their lives disrupted by race riots, lynchings, and the destruction of towns and communities, such as the Greenwood district of black homes, businesses, and churches in Tulsa, Oklahoma, on May 31, 1921. The challenge for black America and the conflict for its story, then, was how to force a nation that excluded black people from its promise of "Life, liberty and the pursuit of happiness" after the Revolutionary War, and failed to redress this grievance after Reconstruction, to honor these principles enshrined in its most sacred documents.

What I have described defines the general shape of the black American group narrative before the beginning of the Civil Rights Movement, the most important and transformative domestic event in American history after the War between the States. The conflict of this story is first slavery, then segregation and legal disenfranchisement. The meaning of the story is group victimisation, and every black person is the story's protagonist. This specific story was not about ending racism, which would be a wonderful thing; but ending racism entirely is probably as impossible for human beings as ending crime, or as quixotic as President Bush's "war on terror." No, the black American story was not as vague as that. It had a clearly defined conflict. And our ancestors fought *daily* for generations, with courage and dignity, to change this narrative. That was the *point* of their lives, their sacrifices, each and every day they were on this earth. We cannot praise enough the miracle they achieved, the lifelong efforts of our leaders and the anonymous men and women who kept the faith, demonstrated, went to jail, registered black people to vote in the Deep South, changed unjust laws, and died in order that Americans of all backgrounds might be free. I have always seen their fight for us as noble.

Among those I pay special tribute to is W.E.B. Du Bois, one of the founders of the NAACP, who deeply understood the logic and structure of this narrative as it unfolded from Reconstruction through the 1950s. It was a sign of his prescience that he also could see *beyond* this ancient story while still in the midst of it and fighting mightily to change it.

In 1926, Du Bois delivered an address titled, "Criteria of Negro Art" at the Chicago Conference for the NAACP. His lecture, which was later published in *The Crisis*, the official publication of the NAACP, which Du Bois himself edited, took place during the most entrenched period of segregation, when the opportunities for black people were so painfully circumscribed. "What do we want?" he asked his audience. "What is the thing we are after?"

Listen to Du Bois 82 years ago:

> What do we want? What is the thing we are after? As it was phrased last night it had a certain truth: We want to be Americans, full-fledged Americans, with all the rights of American citizens. But is that all? Do we want simply to be Americans? Once in a while through all of us there flashes some clairvoyance, some clear idea, of what America really is. We who are dark can see America in a way that white Americans cannot. And seeing our country thus, are we satisfied with its present goals and ideals?...
>
> If you tonight suddenly should become full-fledged Americans; if your color faded, or the color line here in Chicago was miraculously forgotten; suppose, too, you became at the same time rich and powerful;—what is it that you would want? What would you immediately seek? Would you buy the most powerful of motor cars and outrace Cook County? Would you buy the most elaborate estate on the North Shore? Would you be a Rotarian or a Lion or a What-not of the very last degree? Would you wear the most striking clothes, give the richest dinners, and buy the longest press notices?
>
> Even as you visualise such ideals you know in your heart that these are not the things you really want. You realise this sooner than the average white American because, pushed aside as we have been in America, there has come to us not only a certain distaste for the tawdry and flamboyant but a vision of what the world could be if it were really a beautiful world; if we had the true spirit; if we had the Seeing Eye, the Cunning Hand, the Feeling Heart; if we had, to be sure, not perfect happiness, but plenty of good hard work, the inevitable suffering that comes with life; sacrifice and waiting, all that—but, nevertheless, lived in a world where men know, where men create, where they realise themselves and where they enjoy life. It is that sort of world we want to create for ourselves and for all America.

This provocative passage is, in part, the foundation for my questioning the truth and usefulness of the traditional black American narrative of victimisation. When compared with black lives at the dawn of the 21st century, and 40 years after the watershed events of the Civil Rights Movement, many of Du Bois' remarks now sound ironic, for all the impossible things he spoke of in 1926 are realities today. We are "full-fledged Americans, with the rights of American citizens." We *do* have "plenty of good hard work" and live in a society where "men create, where they realise themselves and where they enjoy life." Even more ironic is the fact that some of our famous rappers and athletes who like "living large," as they say, seem obsessed with what Du Bois derisively called "the tawdry and flamboyant" (they call it "bling"). Furthermore, some of us *do* use the freedom paid for with the blood of our ancestors to pursue conspicuous consumption in the form of "powerful motor cars," "elaborate estates," "striking clothes," and "the richest dinners."

To put this another way, we can say that 40 years after the epic battles for specific civil rights in Montgomery, Birmingham, and Selma, after two monumental and historic legislative triumphs—the Civil Rights Act of 1964 and the Voting Rights Act of 1965—and after three decades of affirmative action that led to the creation of a true black middle class (and not the false one E. Franklin Frazier described in his classic 1957 study, *Black Bourgeoisie*), a people oppressed for so long have finally become, as writer Reginald McKnight once put it, "as polymorphous as the dance of Shiva." Black Americans have been CEOs at AOL Time Warner, American Express, and Merrill Lynch; we have served as secretary of state and White House national security adviser. Well over 10,000 black Americans have been elected to offices around the country, and at this moment Senator Barack Obama holds us in suspense with the possibility that he may be selected as the Democratic Party's first biracial, black American candidate for president. We have been mayors, police chiefs, best-selling authors, MacArthur fellows, Nobel laureates, Ivy League professors, billionaires, scientists, stockbrokers, engineers, theoretical physicists, toy makers, inventors, astronauts, chess grandmasters, dot-com millionaires, actors, Hollywood film directors, and talk show hosts (the most prominent among them being Oprah Winfrey, who recently signed a deal to acquire her own network); we are Protestants, Catholics, Muslims, Jews, and Buddhists (as I am). And we are not culturally homogeneous. When I last looked, West Indians constituted 48 percent of the "black" population in Miami. In America's major cities, 15 percent of the black American population is foreign born—Haitian, Jamaican, Senegalese, Nigerian, Cape Verdean, Ethiopian, Eritrean, and Somalian—a rich tapestry of brown-skinned people as culturally complex in their differences, backgrounds, and outlooks as those people lumped together under the all too convenient labels of "Asian" or "European." Many of them are doing better—in school and business—than native-born black Americans. I think often of something said by Mary Andom, an Eritrean student at Western Washington University, and quoted in an article published in 2003 in *The Seattle Times*: "I don't know about 'chitlings' or 'grits.' I don't listen to soul music artists such as Marvin Gaye or Aretha Franklin....I grew up eating *injera* and listening to *Tigrinya* music....After school, I cook the traditional coffee, called boun, by hand for my mother. It is a tradition shared amongst mother and daughter."

No matter which angle we use to view black people in America today, we find them to be a complex and multifaceted people who defy easy categorisation. We challenge, culturally and politically, an old group narrative that fails at the beginning of this new century to capture even a fraction of our rich diversity and heterogeneity. My point is not that black Americans don't have social and cultural problems in 2008. We have several nagging problems, among them poor schools and far too many black men in prison and too few in college. But these are problems based more on the inequities of class, and they appear in other groups as well. It simply is no longer the case that the essence of black American life is racial victimisation and disenfranchisement, a curse and a condemnation, a destiny based on color in which the meaning of one's life is thinghood, created even before one is born. This is not something we can assume. The specific conflict of this narrative reached its dramatic climax in 1963 in Birmingham, Alabama, and at the breathtaking March on Washington; its resolution arrived in 1965, the year before I graduated from high school, with the Voting Rights Act. Everything since then has been a coda for almost half a century. We call this long-extended and still ongoing anticlimax the post-civil-rights period. If the NAACP is struggling these days to recruit members of the younger generation and to redefine its mission in the 21st century—and it *is* struggling to do that—I think it is a good sign that the organisation Du Bois led for so long is now a casualty of its own successes in the 1960s.

Yet, despite being an antique, the old black American narrative of pervasive victimisation persists, denying the overwhelming evidence of change since the time of my parents and grandparents, refusing to die as doggedly as the Ptolemaic vision before Copernicus or the notion of phlogiston in the 19th century, or the deductive reasoning of the medieval schoolmen. It has become ahistorical. For a time it served us well and powerfully, yes, reminding each generation of black Americans of the historic obligations and duties and dangers they inherited and faced, but the problem with any story or idea or interpretation is that it can soon fail to fit the facts and becomes an ideology, even kitsch.

This point is expressed eloquently by Susan Griffin in her 1982 essay "The Way of all Ideology," where she says, "When a theory is transformed into an ideology, it begins to destroy the self and self-knowledge....No one can tell it anything new. It is annoyed by any detail which does not fit its worldview....Begun as a way to restore one's sense of reality, now it attempts to discipline real people, to remake natural beings after its own image."

In his superb book *In My Father's House*, philosopher Kwame Anthony Appiah writes, "There is nothing in the world that can do all we ask race to do for us." We can easily amend or revise this insight and apply it to the pre-21st-century black American narrative, which can do very little of the things we need for it to do today.

But this is an enduring human problem, isn't it? As phenomenologist Edmund Husserl revealed a hundred years ago, we almost always perceive and understand the new in terms of the old—or, more precisely, we experience events through our ideas, and frequently those are ideas that bring us comfort, ideas received from our parents, teachers, the schools we attend, and the enveloping culture, rather than original ones of our own. While a story or model may disclose a particular meaning for an experience, it also forces into the background or conceals other possible meanings. Think of this in light of novelist Ralph Ellison's brilliant notion of "invisibility," where—in his classic *Invisible Man*—the characters encountered by his nameless protagonist all impose their ideologies (explanations and ideas) on the chaos of experience, on the mysterious, untamed life that forever churns beneath widely accepted interpretations and explanations of "history" and "culture," which in our social world, for Ellison, are the seen. I know, personally, there is value in this Ellisonian idea because in the historical fictions I've been privileged to publish, like "Martha's Dilemma" in my second collection, *Soulcatcher and Other Stories*, I discovered that the most intriguing, ambiguous, and revealing material for stories can often be found in the margins of the codified and often repeated narrative about slavery. In this case, I dramatised a delicious anecdote about what happened to Martha and her slaves right after the death of George.

What I am saying is that "official" stories and explanations and endlessly repeated interpretations of black American life over decades can short-circuit direct perception of the specific phenomenon before us. The idea of something—an intellectual construct—is often more appealing and perfect (in a Platonic sense) than the thing itself, which always remains mysterious and ambiguous and messy, by which I mean that its sense is open-ended, never fixed. It is always wise, I believe, to see all our propositions (and stories) as provisional, partial, incomplete, and subject to revision on the basis of new evidence, which we can be sure is just around the corner.

Nevertheless, we have heavily and often uncritically invested for most of our lives in the pre-21st-century black American narrative. In fact, some of us depend upon it for our livelihood, so it is not easy to let go, or to revise this story. Last October, Nation of Islam minister Louis Farrakhan spoke for two and a half hours at the Atlanta Civic Center. He and his mentor, black separatist Elijah Muhammad, provided black Americans with what is probably the most extreme, Manichean, and mythological version of the black American narrative, one that was anti-integrationist. In this incomplete and misleading rendition of the black American story, the races are locked in eternal struggle. As a story, this narrative fails because it is conceived as melodrama, a form of storytelling in which the characters are flat, lack complexity, are either all good or all bad, and the plot involves malicious villains and violent actions. Back in the 1930s when Elijah Muhammad shaped his myth of Yacub, which explained the origins of the white race as "devils," he sacrificed the credibility of both character and plot for the most simplistic kind of dramatic narrative. Farrakhan covered many subjects that day last October, but what I found most interesting is that he said successful black people like Oprah Winfrey, Senator Obama, Colin Powell, and Condoleeza Rice give black Americans a false impression of progress. In other words, their highly visible successes do not change the old narrative of group victimisation. Minister Farrakhan seems unwilling to accept their success as evidence that the lives of black Americans have improved. He seems unwilling to accept the inevitability of change. He was quoted in the press as saying, "A life of ease sometimes makes you forget the struggle." And despite the battles for affirmative action that created a new middle class, he added, "It's becoming a plantation again, but you can't fight that because you want to keep your little job."

I beg to differ with Farrakhan, with his misuse of language, his loose, imprecise diction, because we obviously do *not* live on plantations. And wasn't job opportunity one of the explicit goals of the black American narrative? Farrakhan's entire life has been an investment in a story that changed as he was chasing it. So we can understand his fierce, personal, and even tragic attachment to dusty, antebellum concepts when looking at the uncharted phenomena in the early 21st century that outstrip his concepts and language.

However, it is precisely because Farrakhan cannot progress beyond an oversimplified caricature of a story line for racial phenomena that the suddenly notorious Rev. Jeremiah Wright praises him, saying "His depth of analysis...when it comes to the racial ills of this nation is astounding and eye-opening," and, "He brings a perspective that is helpful and honest." Recently Wright called the Nation of Islam leader, "one of the most important voices in the 20th and 21st centur[ies]." I do not doubt that Wright and Farrakhan are men who have experienced the evil of racism and want to see the conditions of our people improve, or that both have records of community service. But it is the emotional attachment to a dated narrative, one leavened with the 1960s-era liberation theology of James Cone, that predictably leads Wright to proclaim that the U.S. government created the AIDS virus to destroy blacks (he invokes the old and proven, the ghastly Tuskegee syphilis experiment, in an effort to understand a new affliction devastating black people, and thus commits the logical fallacy known as misuse of analogy); that Jesus was "a black man"; and that the brains of blacks and whites operate differently. The former pastor of Trinity United Church of Christ in Chicago has made these paranoid and irresponsible statements publicly again and again without offering the slightest shred of evidence for these claims. "A bunch of rants that aren't grounded in truth" was how Barack Obama described his former minister's incendiary oratory, which is clearly antithetical not only to the postracial spirit of the Illinois senator's own speeches but also to his very racially and geographically mixed background. For in the realm of ideological thinking, especially from the pulpit, feeling and faith trump fact, and passion (as well as beliefs based on scripture) replaces fidelity to the empirical and painstaking logical demonstration.

Furthermore, such obsolete stories can also lead to serious mistakes in scholarship. I'm thinking now of Henry Louis Gates Jr., who in 1988 directed the publication of Oxford University Press's 40-volume *Schomburg Library of Nineteenth-Century Black Women Writers*. In his foreword, Gates praised the lost works of these black women writers as being the literary ancestors of Zora Neale Hurston, Toni Morrison, and Alice Walker. Furthermore, he said it was the discovery of a particular lost black novel, called *Four Girls at Cottage City*, published in 1895 by Emma Dunham Kelley-Hawkins, that inspired him to direct this Schomburg series in the first place so, he said, "I can read them myself."

Okay, so far so good.

But in 2005, Holly Jackson, then a doctoral student of English at Brandeis University, was given the academically pedestrian, grunt-work assignment of writing an entry about Kelley-Hawkins for the *African American National Biography*. At the time very little was known about Kelley-Hawkins. After checking birth records in the Massachusetts Vital Records, and other documents, Jackson realised that Kelley-Hawkins was not black—as five decades of scholars had assumed—but white. Yet all the evidence to suggest her whiteness was clearly present in the books she wrote. Something that had always puzzled scholars, Jackson said, was "the apparent whiteness of her characters, who are repeatedly described with blue eyes and skin as white as 'pure' or 'driven' snow." Even more fantastic are the theories that literary scholars came up with to explain why Kelley-Hawkins, supposedly a black woman, made no references to race or blackness in her two novels written in the 1890s. Jackson says, "Scholars have explained this away by arguing that the abundance of white signifiers is actually politically radical, with some even going so far as to argue that this extremely white world depicts a kind of post-racial utopia," a modern world where, according to critic Carla L. Peterson, "racial difference no longer existed."

Obviously, all these explanations are hogwash. Fifty years of scholarship based on these mistakes—articles, dissertations, courses in African American women's writing that include the work of Kelley-Hawkins—turns out to be an illusion created by the blinding intentionality of those who wrote about this white author based on a tangled knot of beliefs and prejudices, their concept of her completely distorting the facts.

Once Gates learned of this research by Jackson and also investigations by Katherine Flynn, a genealogist, he immediately went into the mode of damage control. He told a reporter that the work of Kelley-Hawkins would at least be removed from future editions of the Schomburg series, and he downplayed the significance of these discoveries by Jackson and Flynn. But Jackson, being a true scholar, would not allow this intellectual scandal to be swept under the rug. Of this "enormous historical misconception," she said, "there is so much at stake here, because of all the writing that has been done based on a false assumption about race." She asks us to wonder, "How have her [Kelley-Hawkins's] overwhelmingly 'white' texts successfully passed as black for so long in the absence of any corroborating historical data? How does this discovery change our understanding of African American literary history?" Finally, she said, "We have stretched our understanding of how black women have written in America to incorporate texts that do not fit."

I've gone into great detail about the Kelley-Hawkins story because it is a cautionary tale for scholars and an example of how our theories, our explanatory models, and the stories we tell ourselves can blind us to the obvious, leading us to see in matters of race only what we want to see based on our desires and political agendas. When we confront phenomena of any kind, we are wise if we assume the position phenomenologist Herbert Spiegelberg called epistemological humility, which is a healthy skepticism about what we think we already know. When constructing our narratives, it would also help if we remember a famous and often-quoted statement by C.S. Lewis on the characteristics of the human mind: "Five senses; an incurably abstract intellect; a haphazardly selective memory; a set of preconceptions and assumptions so numerous that I can never examine more than a minority of them—never become conscious of them all. How much of total reality can such an apparatus let through?"

How much, indeed.

But if the old black American narrative has outlived its usefulness as a tool of interpretation, then what should we do? The answer, I think, is obvious. In the 21st century, we need new and better stories, new concepts, and new vocabularies and grammar based not on the past but on the dangerous, exciting, and unexplored present, with the understanding that each is, at best, a provisional reading of reality, a single phenomenological profile that one day is likely to be revised, if not completely overturned. These will be narratives that do not claim to be absolute truth, but instead more humbly present themselves as a very tentative thesis that must be tested every day in the depths of our own experience and by all the reliable evidence we have available, as limited as that might be. For as Bertrand Russell told us, what we know is always "vanishingly small." These will be narratives of individuals, not groups. And is this not exactly what Martin Luther King Jr. dreamed of when he hoped a day would come when men and women were judged not by the color of their skin, but instead by their individual deeds and actions, and the content of their character?

I believe this was what King dreamed and, whether we like it or not, that moment is now.

8

Master-Slave Dialectics in Charles Johnson's "The Education of Mingo"

— Linda Furgerson Selzer

> The slave is a part of the master, a living but separated part of his bodily frame.
>
> —Aristotle, *Politics* (1255b-10)

In a postscript to "The Phenomenology of the Black Body" (1993), Charles Johnson describes the difficult circumstances under which he originally composed that essay in 1975. A graduate student in philosophy at SUNY Stony Brook, Johnson was in the midst of one of the most difficult years in his life—a year marked by "unemployment and hardship," as well as by the birth of his son, Malik (611).[1] During this year of increased family responsibilities and decreased financial resources, Johnson nevertheless found time to write the first complete draft of *Oxherding Tale*, a novel that he would see published seven years—and several revisions—later. More surprising, perhaps, is that Johnson somehow made time during this difficult year to read Sartre's *Being and Nothingness*, Heidegger's *Being and Time*, and Merleau-Ponty's *The Phenomenology of Perception*—all in little over a single month. Thus if 1975 was a year in which Johnson was to draft what some believe to be his finest novel, it was also a time in which he solidified an interest in philosophical descriptions of intentionality and subject-object relations—what Johnson describes as "the correlate of consciousness and its content, noesis-noema, or subject and object" (600).[2]

Johnson draws upon several philosophical accounts of subjectivity in "The Phenomenology of the Black Body," citing—among others—Hegel, Husserl, Heidegger, Ricoeur, Fanon, Merleau-Ponty, Sartre, and DuBois. He concludes that the experience of black embodiment should be understood as a distinctive variation on subject-object relations—one that develops within and out of a color-caste system. As Johnson explains, "the experience of the Black body becomes, not merely a Self-Other conflict, nor simply Hegel's torturous master-slave dialectic, but a variation on both these conditions, intensified by the particularity of the body's appearance as black...[and] as lacking interiority"(605). Within a color-caste system, Johnson suggests, the subjectivity of Blacks is denied as they are "one-sidedly seen" by Whites and appear as "body *sans* mind for the Other" (608). The ambiguity of the lived body—as both subject and object—is thus reduced by the white Other to the status of a thing.

Influenced by various twentieth-century responses to Hegel's phenomenological analysis of the encounter with the Other, Johnson's reading of the phenomenology of the black body as a special variation on subject-object relations anticipates more recent inquiries into what bell hooks calls "looking relations" (125) and Gayatri Spivak identifies as "the mechanics of the constitution of the Other" (294). Johnson's understanding of the phenomenology of the Black body also provides an important context for understanding his early short story, "The Education of Mingo." Originally published in *Mother Jones* shortly after the first appearance of "The Phenomenology of the Black Body," the tale's direct allusion to the "structures of intentional consciousness" (6) serves as a textual invitation to read this philosophical fable in the context of that earlier essay.[3] Indeed, "The Education of Mingo" can be read as Johnson's fictional engagement with—and self-conscious re-writing of—various philosophical analyses of subject-object relations, including Hegel's well-known master-slave dialectic.

Masters and Slaves

> ...just where the master has effectively achieved lordship, he really finds that something has come about quite different from an independent consciousness. It is not an independent, but rather a dependent consciousness that he has achieved. —Hegel, *The Phenomenology of Mind* (236-37).

The central character in "The Education of Mingo" is Moses Green, a poor white southerner living in antebellum America. Although he inhabits a country shaped by historical diversity—a fact made clear when he pays for his purchases with "Mexican coin" and eats "hominy made from Indian corn"—Moses nevertheless feels threatened by what he perceives as an increasing American pluralism.[4] Labeling anyone who thinks differently from himself an "outrageous liar" (4), he includes in that category "abolitionists,... Red Indians," and "nearly everybody in the New World from Anna Baptists to Whigs" (4). Ironically—yet appropriately—named after the Old Testament patriarch who set God's laws in stone, Moses is singularly unable to tolerate ambiguity. Fearing the ability of others to "twis[t] the truth... until nothing is clear anymore," he is intimidated by beliefs that differ from his own "common sense" opinions (4). Indeed, Moses fits Johnson's description in "The Phenomenology of the Black Body" of the person who is blind to new ideas because he is "locked within the Natural Attitude... and has been conditioned... to fix himself upon certain 'meanings'"(603). Thus the diversity of opinion Moses encounters not only threatens to unsettle his own fixed notions, but also seems to destabilise God's creation itself.

Johnson's probing investigation of master-slave dialectics unfolds when Moses decides to buy a slave. He attributes his desire to purchase Mingo, a young African man of about twenty, to his need for "a field hand, a help mate—a friend" (3). But in fact Moses decides to buy a slave in order to shore up his own threatened identity. In *The Phenomenology of Mind*, Hegel makes the celebrated claim that any attempt to fix the truth of one's own self-consciousness demands an Other. Or, as he explains, "Self-consciousness exists in itself and for itself, in that, and by the fact that it exists for another self-consciousness; that is to say, it is only by being acknowledged or 'recognised'" (229). By purchasing Mingo and especially by educating the African in his own common-sense point of view, Moses seeks precisely that recognition—a way to fix the self and simultaneously to escape the plurality of opinion that unsettles him. Thus even though Moses initially realises that "*every*thing about him and the African was as different as night and day"—including the "structures of intentional consciousness" (6)—he comes to prize Mingo precisely because the enslaved young man begins to function as a mirror for Moses himself, as his "own emanation, but still... [Mingo]. Different enough from Moses so that he could step back and admire him"(11). Mingo's subordination to Moses provides the personal recognition that Moses seeks, because the master sees himself reflected in the slave according to his own intentions and will. Significantly, Moses also sees in the African a way to fight the larger instability of creation: by making Mingo a reflection of his own opinions, Moses intends to aim "a shotgun at the whole world through the African, blasting away at all that Moses, according to his own lights, tagged evil, and cultivating the good"(5). In short, Moses Green buys Mingo in order to use the slave as a tool for "remaking the world so that it looked more familiar" (5-6).

Moses' attempt to use his relationship with Mingo to flee the unfamiliar and to fix the self at first seems successful. Under his tutelage, Mingo appears to become a reflection of Moses' own thoughts and actions, right down to the smallest detail. Mingo begins to walk and talk like Moses: he even reproduces Moses' limp, although there is nothing wrong with Mingo's leg at all. Pleased with the results of his instruction, Moses comes to believe that Mingo is "exactly like him, exactly the product of his own way of seeing, as much one of his products and judgments as his choice of tobacco... a homunculus, or a distorted shadow... his own spitting image"(7). Hegel suggests that as part of his project to secure his own identity, the master attempts to force the slave into conformity with his objectifications. Similarly, Moses convinces himself that Mingo is nothing more than a "product" of his own desires and choices—just like his choice of tobacco. But Moses' purchase of Mingo actually propels him headlong into an encounter with just what he would avoid: difference and the Other. For as Moses Green learns through his own education over the course of this philosophical tale, the dialectic between master and slave is inherently unstable.

When the master has achieved superiority though the subordination of the Other, Hegel suggests, it is ironically "not an independent, but rather a dependent consciousness that he has achieved" (236-37). This dependency arises because the relationship between self and Other is not fixed, but dialectical. Because the master's status depends upon the recognition of the Other, he attempts to secure that status by fixing the Other as the object of his own intentions and will. But the slave is not identical to the master's objectifications, and he is fated to betray them. Indeed, the Other as subject is capable of appropriating and transforming the master's objectifications. These transformations generate new recognitions, which in turn lead to further appropriations and transformations in a dialectical process. Moreover, if Moses understands Mingo's body as a mere extension of his own, he is in danger of losing the recognition Mingo's subjectivity provides him, since another subject is needed to help constitute one's own self consciousness. On the other hand, if Moses recognises Mingo as another subject, he must also eventually recognise that Mingo is capable of his own objectifications—that the slave has the latent power to objectify the master.[5]

In "The Phenomenology of the Black Body" Johnson locates the power of the Other to objectify the self in the ambiguity of the lived body. As he explains, "the body is experienced as having an ambiguity or non coincidence of consciousness and matter....I know that I cannot see myself as others see me, white and black, as if the secret of my body and the objectivity of its 'outside' belongs, not to me, but to everyone else" (603). As a body, one is able to be seen by, to be taken as an object by, the Other. Through this process of objectification, the ambiguity of the lived body as an "embodied subject" is reduced by the Other to the status of a thing. Because the "objectified self" one confronts in this process may not correspond to the self one attempts to secure through the recognition of the Other, being taken as an object is experienced as an alienation. Furthermore, this "objectified self" is experienced as dependent upon the intentions or will of the Other. As Hegel suggests, "just where the master has effectively achieved lordship, he really finds that something has come about quite different from an independent consciousness" (236). (Johnson draws heavily on theories of subject-object relations expressed in the language of consciousness and intentionality. It should be noted that many contemporary theorists of difference have increasingly criticised such language for privileging the individual subject and for ultimately reducing the other to an epistemological problem for the self. For example, Derrida, Levinas, and Lyotard redirect the discussion of the Other to the language of alterity in an effort to place more emphasis upon the encounter with difference and less upon an epistemological understanding of the Other.)

Mingo's ability to objectify Moses, as well as to be objectified, is hinted at early in the short story. Soon after Moses has purchased Mingo, the southerner laughs at the slave's strange speech, which he defines as "half grunt, half whinny" (5). But Moses' objectification of Mingo's speech as bestial is not the end of a process. When Moses laughs, Mingo is struck by the white southerner's "strangely unfiled" teeth, and he laughs at Moses in return. Moses' laughter is part of a dialectical process through which both Mingo and Moses objectify the other as uncivilised. This exchange underscores the true nature of the relationship Moses has entered into with Mingo: because of the ambiguity of the lived body, Mingo can never completely become the product Moses tries to make him. Instead, through his dialectical relationship with Mingo, Moses himself begins to change. First he consciously starts to police his own bad habits—like cussing and sopping cornbread in his coffee (5)—in order that Mingo doesn't pick them up. Later Moses reveals more subtle changes in character, as when in reaction to a shock, he begins to dance, "half juba, half jig" (13). Rather than functioning to fix Moses' sense of self, the slave ironically causes Moses to "constantly revis[e] himself" (5), for—as Johnson points out in "The Phenomenology of the Black

Body"—to 'intend' an object or content of consciousness is to be 'informed' by it as well as to 'give form to it'" (602).

Because Moses fails to understand the structure of the relationship he has entered into with Mingo, he mistakenly believes that he has succeeded in stripping the slave of his own interiority and in reducing Mingo to a mere extension of his own will. As Moses explains to Harriet Bridgewater, a retired schoolteacher to whom he contemplates proposing, "It's like I just shot out another arm and that's Mingo" (10). When she hears him bragging about his success in "educating" Mingo, Harriet cautions Moses, "There's only so much [Mingo] can learn, being a salt-water African and all, don'tchooknow?" (9). Harriet's counsel has been read as a needed corrective to Moses' attempts to reshape Mingo in his own image, and Jonathan Little identifies her as the "the voice of wisdom in the story" (110). But although Harriet does serve a positive function in the tale, her understanding of Mingo ultimately turns out to be as misguided as that of Moses.

Harriet is a positive influence upon Moses precisely to the extent that she offers him the opportunity to overcome his fear of difference and to establish a meaningful relationship with an Other. Certainly Moses finds Harriet attractive in several respects. With a class longing that grows out of his own lowly economic status, he even admires Harriet's "three decked stove, sheet iron stovepipe, and large wooden cupboard"—all of which stands against his own "rude, whitewashed cabin" (9). More importantly, Moses is attracted to Harriet's voice, which sounds like song. Thus, even though Moses doesn't always agree with Harriet's opinions, he finds that he can be so taken by the "sound" of her voice, that he doesn't hear what she is "saying" (9). The music of Harriet's voice figures for Moses a positive encounter with difference not conceivable when he concentrates on what is "said"—or upon his differences of opinion with her and with others. Lonely, Moses seeks out Harriet for companionship, finding a "warmth, well-being, and wonder" as he only "half listens" to her "chatter" (9). Significantly, what Moses finds most attractive about Harriet is an elusive interiority: "a certain silvery beauty intangible, elusive, inside" (8). Harriet functions positively in the tale, then, by offering Moses the opportunity to embrace difference, as it is represented in particular through her gender, education, and class standing. But in spite of her many attractions, Moses "thinks better" of asking Harriet to marry him when he remembers "how married folks... got to favoring each other... like they was wax candles flowing tergether" (20). This image of familiarity stops his plans cold by reminding Moses of exactly what he most fears: an intimacy with difference that requires a transformation of the self. When Moses later considers proposing again, he abandons his imaginings of shared intimacy in favor of the language of ownership, reasoning with himself, "I got to *have* somebody, don't I?" (18, emphasis mine). Moses' rationalisation reveals a confusion of values similar to the one that leads him to buy Mingo in the first place: by thinking in terms of *buying* a slave in order to have a friend or of marrying a woman in order to *have* a wife, Moses conflates—in Johnson's phenomenological terms—"being with having" (8).

But if she inspires the vision of a relationship with the Other built on something other than an oppositional dialectic, Harriet ultimately reveals that she, too, confuses being and having. Indeed, it is Harriet who explains the Reverend Liverspoon's sermon on "property" to Moses, by "spell[ing] out how being and having were sorta the same thing: "'You kick a man's mule, for example, and isn't it just like ramming a boot heel in that man's belly?'" (8). Liverspoon's example forcefully makes a point opposite to the one he intends: one's own being is *not* identical to what one owns. Nor, Johnson's philosophical tale is designed to suggest, is the being of the Other reducible to one's possession or an object of one's perception. During their discussion of whether or not Moses can successfully transform Mingo, Harriet draws upon Aristotle to explain that "slaves are tools with life in them, Moses, and tools are lifeless slaves" (10).[6] Her comments reveal that her warning to Moses about the dangers of trying to educate Mingo come not from her perception that Moses sees too little in the young man, but that he sees too much. By arguing that slaves are nothing but living tools, Harriet also refuses to draw the distinction between being and having that would require her to recognise Mingo as more than a mere extension of self.[7] Taken as mirror, gun, or any other tool, Mingo is denied interiority. Already institutionalised in the Reverend Liverspoon's sermon on property, Harriet's and Moses' personal views on slavery thus reinforce the underlying confusion of being and having that sustains the institution of slavery in the antebellum South.

The Other as Object

> Now instruments are of various sorts; some are living, others lifeless... a slave is a living possession... and the servant is himself an instrument.—Aristotle, *Politics* (1253b-2)

The elusive interiority that accounts for Harriet's attractiveness but is invisible in Mingo is ultimately put at issue in Johnson's short story through two climactic events: Mingo's violent confrontations with Harriet and with Isaiah Jenson, a neighbor on a nearby farm. Like a proud father or an artist pleased with his creation, Moses leaves Mingo to work at Isaiah's one day, certain that the slave will prove how much Moses has taught him. But when Moses returns to pick Mingo up that evening, he is shocked to discover his slave eating calmly in the kitchen—while Isaiah's bloody body lies nearby. As Moses struggles to understand what could have gone so wrong—how it is possible that Mingo could have buried a meat cleaver "deep in Isaiah's forehead" (12) and why it is that the slave seems so indifferent to Isaiah's death—he suddenly remembers back to what he had taught Mingo about chicken hawks: "Months ago, maybe five, he'd taught Mingo to kill chicken hawks and be courteous to strangers" (13). Moses now realises that Mingo has misinterpreted his admonition: in a violent—but comic—reversal of Moses' law, Mingo is kind to chicken hawks and kills strangers. Distraught, Moses goes immediately to Harriet's for solace. But while he is inside looking for a drink to calm his nerves, Mingo kills Harriet out in the yard. In a single afternoon, Mingo has turned Moses' world upside-down.

By raising the question of how Mingo's murderous actions are to be interpreted, Johnson's tale focuses the reader's attention upon the hidden nature of the slave's interiority. Asfraf Rushdy reads Mingo's killing of Harriet and Isaiah as an "outpicturing" of Moses' innermost desires, which Mingo—as a descendent of the Allmuseri nation of sorcerers—would be able to divine. Indeed, Moses himself admits that his feelings for both Isaiah and Harriet are mixed, and he confesses, "Jenson was so troublesome, always borrowing tools and keeping them, he hoped he'd go to Ballyhack on a red-hot rail" (14). Rushdy concludes that because Mingo has "lost his desiring function" his murders reflect the "half understood desires of his master" (376). One way of reading Mingo's actions, then, is as fulfillment of Moses' unstated intentions.

But Mingo's actions can also be understood as an indication of the instability of the master/slave dialectic and as the expression of Mingo's own latent powers of objectification. Hegel argues that the slave's own labor moves him in the direction of liberation: by transforming recalcitrant nature, the slave develops mastery—or the ability to transform the world in ways more responsive to his own needs. Unlike the master, the slave is not content with the world as it is. Although Mingo's interiority may be hidden to Moses, the slave's interests are clearly served when he strikes back at whites, reversing the power relations Moses has dictated. Indeed, Mingo's attack on Isaiah—who, like Moses, is named after an Old Testament figure—can be read as an act of resistance to the larger patriarchal position that whites occupy in the American South, a position also implicit in Moses' suspiciously paternal attitudes toward the enslaved youth. The fact that Moses is "careful not to look [Mingo] in the eye" (15) after the murders signals a change in their relationship, and the tale's historical allusion to "free soilers" implies that power relations between master and slave are also becoming unstable in the country at large. Significantly, when Moses examines Isaiah's dead body, he finds Mingo's image fixed on his neighbor's retina—a reflection that suggests that Mingo has been successful in turning the Other into a mirror for his own objectifications.

Mingo's murders of Harriet and Isaiah suggest that the invisibility of the slave's interior masks hidden and potentially powerful depths. In "The Phenomenology of the Black Body," Johnson argues that it is precisely the denial of interiority that is characteristic of the lived experience of African Americans within a color-caste system. He also suggests three common stances that Blacks take in the face of white objectification of Blacks as "body *sans* mind." The first of these is to "use the invisibility of interior" to deceive, in trickster fashion, by leading Whites to believe that their objectifications of Blacks are accurate.[8] This is precisely the strategy that Mingo deploys in order to escape punishment for his murders. Thus when Moses tells him, "I gave you thought and tongue, and looka what you done with it—they gonna catch and kill you, boy, just as sure as I'm sitting here" (14), it is Mingo who educates Moses in the logical consequences of the master's definition of the slave as tool:

> "What Mingo know, Massa Green know. Bees like what Mingo sees or don't see is only what Massa Green taught him to see or don't see. Like Mingo lives through Massa Green, right?"
>
> Moses waited, suspicious, smelling a trap. "Yeah, all that's true."
>
> "Massa Green, he owns Mingo, right?"
>
> "Right," snorted Moses. He rubbed the knob of his red, porous nose. "Paid good money—"
>
> "So when Mingo works, it bees Massa Green workin right? Bees Massa Green workin', thinking' doin' through Mingo—ain't that so?"

Punctuating his argument with questions carefully designed to prompt Moses' agreement, Mingo through his speech recalls both Socratic dialogue and African-American trickster tales. Logically and craftily, Mingo leads Moses step-by-step to the conclusion that follows unavoidably from his definition of the slave as a tool or an extension of self: the recognition that according to his own logic, Moses must assume the responsibility for Mingo's "workin" and "doin"—or the murders of Isaiah and Harriet. Mingo's carefully constructed argument advances his own interests rather than those of the master's.

Indeed, because Mingo is successful at convincing Moses of his own culpability, Moses eventually decides not to kill Mingo or even to turn him in, but to set out "thataways" (23) with the slave, to head West in the "general direction" of Missouri. Moses' uncertainty about the exact location of Missouri and the tale's reference to "free soilers" may indicate that Mingo has successfully tricked his master into heading for free territory. In any case, the slave's appropriation of the master's discourse effectively subverts the epistemic hegemony that Moses attempts to maintain.

Through Moses' ultimate failure to fix his opinions in stone, Johnson calls attention to the unstable and equivocal nature of language itself. Although Moses imagines the American landscape to be a place where definitions can be clearly and authoritatively established, his relationship to Mingo demonstrates that he in fact inhabits a realm in which meanings are continually subject to challenge and revision. Indeed, from the outset of the narrative, language is portrayed as a contested site of intersubjective exchange: Moses intends to counter the "lies" of others with his own "common sense" views; Harriet sings the promise of reciprocal dialogue even as she rationalises slavery; Mingo speaks at times with a voice that sounds exactly like Moses' nasal twang and at other times with the exaggerated dialect of a Sambo character. Moses, in particular, exhibits language difficulties. He searches unsuccessfully for the names of commonplace objects (for example, he calls fences, "watchermercallems" [10]), agonises over how best to explain lightening to Mingo, and avoids proposing to Harriet until he ties one on. And although Moses claims to have given "thought and tongue " to Mingo, it is clear that the slave's use of language far outstrips his own. Through Moses' language problems, Johnson effectively dramatises the slippage in meaning characteristic of dialectic and underscores Moses' refusal to recognise the interdependency that characterises his relationships with others—both linguistic and otherwise.

In explaining his theory of conversation, Hans-Georg Gadamer has suggested that "to be in a conversation... means to be beyond oneself, to think with the other and to come back to oneself as if to another" (110). Instead of entering into such conversation, Moses offers his own opinions as pre-existing law—a common sense, ready-made language that requires no contribution from the Other. Merleau-Ponty—perhaps the philosopher most influential upon Johnson—describes such "commonplace utterance" as language that has already been institutionalised: the language of "a world already spoken and speaking what we think" (184). From the tale's outset, Moses relies upon common-sense views to neutralise difference. But the linguistic acts of others repeatedly transgress the boundaries of Moses' perceptions throughout the story, and they build to Mingo's climatic reversal of Moses' admonition to "Kill chicken hawks and always be courteous to strangers." Ironically, it is through Moses' own pronouncements that his objectifications are ultimately appropriated and transformed. The master's attempt to claim language as a site of control over the slave fails to account for language as a site where control is also contested and modified. Rather than effectively silencing the "liars" who oppose his common-sense views, Moses finds that by the end of the tale his own voice has been reduced to "a rasp and a wheeze" (23).

By undermining the hegemony that Moses seeks to maintain, the dialectical relationship he enters into with Mingo would seem to hold out the possibility for improved relations. By the end of the short story there is some evidence that Moses has begun to recognise Mingo as more than a mere extension of self. After the murders, Mingo suddenly strikes him as "strangely elemental," and Moses becomes aware that the young man appears changed. When he is away from "the familiar setting of the farm," Mingo's skin takes on "the texture of plant life" and "the stones of his eyes" take on "an odd, glassy quality like those of a spider, which cannot be read" (21). Moses' association of Mingo with plant and animal life might be judged as another failure on his part to recognise the slave's interiority, but actually his new appreciation of the slave's physicality reveals the master's nascent perception of alterity. Rather than perceiving Mingo as merely an extension of the self, Moses now senses a strange, embodied Otherness to the slave. Johnson suggests that such embodiment does not deny the subjectivity of the Other, but in fact is a condition for it. Thus at the same time that Moses associates Mingo's appearance with a spider (a traditional trickster figure in African folklore), he also begins to suspect that the slave has depths—depths that "cannot be read" (21). As a result of his own education, then, Moses momentarily perceives Mingo as radically Other and as possessing a mysterious interiority, if one that is "faintly innocent, faintly diabolical" (21).

But in this tale of "monstrosity and existential horror" (17), Moses' few, momentary glimpses of the basis for a more complex intersubjectivity—either through an identification with the Other as figured by Harriet's language or through an acknowledgement of difference as encountered through embodiment—are ultimately overwhelmed by nightmare visions of an obstinate, destructive dualism.[9] In one "night vision," Moses imagines that he and Mingo are "wired together" like "two ventriloquist's dummies" (15-16). When Moses tries to run away, so does the illusory Mingo, "pumping his knees right alongside Moses, shrieking, their voice inflections identical" (16). Moses' second vision is of a coin, with his own image engraved on one side and Mingo's on the other. Both visions suggest that what is etched in stone is not Moses' own precepts, but his inescapable relation to the Other. Like two ventriloquists' dummies or two sides of the same coin, both master and slave are locked in association. Moses' visions demonstrate that he now senses the truth of Hegel's claim that "it is not an independent, but a dependent consciousness that the Master achieves" (236-237). Recognising that "It was a bitter thing to siphon your being from someone else" (18), Moses finds that he is unable either to turn Mingo in or to manumit him, precisely because the slave "shores up, sustains, lets be [Moses'] world... every time he opens his oily black eyes" (13).

In "The Education of Mingo," Johnson uses Moses' disturbing and complicated relationship with Mingo to signify a subject-object relations in general, and on Hegel's master-slave dialectic in particular, positioning them within the historical institution of American chattel slavery.[10] By doing so, he crafts a devastating satire of what some historians have identified as the central "deception" upon which chattel slavery rested: "the notion that in fact, as well as in one's fantasy life, some human beings could become mere extensions of another person's will" (Genovese 30). Originally Moses intends to use Mingo to neutralise difference by "aiming a shotgun at the whole world through the African" (5), but by the end of the tale Moses' intentions have backfired. He has learned—as Sartre warns—that the Other treated as object is an "explosive instrument" that must be "handled carefully":

> Thus the Other-as-object is an explosive instrument which I handle with care because I foresee around him the permanent possibility that they are going to make it explode and that with this explosion I shall suddenly experience the flight of the world away from me and my being.[11]

The Other taken as object is an explosive instrument because the invisibility of the interior hides a latent power. The Other is never reducible to a mere extension of self. As embodied subject, Johnson suggests, the Other is capable of his own objectifications—of transgressing the boundaries of self and of remaking the world according to his own needs, aims, and desires.

Through Moses Green's attempts to use Mingo as a tool, Charles Johnson probes the singular variation of subject-object relations that he identifies as developing within a color-caste system, wherein a black Other is denied the *interiority* that would make him capable of his own *intentionality*. Through Mingo's unanticipated and violent attacks upon Harriet and Isaiah, Johnson dramatises the explosive force of the Other taken as object, who—contrary to the Rev. Liverspoon's sermon equating being and having—is never completely reducible to an object of one's knowledge or will. Moses Green's attempt to use Mingo as a tool for neutralising difference leads to the loss of friends, farm, and all that is commonplace. Ironically, Johnson's narrative closes as Moses—who initially purchases a slave in hopes of making his world look "more familiar"—rides out with Mingo into unfamiliar territory.

Notes

1. All references to "The Phenomenology of the Black Body" are to "The Phenomenology of the Black Body," *Michigan Quarterly Review* 32 (Fall 1993): 590-614; page numbers are indicated parenthetically in the text. Johnson's essay was originally composed in 1975 as a "style paper" for his graduate program in philosophy. The article first appeared in print in the Winter 1976 issue of *Ju-Ju: Research Papers in Afro-American Studies.*
2. Johnson names Hegel as one of the writers whom he most admires (Boccia 615).
3. For other readings of "The Education of Mingo" see Benesch (173-177), Byrd (340-344), Griffiths (536-538), Little (*Spiritual* 109-11), and Rushdy ("Phenomenology" 378-380). Benesch reads the tale as a philosophical parable that criticises the Cartesian notion of an autonomous self and dramatises Johnson's understanding of universal connectedness. Byrd analyses the tale in light of Whitehead's theory of organism. Placing Johnson in an intertextual dialogue with Toomer and Plato, Griffiths reads the story as an "antebellum parable about education and slavery" (527). Little stresses the many layers of meaning available in the parable form and focuses on the tale as a "shocking allegory of artistic creation gone awry" (109). Finally, Rushdy approaches the tale from the perspective of the version of phenomenology he identifies as figured by the Allmuseri tribe in Johnson's fiction. By approaching the short story from the perspective of Johnson's article on the phenomenology of the black body, I also offer a phenomenological reading of the tale, but draw different conclusions about the precise nature of the relationship between Mingo and Moses and, especially, about the significance of Mingo's actions.
4. All references to "The Education of Mingo" are to "The Education of Mingo," *The Sorcerer's Apprentice: Tales and Conjurations.* New York: Plume Books, 1994, 3-23, 3. Subsequent page numbers are included parenthetically in the text.
5. See Leiberman's description of the structures of epistemic domination and racial objectification in "The Dialectics of Oppression."
6. See Aristotle, section 1253b, 23-32, and 1255b.
7. The fact that Harriet keeps a gun in her cupboard "on account of slaves who swore to die in the skin of freemen" (22) suggests that even she does not truly believe in her definition of slaves as tools.
8. Although Mingo uses this strategy effectively, Johnson seems not in general to view such deceptions positively, but rather as a form of bad faith. In "The Phenomenology of the Black Body," Johnson describes those who use such strategies as "cynically" playing with "frozen intentions, presuppositions, and stereotypes" (608).

9. Harriet is seen reading Shelley's *Frankenstein,* described as a tale of "monstrosity and existential horror."
10. By suggesting that "The Education of Mingo" 'signifies' upon theories of subject-object relations, I want to stress the "double-voicedness" through which Johnson both calls up and revises such theories from a specifically African American perspective. For the vernacular origin of signifying as a linguistic practice and for its importance to African-American literature, see Bernard Bell. For an analysis of linguistic signifying as a metaphor for other African American "signifyin(g) revisions" of dominant cultural theories and practices, see Henry Louis Gates.
11. Jean-Paul Sartre, *Being and Nothingness*, 364. The conclusion to Johnson's short story is in fact reminiscent of Sartre's pessimistic revision of Hegel in his analysis of "The Look" in *Being and Nothingness*. See, for example, Sartre's claim that the relationship between consciousnesses is essentially "a conflict" (502). See also Liberman's discussion of Sartre (272-273).

Works Cited

Aristotle. *The Politics*. Ed. Stephen Everson. Cambridge: Cambridge UP, 1986.

Bell, Bernard. *The Afro-American Novel and Its Traditions*. Amherst: U of Mass P, 1987.

Benesch, Klaus. "Charles Johnson: 'The Education of Mingo.'" *The African American Short Story 1970-1990.* Ed. Wolfgang Karrer and Barbara Pushmann-Nalenz. Trier: Wissenschaftlicher, 1993. 169-179.

Boccia, Michael. "An Interview with Charles Johnson." *African American Review* 30 (Winter 1996): 611-618.

Byrd, Rudolph P. "It Rests By Changing: Process in *The Sorcerer's Apprentice.*" *I Call Myself an Artist: Writings by and about Charles Johnson.* Ed. Rudolph P. Byrd. Bloomington: Indiana UP, 1999. 333-352.

Gadamer, Hans-Georg. "Destruktion and Deconstruction." *Dialogue and Deconstruction: The Gadamer-Derrida Encounter.* Eds. Diane P. Michelfelder and Richard Palmer. Albany: State U of New York P, 1989. 102-125.

Griffiths, Frederick T. "'Sorcery is Dialectical': Plato and Jean Toomer in Charles Johnson's *The Sorcerer's Apprentice.*" *African American Review* 30 (Winter 1996): 527-528.

Gates, Jr., Henry L. *The Signifying Monkey: A Theory of African American Criticism.* New York: Oxford, UP, 1988.

Genovese, Eugene. *Roll, Jordan, Roll: The World the Slaves Made.* New York: Random House, 1976.

Hegel, G. W. F. *The Phenomenology of Mind.* Trans. J. B. Ballie. New York: Harper and Row, 1967.

hooks, bell. *Black Looks*. Boston: South End Press, 1992.

Johnson, Charles. "The Education of Mingo." *The Sorcerer's Apprentice*. New York: Plume Books, 1994, 3-23.

_______."A Phenomenology of the Black Body." *Michigan Quarterly Review* 32 (Fall 1993): 590-614.

Liberman, Kenneth. "The Dialectics of Oppression." *Philosophy Today* 43 (Fall 1999): 272-282.

Little, Jonathan. *Charles Johnson's Spiritual Imagination*. Columbia: U of Missouri p, 1997.

Merleau-Ponty, Maurice. *Phenomenology of Perception*. Trans. Colin Smith. London: Routledge and Kegan Paul, 1962.

Rushdy, Asraf H. A. "The Phenomenology of the Allmuseri: Charles Johnson and the Subject of the Narrative of Slavery." *African American Review* 26 (Fall 1992): 373-94.

Sartre, Jean-Paul. *Being and Nothingness*. Trans. Hazel E. Barnes. New York Philosophical Library, 1956.

Spivak, Gayatri Chakravorty. *Marxism and the Interpretation of Culture*. Urbana: U of Illinois p, 1988.

9

To Transcribe and Transfigure: An Interview with Charles Johnson

— Shayla Hawkins

He is a minority among minorities, a genius among even the keenest of intellectuals. He is Dr. Charles Johnson, the only African American novelist to have a Ph.D. in philosophy and one of only two black men ever to win the National Book Award (The other was Ralph Ellison, one of Johnson's greatest literary influences). In a career that spans over 40 years, Johnson has channeled his perspective of the world into a dazzling multitude of incarnations. He is a philosopher, essayist, book critic, martial arts practitioner, cartoonist, MacArthur Fellow, lecturer and the S. Wilson and Grace M. Pollock Professor of Creative Writing at the University of Washington in Seattle. It is, however, through his vocation as a fiction writer that Johnson has made the most resonant impact on America's aesthetic landscape.

In 1974, with the tutelage and support of his mentor, novelist and famed fiction teacher John Gardner, Johnson published his first novel, *Faith and the Good Thing*. Johnson followed this critically acclaimed debut with *Oxherding Tale* (1982), *Dreamer* (1998) and the short story collections *The Sorcerer's Apprentice* (1986), *Soulcatcher and Other Stories* (1998) and *Dr. King's Refrigerator and Other Stories* (2005). But it was *Middle Passage* (1990), Johnson's third novel, which gave him immortality and assured his seat in the lineage of great American writers. The novel's protagonist, a newly freed slave named Rutherford Calhoun, undergoes a profound and traumatic psychic metamorphosis when, in a desperate bid to flee his debtors and a forced marriage, he unknowingly makes himself a stowaway on the *Republic*, a slave ship bound for Africa. Calhoun is one of only five characters aboard the ship to survive its doomed return voyage. In an effort to understand the atrocities he witnessed and maintain his sanity, Rutherford writes a detailed account of everything that happened on the *Republic*. Concerning his compulsion to write, Rutherford notes that he "came to it with ... a need to transcribe and thereby transfigure all we had experienced, and somehow through all this I found a way to make my peace with the recent past by turning it into Word."

In the following interview, conducted in the late spring of 2006, Dr. Charles Johnson offers, among other insights, his candid considerations about women, retirement, the pursuit and possession of real happiness and his own mastery at taking his life experience and molding it into luminous, immutable Word.

Hawkins: Most readers and critics think *Middle Passage* is the crown jewel of your literary works. Do you agree? Or do you feel that you have yet to produce your greatest writing? Is such a notion even important to you?

Johnson: My second novel, *Oxherding Tale*, is the work I always whimsically refer to as my "platform novel" (borrowing that phrase from the Platform Sutra of the Sixth Patriarch in Buddhist history). It is somewhere around 25 per cent more complex and ambitious than *Middle Passage*, a work where I addressed similar issues—for example, "What is the nature of the self?" If I hadn't written *Oxherding Tale*, I'm sure I wouldn't have been interested in writing anything else. So I have a special affection for that novel; when I was writing it, I felt everything important for my life was at stake, while with *Middle Passage* my basic intention was to address some of the same issues, yes, but also to create a rousing good sea adventure story that would be more accessible than my second novel. Comparing one's works is always difficult—it's like trying to compare one's children, and just as futile as an exercise, in my view.

Hawkins: In *Middle Passage*, Rutherford's mother's name is Ruby and his brother's name is Jackson. Your mother's name was Ruby and her maiden name was Jackson. Given that, how much is Rutherford—or any of your protagonists (or antagonists, for that matter)—not just a product of your imagination, but also a reflection or extension of who you are?

Johnson: Every writer I'm acquainted with draws upon the world that envelops him (or her), and their own personal history sometimes for character names, sometimes for anecdotes or incidents that they re-invent in their stories. "Real" life is always grist for the mill of storytelling.

Hawkins: In a 1996 interview, you said that you had completed two screenplays for the film adaptation of *Middle Passage* and were confident that Hollywood would eventually produce it. Are you still confident *Middle Passage* will become a movie, considering that it's been over 10 years since you made that statement and Hollywood has already released a slave rebellion epic with Steven Spielberg's *Amistad* ?

Johnson: As I utter these words, a theatrical version of *Middle Passage* is being prepared for next year. I think some day a film adaptation will be done. We came close ten years ago, but the people involved just couldn't carry the project through. It would be an expensive film—it takes place on the water (always hard to control) and is a costume drama (every prop has to be period)—which would place its cost today, I believe, at around $100 million. Warrington and Reginald Hudlin simply couldn't get it green-lighted at first Tri-Star, then Interscope with themselves attached as directors. Not that long ago (two years, I think), John Singleton contacted me again (He optioned the film rights for Warner Brothers) since he felt he finally had the perfect actor to play Capt. Falcon. I haven't heard from him since then. It's important to remember that *Middle Passage* is an epic sea adventure story, and Hollywood has never done a black epic. Its cost would be a great risk (most black films are budgeted around $15-20 million), one that could break (or make) a studio for the year of its release. The film *Amistad* is, at best, a courtroom drama—there's only one significant on-board montage of slaves being dumped into the ocean. But I suspect it will get done one day; my second script for the adaptation (written at Interscope) opens up the story even more dramatically, including a section where the sailors on the *Republic* (but not Rutherford) raid and destroy the village of the Allmuseri. Very powerful stuff in that new material.

Hawkins: Did you have any idea while you were writing it that *Middle Passage* was the book that would place you in the pantheon of great American authors?

Johnson: All I can really say is that from the beginning of my work as a fiction-writer I knew the significance of what I was doing with those two sister disciplines, fiction and philosophy, and that these works filled an aesthetic void in American literature.

Hawkins: Some of your fiction, particularly the hilarious and tender love scene between Rutherford and Isadora at the end of *Middle Passage*, is highly reminiscent of John Donne (one of my favorite poets) and his simultaneously metaphysical, religious and erotic love poetry. Although you're a Buddhist and Donne was a Christian minister, you both are incredibly adept at wedding the flesh with the spirit in your writings. What would you say to critics who think sex and divinity should stay segregated in literature?

Johnson: I would simply say that an expansive work of fiction treats *all* of human experience, or as much as an artist can possibly render. One wishes to be, as one person put it (whose name I forget at the moment) a writer on whom nothing of significance in the world around him is lost. Naturally, that includes all kinds of love—eros, philias, and agape, all three of which I believe my novels and stories treat.

Hawkins: The magical realism in your fiction is reminiscent of the magical realism in Gabriel García Márquez's novels and short stories. Was Marquez an influence for you with that technique? If not, how did you acquire your skills using magical realism in your stories?

Johnson: Actually, Márquez was not an influence. My work has sometimes been called "magical realism," but that critical term would apply to only a few works, not to the strictly "realistic" stories, say, in *Soulcatcher and Other Stories*.

Hawkins: When I was in college in the mid and late 90s, there was only one black male in the undergrad English program. Almost without exception, every other black male student on campus majored in Math, Engineering or Business Administration. What, if anything, would you say to a black male college student who likes to write and is considering getting an English degree, but also has the talent to become (and knows he'll make a whole lot more money as) an engineer or corporate executive?

Johnson: I truly believe we, as black people, need more scientists and engineers. (See my October 14, 2005 op-ed piece on "The Crisis in Black America" in *The Wall Street Journal.*) If a young black male (or anyone) is interested in a degree in English (which, incidentally, I don't have, my two advanced degrees are in philosophy), I would suggest they pursue that discipline passionately, as my own teacher John Gardner did, learning everything there is to know about classical and contemporary literature in order to determine what he (or she) might do to *advance* that body of literature, thematically and technically. Yes, it's true: they won't make as much money as an engineer, but this isn't about money. It's about passion and, as Horace Mann once said, "Being ashamed until you have won some great victory for humankind."

Hawkins: There's a strong undercurrent of romance and love (erotic and otherwise) in many of your stories. I'm thinking especially of the bond between Rutherford and Isadora (and Squibb and Maud) in *Middle Passage*; between Moses and Harriet (that is, before she's murdered) in "The Education of Mingo" and the sweet and suggestive dialogue between the newlywed Martin Luther and Coretta Scott King in "Dr. King's Refrigerator." (Even in your story "China," Rudolph tells Evelyn that he'll fight better in his first martial arts match if she's there.) And then there's this wondrous excerpt about Felicia's feelings for Fortunata in your story "Cultural Relativity": "Everyone knew animals didn't kiss. They licked. The reason for having lips in the first place, Felicia decided just before daybreak, was so people could use their God-given soup coolers as the most romantic, the most erotic, and the most natural way to show they loved someone."

No man—gifted writer or not—could describe a feeling so beautifully or romantically unless that feeling was already buried somewhere inside of him. Most readers of your work know something of how you evolved into Buddhism. But where did your depth and clarity about love, romance and the complex web of erotic feelings between a woman and a man come from?

Johnson: Well, I guess the answer is that I've always loved women. I think no beings on earth are as beautiful as women. Growing up, I had a very old-fashioned, even romantic view of women—especially the woman one loved—that resembles the idea of the perfect wife in the *Book of Psalms* (my wife loves that description), someone a man could ride into battle for, revere and dedicate himself completely to. But, like I said, I'm very old-fashioned in that way.

Hawkins: Because the characters' accumulation of money without having earned it has such deadly consequences in your short story "Exchange Value," I can't help but wonder: What are your thoughts on the issue of reparations for the descendants of African and African American slaves?

Johnson: Right now what I think is that reparations for black Americans, after 9/11, is unlikely to happen since this nation has generated a debt in the war on terrorism that won't be paid off until our grandchildren are very old.

Hawkins: What's the secret to writing good moral/philosophical fiction without proselytising and/or boring a potential reader to tears with one's particular ideology?

Johnson: As a phenomenologist, I've always been opposed to ideology (which, by the way, Buddhism is not) and explanatory models for human experience. Philosophical ideas do not begin in some far away, airy realm of Forms. Rather, they emerge from the grit and mud and sweat of human beings living their lives. A philosophical writer does nothing more than return those ideas to the messy, quotidian context of lived-experience in which they initially arose, examining them through the dramatic possibilities inherent in character and event.

Hawkins: What is your advice to writers who cannot and/ or have no desire, to be as profoundly philosophical and, to borrow a phrase from your novel *Dreamer*, go "from surface to seabed" in their writings as you do, but still want their work to be powerful, poignant and taken seriously?

Johnson: Take emotional risks. Honestly explore the things you fear most. Make each of your stories a private act in a public place. Show us the naked workings of the human heart, uncensored. That approach is best, as Saul Bellow once said, because no community altogether knows the secrets of its own heart.

Hawkins: You're at a point in your writing career where you can write anything you want without reprisal or compromise. But was there ever a time when you felt pressured to choose between your literary vision and the demands of the marketplace? If so, how did you handle that?

Johnson: I simply ignored the marketplace. My agent of 33 years, Georges Borchardt, once remarked that "Charles never sold out." I never did. I didn't know how to do that. I'm a college prof, so early in my career I didn't have to pay my bills through what I wrote—I was free to simply do what I felt was best for me to do. I admire my writer friends who literally write their next meal onto the table, because I value productivity and creative pressure, but I don't admire some of the things they feel they had to write to pay the bills, and I wouldn't want my name on those books. They write, say, a book a year, and have no time for revision, for deepening their text through massive research and prodigious re-writing. Me, I'll spend five or seven years on a novel because I know a new work may wind up being my literary last will and testament if I die right after it's done. So, no, there was no way I could ever sell out—writing for short-term monetary goals to satisfy literary fads and fashions—when what was at stake with each book was an intellectual and artistic declaration, one that my children possibly might turn to in order to answer the question, "What was Dad's vision of the world?"

Hawkins: Your birthday (April 23rd) is the same day as William Shakespeare's. Do you have any thoughts about Shakespeare's literary prominence and immortality and/or your own literary legacy?

Johnson: I always give proper respect to the Bard, and I've enjoyed his plays since my early teens. As for my own literary legacy, well, future generations will have to determine that. An old rule of thumb is that a literary work should be around for about 50 years, and have influenced two or three generations, before we say it is an important cultural artifact.

Hawkins: Speaking of great playwrights, you were friends with the late August Wilson. Do you care to share any thoughts about Mr. Wilson, his literary impact and/or the friendly competition between you two?

Johnson: August was my good friend for the 15 years he lived in Seattle. I miss him greatly. We used to have 7 to 10 hour dinner conversations. I've given two tributes to him in Seattle since last Thanksgiving. We couldn't exactly be in competition since he was a playwright and I work primarily in prose (novels, short fiction, essays, philosophical articles, TV scripts for PBS, comic art) and have little experience with theater.

Hawkins: You have a nonfiction book called *Turning the Wheel: Essays on Buddhism and Writing*. But I'd like to ask you about another symbolic wheel: the hamster wheel that so many Americans are stuck on. Every morning, tens (and perhaps hundreds) of millions of people in this country wake up and trudge through the day with no joy, no fulfillment and no sense of their divine purpose. As a man with an abundant and purpose-driven life, what would you suggest for someone who wants to get off the "hamster wheel" and live better and more deeply?

Johnson: The best way to get off the "hamster-wheel" is to find something you love and are passionate about, and pursue it with all your heart and soul. My 24-year-old daughter Elisheba is doing that right now with her first business, Faire Gallery/Cafe in Seattle. Two years ago she graduated from Cornish College of the Arts, and she is a conceptual artist. She worked a few jobs she hated after graduation. Then she came up with the idea for Faire (French for "to make, to do"). She's combined art showings (monthly) with commerce (a well-stocked cafe). Faire has been open now for two months, and she's having the time of her life creating a space for Seattle folks (and especially young artists) to come together as a community. I handle all my meetings and appointments there, at Faire, because the ambience is very comfortable, her customers nice people, and there's a new art show to look at every 30 days. She's sold a lot of art there. You can visit her website at www.fairegallerycafe.com. The just out May issue of *The International Journal of African American Art*, edited by Juliette Harris, has a nice little notice for the gallery/cafe.

Hawkins: You have so many talents; you're like the Russian matryoshka dolls that are stacked inside of each other. You're a writer, of course; then there's your role as a philosopher, professor and cartoonist. You're also a lecturer and a book critic. Are there any talents you don't have that you wish you did? Or is there something you haven't done yet but still want to accomplish?

Johnson: I think I've accomplished everything in life that I set out to do. I love science and technology, so I wish I had a better background in math, but it's not possible to do everything in one lifetime. I just have to be content as a lay reader of science.

Hawkins: I went to Rosa Parks's funeral last year, and at the service, I noticed something. It hit me that of all thousands of people in that sanctuary, and of all the bishops, senators, judges, so-called black leaders (Farrakhan, Sharpton and Jackson), celebrities, former presidents and presidential candidates, the best leader and the one person who had brought about the most good and the most significant change in this world was the woman lying in the casket. I remember thinking that the age of the great black American civil rights leaders died with Mrs. Parks and would never return. What do you think about the notion of great black civil rights leaders in the 21st Century United States?

Johnson: As I said in that op-ed article called "The Crisis in Black America," in *The Wall Street Journal*, in the 21st century we all must become, each and every one of us, the intellectual and spiritual leaders we have been looking for.

Hawkins: What hobbies or major time-consuming activities do you have outside of writing, teaching, practicing Buddhism and studying Sanskrit? What, if any, kinds of music do you listen to? Do you like any major league athletes or sports teams?

Johnson: I've never been interested in spectator sports. But I do enjoy listening to soft jazz, especially when I'm drawing.

Hawkins: As the human body ages, it becomes more difficult to command the dexterity, power and discipline the martial arts require. You'll be 60 in a couple of years. Has your body rebelled against practicing the martial arts yet? If so, are you sad or melancholy about it, considering all that you've achieved as a martial artist?

Johnson: I still practice my sets—empty hand and with traditional weapons—to keep them polished. And now I find myself doing more Tai Chi Chuan than kung-fu. As one gets older, it's natural (and also traditional) to shift to a "softer," internal system like Tai Chi.

Hawkins: Do you think you'll ever retire from teaching and/or writing?

Johnson: Nope. Unlike a job or a career, art (creating) is a life-long passion. August Wilson worked on revising his last play, *Radio Golf*, until he was too weak last fall to go on. And the great painter Jacob Lawrence was working on his canvasses until the day of his death.

Hawkins: After your physical body dies and your spirit is released into the next realm, if you're able to look back at your life on this earth, what might be the epitaph you assign to it?

Johnson: Long ago I advised my family to place on my tombstone, not words, but the simple Taoist symbol for a person traveling the Path. That symbol appears on the title page of my novel *Oxherding Tale*.

10

Four Years of Adventure*

— Charles Johnson

Good morning and welcome to the *University of Washington.*

First, I would like to congratulate those of you who begin this week as freshmen, and I would like to also congratulate your families, your counselors and your mentors for helping you to begin what we hope will be four years of adventure. The very fact that you are in this audience means that you have distinguished yourselves already. As a class, you have a grade-point average of 3.6. Your average SAT store is 567 for the verbal exam and 581 for math. Only 25 per cent of this country's population go to college. Tomorrow, on Monday, you will become part of an institution that is 135-years-old and the size of a small city, a school that has over a billion dollar operating budget each year and 20,000 faculty and staff —a school that receives more federal research funds than any other public university in the country. Eleven graduate departments at this university are rated in the top 10 in their field in the nation. On an average day 27,000 vehicles travel across UW's 703 acres.

At first glance, a university this size can seem overwhelming to faculty as well as students, and sometimes one wonders if so many departments, and so many courses, and so many people have a common purpose. As one teacher put it in a now famous definition, "The university is a collection of

---

**Keynote address delivered by Charles Johnson on September 29, 1996, at the Freshman Convocation Ceremonies at the University of Washington, Seattle, U.S.A.*

departments held together by a heating system." When I graduated from college many years ago I had a friend who probably agreed with this definition. The day after we graduated, after we'd taken back our caps and gowns, he made an appointment to see our college president. And he brought along his grade transcript. Sitting in the president's office, he spread the transcript out on his desk, and he said, "You made me take all these classes. What I want to know is, how do they all fit together?" Our school president looked over his transcript, he thought for a moment, and at last he said, "I don't know."

Before my address today is over, I'd like to give you one possible answer to that question, "How do these four years fit together?"

This fall begins my 20th year of teaching at UW—some of you probably weren't born when I arrived on this campus in 1976 as a 28-year-old assistant professor. Over the last two decades I've worked with thousands of students. Most of them were aspiring writers, and I'm pleased to say that some of them have gone on to become bestselling authors like David Guterson, whose first novel *Snow Falling on Cedars* won the 1995 PEN/Faulkner Award for fiction—and has over a million copies in print. My former students have spread out to all four corners of the earth. They are editors now and teachers, published novelists, poets, screenwriters, and short story writers. One whose name is Katherine Phelps is one of the leading writers on computer technology in Australia. And, of course, some of my students became bankers and partners in mid-sized law firms—but they are bankers and lawyers who still write fiction and have an insatiable love for literature and the arts. (One of them just wrote last week, after 10 years, to see if I'd read his new novel manuscript.)

Having worked with these very successful students, I can say that some of them knew from the very moment they set foot on campus what they were and they knew what they wanted to be. But the vast majority of my students were not so prescient. And neither was I when at 18 I left home for the first time to go away to a large, state school in Illinois—

Southern Illinois University—a school much like UW in its size and in what it offered.

Like many of you, I was the first person in the history of my family to go to college. My earning a degree was the dream of my mother, who went as far as high school, and of my father, who went only as far as the fifth grade. My parents—like yours—were my *first* and most important teachers. An Italian friend of mine once told me that when he went off to college his mother said to him, "Don't get too smart and forget about your family." Her words were full of wisdom and could well be a motto for all of us in higher education.

In 1966, I went off to college as eager for education and as idealistic and naive as any young man could be. But like my Italian friend, I was very conscious of the fact that my parents and all my relatives were counting on me to fulfill the dreams they had been denied. The summer before my freshman year Martin Luther King Jr. brought his campaign against discrimination to Chicago, where my family lived in Evanston, a nearby suburb. I was acutely aware that thousands of civil rights workers had risked their lives, and some gave their lives, so that I would have the simple opportunity to study and grow, and maybe one day repay others for the great sacrifices *they* made to realize a more integrated and just society. In those days this country was in turmoil, changing, and the ground beneath our feet felt as if it was constantly shifting. And college campuses were changing too.

It was impossible for a student not to be interested in politics, but my greatest concern at age 18 was answering the question, what was I going to be? My dream when I was a teenager was to be an artist. Drawing was the only passion that I knew since childhood. In high school when I was 17 I published my first drawings and stories and I worked on the school newspaper. So it seemed logical to me that in college I should pursue the vocation of journalism. I thought newspaper work would allow me to continue publishing my writing and my drawings. I anticipated that after four years I might work on a newspaper like *The Chicago Tribune*, which would have made my mother very happy—her son's by-line in the hometown paper.

So within a few days of unpacking in my dormitory room I found my way to the college newspaper, showed them my samples from high school, and I got hired drawing cartoons. A little bit later I talked my way onto the town newspaper and got regular work as a political cartoonist. On campus, I later taught a drawing class in what was called "The Free School," where *anyone* could teach whatever they wanted—for free, of course. And for the campus TV station I created a television series on how-to-draw, which went nationwide on PBS the next year. Remember, these were the '60s. New programs were being created, like Black Studies, and because there were so few Black Studies teachers, I found myself recruited to be one of 30 undergraduate discussion-group leaders for a big survey course on black history. College, as it turned out, fed my creativity and supported my early passion to draw.

But I would be less than honest if I said that all the students I went to school with felt as I did. Many of the friends I made in my freshman year said with no hesitation that all they wanted to do was "get that piece of paper," and to get out of school as soon as they could. I think I understood their feelings. Then, as now, a college degree translates into greater earning power in the marketplace. As a matter of fact, I recently read that for every year of college education you complete, you raise your future salary or wages by 10 per cent. The premium for a college education is at its highest level in more than 50 years.

This is good news, because we all want to make money. But I think the freshmen I knew who only saw a degree in financial terms, and who failed to open themselves to the university's dazzling array of opportunities, cheated themselves and today many of them regret that. It was as if they were wearing blinders that shielded out anything that might distract them from the dogged pursuit of their diploma and finding a high-paying job after graduation. But what most people don't know is that after getting a degree, the average student reads only *one* book a year. Most likely that book is a bestseller his (or her) friends and co-workers are reading, and he's too embarrassed to admit that he hasn't read it too. Sadly, some of my old college friends fall into that category today.

However, other freshmen I met took full advantage of the new resources at their disposal. One of my fellow students in journalism was a man from Ghana who had one of the most poetic names I think I've ever heard—Fortunata Massa. And I remember Fortunata saying to me something I've never forgotten. He said, "Do you know what I like most about America? No matter *what* you want to learn, there is someone here who can teach it to you." In a sense, Fortunata Massa understood the spirit of serendipity at American universities better than some of my born-and-raised American friends. He was eager to learn everything, from journalism to automobile repair, from economics to guitar-playing, from karate to physics. Like Henry David Thoreau, Fortunata wanted to "have as many trades as fingers on the hand." And he discovered—as I discovered—a source of enrichment seldom described in your college handbook.

I'm talking about other students, the people you're sitting beside in this room today. I found, as I hope you will find, that the other students with whom you share classrooms and dormitories represent an incredible degree of difference and diversity. My classmates in college were not only from the Midwest. They came from the East coast, from Africa (like Fortunata) and from China, from Chicago's inner-city and from little rural towns in Illinois with names like "Flat Rock" and "Granite City." They came with backgrounds and cultural experiences different from my own. As a matter of fact, a few older students I knew came from prison. Needless to say, each and every one of these students enlarged *my* perspective on life. I believe your fellow students, if you let them, will, do the same for you.

Your other source of serendipity is, of course, the faculty.

I said I started out as a journalism major. As such, I found I was *required* to take a class in—of all things—philosophy. At 18, I knew *nothing* about philosophy. I let my advisor talk me into taking a huge lecture course taught by a professor named John Howie, on the philosophy of the pre-Socratics. Somehow (I don't know how) and with some gift he had (I don't know what), Dr. Howie was able to *sing* the 2,000 year-old ethical problems Democritus and Epicuris wrestled with in such a way that I realised for the first time that many of the political issues I was publishing cartoons about in the late 1960s were issues debated and discussed with sophistication two thousand before the birth of the American republic. He made me see that the questions we ask determine the quality of the answers we get. Sitting in a sea of students in Dr. Howie's class, I realised I simply had to pursue philosophy if I wanted to understand my work as a journalist better. And so, thanks to Dr. Howie, who is today one of my friends and colleagues, I discovered a new passion I didn't realise I possessed until I went to college.

Dr. Howie was a quiet man, in fact, he was a minister. But directly across the street from his office in the Department of Philosophy was the Department of English, and in one of those tiny offices there was a young teacher named John Gardner, who was a novelist, medievalist, and critic. He was destined to become the most influential writing teacher in our time. I came to know John Gardner after I graduated with a degree in journalism, and was by then a graduate student in philosophy while I worked part-time as a reporter for one of the local newspapers. I signed up for his class in novel-writing because I'd heard so much about him, and because after writing and publishing journalism for several years I had the urge to explore what I might accomplish as a writer in a longer form—like the novel. To shorten a long story, John Gardner—who taught thousands of students across America—guided me, sentence by sentence, when I was 24 through the composition of my first published novel. He also provided me with a portrait of what an artist and scholar could be. Gardner knew 12 languages, ancient and modern. He was a Chaucer scholar, and if any of you take a class on the Old English epic *Beowulf*, it's possible that your teacher will also ask you to read Gardner's novel *Grendel*, which retells the story of Beowulf's battle with the monster Grendel from the monster's point-of-view. (It's a bit like *Beowulf* meets Walt Disney.) Gardner so loved the poet Homer that at age 45 he taught himself Greek in order to do his own translation of *The Iliad* for his students, whose work—by the way—Gardner published at his own expense in a magazine he started in the 1950s. He translated Japanese authors whose work he admired, and published over 30 of his own books—novels, short stories, and poetry. He wrote librettos, screenplays, book reviews, *everything* possible in the English language, and on top of all that he played the French horn. He also believed deeply in an artist's and scholar's *duty* to teach what he (or she) has learned, and to prepare the next generation to pick up the torch of creating and educating.

The word "education" has Latin roots. If you look it up, you'll discover that "education" comes from the Latin word *educare*, which means "to lead out or draw out." In other words, education is not simply about pouring information into the head of passive students. No, it is about drawing out each student's individual potential, so that they—the students—can continue to learn and grow long after they have left their professors, and even to contradict their professors in the name of truth, if that becomes necessary.

This was the kind of teacher John Gardner was. He believed the university provided each of us with a rare opportunity to—in the words of Aristotle—"actualise our full potential." I can assure that it wasn't until I went to college that I realised how the arts and sciences were *inter-connected* and *inter-disciplinary* at their very foundation. I discovered that the love of art inevitably led to a curiosity about the history of ideas, and that the history of ideas led to a critical interest in culture, which in turn demanded the study of *other* cultures as well. My teachers like Howie and Gardner helped me discover that the seed of a single passion well pursued can flower into a lifelong commitment to creativity and the quest for knowledge.

As freshmen, you will find educators like these at the University of Washington. The UW has 4 recipients of the Nobel Prize, 36 professors with awards from the National Academy of Sciences, 10 teachers honored by the National Academy of Engineering, 38 by the National Institute of Medicine, 24 who are members of the American Academy of Arts and Sciences, 6 MacArthur fellows, 3 National Medal of Science winners, 42 recipients of Guggenheim fellowships, and one National Book Award winner.

During the next four years it will be to your advantage to regard all of your professors and classes as a resource, as doorways into worlds of knowledge and experience. Some of those yet unopened doors may deliver you to careers and achievements you cannot dream of this morning. But let me give you one warning so that four years from now you don't carry your transcript over to President McCormick and ask him, "How does this all fit together?" The warning is this: You cannot hold the university responsible for your intellectual life. The only person ultimately responsible for the diversity of your skills and the depth of your knowledge is *you*. You must bring the curiosity. You must bring the passion to—as the Greeks put it—"Know thyself." The only thing your teachers can provide is a strong yet flexible foundation for learning, one that we expect you will build upon for the remainder of your days on this earth. I think educator Mortimer Adler sums this up very well when he says:

> What is the real end of learning? What is the ultimate goal toward which every part of schooling or education is directed? I think you all know the word that describes it. It is wisdom. We would all like to be a little wiser than we are—to have a little more understanding, a little more insight, a little more comprehension of the human situation, of the conditions of our lives, of the world in which we live; to know better the difference between good and evil. But how long does it take to become wise? The answer is, a lifetime. Certainly we all know that we cannot become wise in youth. Nothing would be more preposterous than the supposition that a boy or girl graduating from college could be wise.
>
> Nor can you ever have enough wisdom, or too much. No matter how wise we become little by little in the course of a lifetime, we are always less than perfectly wise, nor are we ever as wise as we can be. Hence, if wisdom is the ultimate goal of the whole process of learning, then that process must go on for a lifetime. For any of us to attain even the little wisdom we can acquire in the course of our whole life, there is no stopping short. We can never become wise enough to say 'Now I can stop learning or thinking.' Wisdom is hard to come by and is slowly won....

In closing, let me make one final remark.

I've spoken about the transformative impact the university may have on you. What is equally important is the impact each of you will have on the University of Washington while you are here and after you leave. UW is 135-years-old, but it is not finished. Like you—like me—this school is in a constant process of change and evolution. If your teachers are to realise *their* full potential, they need you and the best that you can give. What Martin Luther King Jr. once said about all Americans is equally true for the relationship between you and the professors you will meet this week. He said, "Strangely enough, I can never be what I ought to be until you are what you ought to be. You can never be what you ought to be until I am what I ought to be."

This is the adventure of the university. All together, each of us possessing what the other needs, we form—as teachers and students—a community which moves toward enlightenment and completion.

Thank you and have a terrific first year.

11

A Tribute to Charles Johnson, Teacher of Writers

— Marc C. Conner

I have been privileged to encounter the work of Charles Johnson in a number of ways: as a student in his fiction writing seminars at the University of Washington in the late 1980s; as a scholar of his work since the late 1990s, publishing numerous reviews and papers and also my book of essays on his work, *Charles Johnson: The Novelist as Philosopher*; and as a teacher of his novels, short stories, and philosophical writings in my literature courses. But although I've written often about his work from multiple literary and philosophical perspectives, I've never addressed—nor have I ever heard anyone else address—the activity that has probably occupied more of his time over the last 30 years than any other: the teaching of writing.

Yet it's peculiarly appropriate to talk of Charles Johnson as simultaneously a writer and a teacher of writing, for this gets at two of the fundamental elements of his identity. He is, first and foremost, a writer—and he is by profession (or was, until his official retirement in June of 2009) a teacher of other writers. But he goes further: Johnson is a theorist of the pedagogies of writing, or, put differently, he has thought long and hard about what we do when we teach others to write. And he has pursued the question that nags many of us: why- -*why on earth?*—do we teach people to write? What motivates this?

Johnson himself was never a product of the university writing workshop approach to teaching writing. He first *taught himself* how to write, having written six novels in the late 1960s and early 1970s, cranking them out at the rate of one novel per ten-week college term—a rate that at least speaks to his work ethic and determination. He then came under the tutelage of the late John Gardner, and so underwent a second level of education in the teaching of writing. Finally, in 1976, Johnson came to the University of Washington to teach writing at the college level, and so he learned to teach writing through the necessity of having to do it on a daily basis. Through these very different experiences in his own learning, Johnson developed his own idiosyncratic method, what he calls his "boot camp" in creative writing.

The best way to describe these fiction workshops run by Johnson is as an all-consuming immersion for the students in the many techniques and skills required to become an accomplished writer of good prose fiction. In a 2003 essay for the *Chronicle of Higher Education*, Johnson describes what he emphasizes in these courses: it is "a labor-intensive 'skill acquisition' course"—he says he is less interested in *what* one writes than in *how* one writes; it must include "capacious" reading and instruction in all styles, genres, and subgenres of fiction; it must train students in a large "repertoire of literary strategies," including the mastery of dozens of writing exercises culled from figures such as Gardner, Weathers and Winchester, and many of Johnson's own invention; students must begin reading a full dictionary—must learn to keep a writer's journal—must outline a half-dozen future stories—and much more. The goal, he states, is for them to master as much as possible the techniques and skills—the toolbox—of fiction writing.

This method is most akin to the medieval apprentice model, whereby one progresses from novice to trainee to journeyman to—if one has sufficient gifts—master's level. Johnson compares it quite rightly to the training undergone by a jazz musician, or a martial artist. For just as the beginner martial artist must master certain basic stances, blocks, and strikes, and then progress into basic kata forms, that themselves will become increasingly complex as the student grows; and only then can the student begin to understand how to apply the kata training in actual combat—so too the beginner artist must move through basic techniques into more advanced forms. And just as the martial arts adage holds that a student must perform a move at least 1,000 times before he has made it his own and can use it in combat, so too the writer must repeat and repeat the basic moves of her craft before it becomes her own and can be employed in creating publishable fiction—the writer's equivalent, perhaps, of tournament sparring... or even real-life fighting?

Yet the training of dozens of prose technicians each year hardly describes Charles Johnson's efforts as a teacher of writing. In another essay, "Storytelling and the Alpha Narrative," he states that "craft is only one side of the story," and that "the *other* side of the story—what craft is in the service of"—is even more compelling. "Why," he asks, "do we write fiction? Why do we read it?... Why are stories so important to us?" It's because this question is so consuming for Johnson that he also has his fiction students read such works as Longinus's classic aesthetics treatise, "On the Sublime," along with Sartre's probing essay, "What is Literature?," Albert Murray's "The Hero and the Blues," and Northrop Frye's elegant study, "The Educated Imagination." The goal is to help students understand the majesty and magic of deep reading experiences. Johnson argues that the true practice of reading has much in common with the phenomenological experience of bracketing one's experience and focusing only on the present moment—much as the Buddhist turns all attention to this present spot of existence and resists the allure of the illusionary past and future. Johnson blocks out all extra-literary concerns—critical ideas, reputations, literary theories, etc.—and seeks only "the same innocent enchantment I had when I was a reader of twelve or thirteen... the experience of mystery and wonder, and needing to know *what happens next*." When a story has sufficient power and magic to so consume the reader that everything disappears except the story—this is what Johnson terms an "Alpha Narrative": "stories that endure," that "liberate our perception." Or more simply: "whopping good stories."

How does one create such a story? Johnson suggests that it is less a matter of conscious creation, more a matter of allowing the story to emerge, much like the old Zen proverb of the sculptor whose main task is to see the stunning statue that resides within the unworked piece of wood or stone (a figure he depicts in Reb the coffinmaker in his novel *Oxherding Tale*). Johnson cites Aristotle in this regard and his concept of *energeia*, or "the actualisation of the potential which exists in character and situation." "The actualisation of the potential"—so a skilled writer must be able, first, to recognise a great story when it appears before her (thus Johnson's insistence on training their skills as readers); and that writer must have the *techne* necessary to help that story emerge into a work of serious craftsmanship, perhaps even art. He writes, "I view the techniques and elements of craft that I've taught writing students simply as tools to prepare them for the time when such a narrative drops into their laps."

All of these ideas—of the reading experience, of the craft and techniques of writing, of the range of voices, styles, and perspectives that the writer must master—are present in Johnson's own creative work, as any reader of his novels and stories can attest. Of particular interest to me is the venture that he began 12 years ago, writing a "Bedtime Story" for the Humanities Washington annual autumn gathering. These 11 stories are incredibly diverse, in every sense of the word—including its Renaissance meaning of "not alike in nature or qualities" or even "different from, or opposed to what is right, good... *perverse, adverse*," particularly if we understand "what is right" as "what our culture today tells us is right." To the standards of today's culture, with its emphasis on hedonism, mediocrity, a flattening of experience and of art, and particularly its moral indifference, Johnson's work is certainly *adverse, perverse*. This is the heart of his teacher John Gardner's credo, "On Moral Fiction"—that fiction calls us to an ethical stance, demands that we engage our moral lives, what Levinas terms the face-to-face confrontation with the other. These imaginative, fanciful stories of bedtime are indeed confrontations with otherness: fairy tales of princes turning to frogs, historical meditations on Descartes's meeting with the

Queen of Sweden, imaginative journeys to Africa or Ancient Greece, science fiction forays; and they exhibit all the formal diversity of an 18th-century narrative, ranging from animal tale to parable to fabula to dream vision to good old-fashioned realism. The best of these stories, for this reader, is "Dr. King's Refrigerator," a delightful re-imagining of the early days of King's work, focusing more on King as man, husband, and philosopher, less on the world-historical figure he would shortly become. The story delights and it instructs, in the best Horatian tradition, but also in the tradition of the *Book of Proverbs*, a text that has fascinated Johnson for at least the past decade. Proverbs is the domain of Wisdom Literature, the teachings that allow a people to survive in the midst of a world that would consume them. If modernity teaches us to disavow a literature that teaches, Johnson insists that only a literature that does teach is finally worthy of our attention. This is his phenomenology of teaching, as all distraction fades and the reader is left in the solitary confrontation with the transcendent written word. To read, to ponder, to create, and to help others in these tasks, this is the word-work of Charles Johnson, and our participation in this exercise is, to me, the most telling tribute we can offer to this superb writer.

12

Walking Meditation: Sangha on Unbound Pages

for Charles Johnson

— Sharyn Skeeter

Along the path you curve black ink,
draw a man's cheek in a box. Gags
move his feet from the page.

May they be free from suffering.

Your sailor gambles, escapes
the bayou, leaves debt onshore,
swims in wakes. Salt
water cleanses his lungs.

May they be free from fear.

The runaway teacher
threadbare and gray, sleeps
in a coffin, one eye open.
Your keystrokes balance
his compass to center.

May they be safe.

You lead the dreamer, walking,
in space between words,
through black and white lines,
on divided streets.

May they be whole.

Your pages breathe, flicker
in light. Gongs vibrate,
pulse, dissolve into silence.

13

The Meaning of Barack Obama

— Charles Johnson

There are many things we can say about the historically unprecedented campaign of Senator Barack Obama to become America's first non-white president, but one thing we can certainly expect the general election in November to do is take the temperature of racial attitudes in America at the dawn of a new century.

For Buddhists, awakening is the goal of our practice. After decades of meditation, daily spiritual practice, and study of the dharma, we find ourselves acutely aware of how intellectual constructs can create illusion or ignorance (*avidya*), and fuel divisiveness and dualism in our lives. Clearly, one of the most toxic of these illusions is the notion of "race." To be sure, it is a political issue. But more importantly, it is an enlightenment issue as well.

By now we know—or *should* know—that race is our grandest lived delusion and grief-causing fiction: "a social construction," says Stanford University historian Richard White, who reminds us that at one time the Irish, Jews, Poles, and southern Europeans were excluded from the exclusive social club of "whiteness." As scientists continue sequencing the genome, they find no biological basis for race. Sharon Begley's 2003 "Science Journal" column in *The Wall Street Journal* reported that, "Geneticists find that when they add up the tiny genetic variations that make one person different from the next, there are more differences within races than between races."

"Race has no basic biological reality," Jonathan Marks, a Yale University biologist, reported in a Knight-Ridder newspaper article. "The human species simply doesn't come packaged that way." Stanford geneticist Luigi Cavalli-Sforza added, "The characteristics that we see with the naked eye that help us distinguish individuals from different continents are, in reality, skin-deep. Whenever we look under the veneer we find that the differences that seem so conspicuous to us are really trivial."

Yet, for all that, we continue to live the lie of race, which according to an article in a 2003 issue of *Science News* literally makes us stupider. "White people who hold biased feelings toward blacks have to work to control their thoughts and behaviors during interracial encounters," said Dartmouth psychologist Jennifer Richeson. "This social strategy depletes the limited pool of mental resources available for monitoring and using various types of information."

Even before the current popular interest in DNA research, Guy Murchie wrote in *The Seven Mysteries of Life* that if we trace our ancestry back fifty generations to C.E. 700, we find we all share a common ancestor. None of us, Murchie insists, can be less closely related than fiftieth cousins. "Your own ancestors," he wrote, "whoever you are, include not only some blacks, some Chinese, and some Arabs, but all the blacks, Chinese, Arabs, Malays, Latins, Eskimos, and every other possible ancestor who lived on Earth around A.D. 700 .... It is virtually certain therefore that you are a direct descendent of Muhammad and every fertile predecessor of his, including ... Confucius, Abraham, Buddha, Caesar, Ishmael, and Judas Iscariot."

Murchie's observation is, for those with dharma-trained eyes, a statement of dependent origination (*pratitya samutpada*), or what Thich Nhat Hahn calls our "inter-being." My point, if it isn't clear yet, is that race is *maya*, a chimera constructed for reasons of social, political, and economic domination, and for the comfort of fragile, insecure egos.

It is easy to recognise in the biography of Barack Obama this interpenetration of backgrounds that transcends dualism.

There is the white mother from that most iconic of states in pop culture (Kansas, for heaven's sake, Toto), the Muslim father from Kenya (which makes him genuinely *African*-American), his formative years spent in Indonesia and his Indonesian half-sister, and Hawaii (a state of considerable multicultural diversity). Indeed, his clearly multiracial background, like that of Tiger Woods, Halle Berry, and, if we scratch ourselves deeply enough, all of us, indicates a demographic that will only vividly increase in the twenty-first century, with the generic and misleading terms "white" and "black" consigned to the dustbin of human history.

In fact, it is primarily this subtext—his cosmopolitan, globe-spanning background and sensitivity—that made the initial public response to Obama after the Iowa primary nothing short of *primal*, and he and his wife Michelle the stuff that dreams are made of, symbols for a new century and its desire to transcend tribalism and the barriers between people. With little political history or baggage to weigh him down (which to his opponents is an Achilles heel), Obama is, as he himself has said, a kind of blank slate onto which Americans have projected their deepest and most visceral social and cultural longings.

For black people, the promise of his becoming president is the "impossible dream" their ancestors had nurtured since the era of slavery. For whites, a presidential candidate of color—especially one who in his speeches transcends decades of Balkanisation along the lines of race, class, and gender—means that the ideals of equality and opportunity enshrined in the nation's most sacred documents are not just fine-sounding words but a tangible possibility that might take place in our lifetime. And across the planet (in a Muslim nation, a man told reporters the freshman senator looked like people he saw every day), Obama's seemingly exotic but in fact very common background is inspirational because, as he told an audience of 200,000 in Germany, he is an American who views himself as "a fellow citizen of the world." At a time when the prestige of the United States has been badly damaged abroad, Obama's approach has not been the disjunctive, polarising "either/or" style of the past eight years, but instead is conjunctive, in the spirit of "both/and," which is far more compatible with the dharma.

Predictably, Obama's universality has triggered both confusion and criticism. As David Brooks said in *The New York Times*, "There is a sense that because of his unique background and temperament, Obama lives apart. He put one foot in the institutions he rose through on his journey but never fully engaged .... This ability to stand apart accounts for his fantastic powers of observation, and his skills as a writer and thinker. It means that people on almost all sides of an issue can see parts of themselves reflected in Obama's eyes. But it does make him hard to place."

Eloquent and elegant, charismatic and holding a degree from Harvard Law, always comfortable in his skin, he and Michelle are also avatars of a new black America of the post-civil rights period: namely, of two generations of high-achieving, disciplined black professionals—historically *transitional* generations—whose accomplishments are everywhere evident in fields as diverse as business, the sciences, education, law, and the entertainment industry. Has the hour arrived, then, for a member of this generation to move into the White House?

Perhaps it would be best to describe the Obama phenomenon as being, from a Buddhist perspective, not so much revolutionary as potentially *evolutionary*. But if so, then one problem Obama faces are people who do not want to evolve beyond the ancient stupidity and error of epidermalising the world, who are attached to the idea of a racial (or geographic) identity as a way of avoiding the experience of their true nature as interconnectedness or emptiness. Or, if you prefer existentialist thought to the buddhadharma, see this in terms of Sartre's famous statement, "Existence precedes essence."

In other words, the meaning of our lives is never pre-given: whatever meaning we find is based on our deeds, actions, and, as Martin Luther King, Jr. once said, "the content of our character." The senator from Illinois, who repeatedly rejects obsolete ways of thinking and talking about race, predictably finds himself walking a cultural tightrope, always performing with balance, remarkable grace, and civility when attacked by those with a tribal mentality (white, black, and otherwise) who feel most threatened by the monumental sea change his presence in American politics represents. If his campaign fails, it may well be for the reason Charles M. Blow identified in an op-ed piece in *The New York Times*: the inability of American voters to "let go" the illusion of race. If he wins, we may have the possibility of a bit of liberation and relief from centuries of racial masks and dissembling.

For Obama understands that a black presidential hopeful can only become the leader of the most powerful nation in human history if he rises above the racially provincial and parochial; if his humanity, empathy, and compassion are strongly felt to be genuine by his "fellow citizens of the world." That is one enduring lesson of this dramatic, unprecedented campaign. And whether he wins or not in November, the truth that excellence is color-blind, and that broad service to others has no tribal affiliation, will live on in our memories long after the general election is over.

14

Philosophy, Perception, Buddhism and Literary Art as Language Performance: A Conversation with Charles Johnson

— Adam Tolbert

Over the last forty years in several novels, essays, interviews, and classrooms, Charles R. Johnson has promoted our universal ability to learn from the best that has been done and said. The engine of his effort as a novelist, scholar, and teacher is to learn from and contribute to what he calls "perennially important questions such as the nature of the self or personal identity; perceptual experience and the polymorphous character of meaning; the relationship between the individual and society as well as that of the individual to history; and, finally, the question of what do we mean exactly—indeed, what *can* we mean—by such terms as freedom and liberation." For such a grand quest, Johnson employs Eastern and Western philosophies of existence to highlight the illusory nature of appearances and to persecute the fallible separation between subject and object. By seeing existence in terms of a we-relation, or what Thich Nhat Hanh calls "Interbeing," Johnson believes that self-limiting concepts of separateness must yield to curiosity and a more fully realised existence based on a variety of philosophies. Ultimately, Professor Johnson sees his novels as "invitations for contemporary readers to interrogate the promise and potential for what it means to be human, and to do so equipped with the fruit of the intellectual and spiritual journeys of our predecessors and ancestors from all over the world."

Tolbert: Professor Johnson, please accept my respectful thanks. I admire your work as a storyteller and your efforts to explore the nature of existence. As a young man growing up in Evanston, Illinois, what set you off on this journey around the philosophical world?

Johnson: It was art, the love of art. In my childhood, nothing delighted me more than drawing, which naturally led to a love of being exposed to artworks in all forms, and from all time periods and cultures. In my teens, I could think of nothing more glorious than being an artist capable of producing work that an audience might experience as good, true and beautiful. That love of doing art led to a deep curiosity about the lives and methods and cultural milieu of other artists (in other words to a broad interest in art criticism and history), the vision behind a particular work of art or cultural product (in other words to philosophy), and since so much Western and Eastern art has been based on religion, that initial seed of loving art progressed to a love of the life of the spirit, and to spiritual practice. It is from that single passion—the love of art—that everything else in my life has grown. So I am especially pleased that my 25-year-old daughter Elisheba, a conceptual artist, created last year her first business, Faire Gallery/Café in Seattle, a space where she features each month the work of a new painter or sculptor (and others), as well as jazz musicians, comedians, poetry readings, and the performance of plays for the community on Capitol Hill.

Tolbert: Pictorial art is one of the oldest expressions of individuality, and yet in the act of being representational, a work of art is the essence of unity. We could look for the foundations of your artistic inspiration in the caves at Lascaux. 30,000 years ago, where a human hand sculpted horses in flight across the Dordogne. Other hands painted and engraved bison at pasture, and still others preferred to draw mammoth. The artist was able, through careful study and attention, to *re*present everyday items through the lens of his perception. This act of individuality gave the tribe another way to "sing the world." That spark lit new fires in their imaginations, and for the next 30,000 years (and counting), men, women, and children of many tribes continued to explore the nature of perception, representation, and existence in relation to this singular act. The artists who worked at Lascaux had no idea that their art would affect so many, and yet the mastery of their craft reverberates across the ages. You mention the desire to produce art that is "good, true, and beautiful," which is a reference to Plato's belief in forms that are universal and therefore capable of being appreciated across races, times, and cultures.

In the *Symposium*, Plato declares: "For herein is the evil of ignorance, that he who is neither good nor wise is nevertheless satisfied with himself: he has no desire for that of which he feels no want." How did you see a role for Plato and other culturally distant thinkers in your life?

Johnson: As a philosophy student, I first encountered the Dialogues of Plato and the philosophy of the pre-Socratics when I was eighteen-years-old. I truly regret that these days a class in philosophy (which literally means, "the love of wisdom") is no longer a requirement for the bachelor's degree. A report released in 1997 by the National Association of Scholars at Princeton, "The Dissolution of General Education 1914-1993," found that a required, mandatory course in philosophy dropped from more than 75 percent of colleges in 1914 to just four percent in 1993. This is tragic insofar as a solid foundation in philosophy gives a student a leg up, so to speak, in almost any other field he chooses to study. All the various disciplines—physics, psychology, ethics, biology, logic, political theory, religion, ethics, aesthetics—have their roots and origins in classical philosophy before they broke away to become separate fields of study. The beautiful thing about the systematic study of philosophy for a writer (or anyone) is that it empowers him (or her) to address or interpret a very wide-range of cultural phenomenon.

As for Plato, it was once the case that every college student had to read Socrates' *Defense* (Apology), if only to appreciate how this "gadfly of the state," put to death by the Athenians, defined through his life the beauty and challenge faced by all men and women who seek truth. "I should reply, Gentlemen," he said, according to Plato, "I am your very grateful and devoted servant, but I owe a greater obedience to God than to you, and as long as I draw breath and have my faculties, I shall never stop practicing philosophy and exhorting you and elucidating the truth for everyone I meet. I shall go on saying, in my usual way, my very good friend, you are an Athenian and belong to a city which is the greatest and most famous in the world for its wisdom and strength. Are you not ashamed that you give your attention to acquiring as much money as possible, and similarly with reputation and honor, and give no attention or thought to truth and understanding and the perfection of your soul?"

Such remarkable eloquence stirred me when I was in my late teens, as it has stirred men and women, regardless of race, class or gender for two thousand years. These are words, I daresay, that our politicians and the general public today should be urged to commit to memory, for if Plato shows us anything through the figure of Socrates, it is that the essence of philosophy is asking throughout our lives the question, "How shall I live?" When we are at our best, intellectually and morally, we are all Platonists.

Tolbert: To value philosophy and the unending pursuit of "truth and understanding and the perfection of the soul" is to approach the world with humility, to wake each morning with more questions than answers, and to exist forever on a journey of discovery. Stripped of simple definitions, we become bearers of complexity and pilgrims of the unknown—seeking what happens in the genesis of the empirical and the spiritual—seeing ourselves always as part and process of the experiment. Though Socrates wore simple clothes and counted few (if any) properties to his name, he was a student of the world and the quest to discover his place in it.

One tends to think of this sort of inquiry as being the sole province of Ivory Towers and wise leaders such as Marcus Aurelius who realised that everyone must "observe constantly that all things take place by change, and accustom thyself to consider that the nature of the Universe loves nothing so much as to change the things which are and to make new things like them." What must be noted here is that Aurelius *chose* to study the wealth of ways that it *can mean to be in the world*, and with that choice he was able to transcend a life limited by any single cultural outlook. A broad interest in knowledge made him more relevant to the multi-faceted people in his charge, and to all of us that read him through the ages. Great philosophers and great kings are forged by a willingness to improve the Self, which is the right and province of all living things.

What role does reading play in your work as a writer, and what is your relationship to *The Educated Imagination* by Northrop Frye?

Johnson: I love your description of the beauty that comes from living an "examined life." Your reference to Marcus Aurelius has touched me on a personal level, because his *Meditations* got me through a rough path of living thirty years ago when I was a poor graduate student with one published novel under my belt, a first baby on the way, my Ph.D. exams to prepare for, and, of course, the book world expecting a second novel. That work by Marcus Aurelius—so wise, so unerring in its interpretation of our experience—has always seemed to me to be a meditation that might well have been written by an advanced student of the Buddhadharma.

As for Northrop Frye, one can hardly say enough about his importance as a literary scholar of insight and imagination. In his lovely radio lectures from the 1960s, *The Educated Imagination* (still in print after all these decades), he makes it very clear that we—as writers—can only learn what writing is from reading others. There is no other way to become a literary craftsman. Others teach us the literary conventions of our moment in cultural history. If one reads, say, murder mysteries it is very likely that person will one day attempt to write a murder mystery. And if one reads deeply in philosophy—and philosophical fiction like that produced by the French existentialists in the 1940s and '50s—it follows, from Frye's observation, that one will most likely be inclined to write a "novel of ideas." In my aesthetic view, it is therefore crucial for a writer to read widely: the classics of Western and Eastern literature, contemporary fiction, and even what is called "pulp" fiction, for in the latter one often sees a spirited and muscular storytelling, and the writer's commitment to entertain. Such a reading regimen, it's clear, will last for an entire lifetime.

Tolbert: Frye's humble approach to life allows one to open numerous doors of perception, and the pursuit of what Matthew Arnold called "the best that has been done and said" is an open invitation to the interdisciplinary and the international. Dogen Zenji (1200-1253), founder of the Soto school of Zen in Japan, offers a similar view when he says that "to forget the Self is to be enlightened by all things."

In *Turning the Wheel: Essays on Buddhism and Writing* (2003), you write that "this thing we call 'self' is, depending on the spiritual angle from which it is viewed, everything. And nothing. It is empty (*shunyata*), possessing no essence or intrinsic reality; it is, at best, a process dependent each and every moment on all other beings" (p.10). So much human strife is a result of ignoring this we-relation. How has Eastern literature informed your life and work, and what are your favorite teachings from the Buddhadharma?

Johnson: Buddhist literature has been my personal refuge since I was 14-years-old and first practiced meditation. In the tempestuous mid-to-late 1960s when there was so much violence—political assassinations, rioting in cities, anger and polarisation of blacks and whites, old and young—the Buddhadharma provided a place where I could always achieve clarity and inner peace, and with that as my basis I could always work toward achieving respect, *metta* (loving-kindness) and generosity as a goal in all my social relations with others—in my relations to my parents and friends, teachers, then my own students and colleagues, indeed, in my relations with all sentient beings. It nurtured my creativity, especially beautiful visual art like the several versions of "The Ten Oxherding Pictures."

There are sutras that I return to again and again, translating them and committing verses from them to memory. Among these are *The Lotus Sutra*, *Heart Sutra*, *Diamond Sutra*, the frequently very funny *Vimalakirti Sutra*,

Nagarjuna's *Seventy Stanzas on Emptiness*, *Alagaddupama Sutra*, *The Dhammapada* and, of course, the essential *Mahasatipatthana Sutra.*

Tolbert: On page one of *Oxherding Tale* (1982), you include four quotations. The first is from St. Augustine: "Noli foras ire in te redi in interiore homine habitat veritas," which means, "Do not wander far and wide, but return into yourself. Deep within man there dwells the truth." The second quotation is from the *Rig Veda* (1500 BCE): "I do not know what I am like here, I do not know in relation to what I can say, 'This I am.' Bewildered and lost in thought, I wander." The third quotation is from the *Ten Oxherding Pictures* (1200 CE): "Desolate through forests and fearful in jungles, he is seeking an Ox he does not find." The fourth and final quotation is from Franz Kafka's *The Great Wall of China* (1933): "There exists in the same human being varying perceptions of one and the same object which differ so completely from each other that one can only deduce the existence of different subjects in the same human being."

What is the significance of these quotations to your worldview as a human being, a philosopher, and a novelist?

Johnson: If we rearrange a bit the epigraphs for this 1982 novel, I think we have a general outline for spiritual progress. Start with the quote from the *Rig Veda*, which describes the state of consciousness when (as an existentialist would say) it is hurled into the world (and rudely at that). At birth we are given no blueprints for living, and we find competing models for morality in a society that is incoherent, inconsistent, and always changing. Next go to the quote from St. Augustine, which is the first bit of wisdom consciousness receives or stumbles upon: namely, that whatever truth it will find must be found, not in the external world, but within the seeker himself (or herself). This starts a spiritual aspirant on the path. I would put the quote from the *Ten Oxherding Pictures* next. The seeker is still "bewildered" and feeling "desolate," because when he looks into what Augustine calls "yourself," he cannot find the Ox (self). Finally, he progresses to the fourth quote, the insight from Kafka that he seems to be several selves or subjects. In other words, as he examines his own mind, his own thoughts and feelings in, say, *vipassana* meditation, he realises that his perceptions, feelings and thoughts (so many of these are not even his own, but instead reflect the conditioning he has received from others, from his parents, teachers, friends, and the enveloping social world) seem to represent many people. Yet he realises that these feelings, ideas and thoughts are just the activity of the restless mind, and he does not identify with any of it. Rather he simply observes these perceptions, ideas and feelings, letting them arise and fall away (for they, too, are impermanent, like all things) until the mind grows quiet, peaceful again, and he realises that an enduring "self" in an illusion.

Tolbert: In *The Art of Fiction* (1983), John Gardner declares that "art produces the most important progress civilisation knows. Restating old truths and adapting them to the age, applying them in ways they were never before applied, stirring up emotion by the inherent power of narrative, visual image, or music, artists crack the door to the morally necessary future. The age-old idea of human dignity comes to apply even to the indigent, even to slaves." This seems to be your goal in *Oxherding Tale* (1982), and especially *Middle Passage* (1990), which was recognised with the National Book Award. If I were to look for a "morally necessary future" implied by your writing in *Oxherding Tale* and *Middle Passage*, it would be that humans must respect each other and choose to study "the best that has been done and said" if we are to be free of the limitations of perception and gain the tools necessary to transcend the physical, spiritual, intellectual, and economic challenges of existence. In both novels, you incorporate Eastern and Western philosophies of existence that demonstrate a concept of identity where the Self is a continuing journey between ports; a nonentity defined more by interrelatedness and transformative change than by a solid sense of an unchanging "I."

What are your thoughts about John Gardner's assertions, and what do you see as America's most significant symbol of interrelatedness and transformative change?

Johnson: Gardner, as you know, was my literary mentor, though not a spiritual or philosophical one since he was rather frightened by the Buddhadharma. Please see my discussion of this and his softening of his initial suspicion of the East in my essay "Literary Culture and Civilisation: Autopsy for a Creative Writing Workshop," which appears in the summer, 2008 issue of *Michigan Quarterly Review*.

If I had to select an American "symbol of interrelatedness and transformative change," I would pick Martin Luther King Jr., who told us that, "It really boils down to this: That all life is interrelated. We are all caught in an inescapable network of mutuality, tied in a single garment of destiny. Whatever affects one directly, affects all indirectly."

Tolbert: With the inauguration of President Barack Obama, we are witnessing a worldwide outpouring of gratitude, respect, and hope for positive change. What is perhaps more striking about this journey is that beyond any single concept of race, religion, culture, or class, President Obama is almost a universal representation of human excellence. He is hardworking, honest, humble, compassionate, rational, practical, imaginative, and inclusive. What are your thoughts about the diverse support that made his election possible, and what are your thoughts about his role as president in relation to aspects of the black American experience and the course of human events?

Johnson: In August of 2008, I wrote two essays on Barack Obama's unprecedented and dramatic campaign to become the first black American president. The first, "The Cultural Challenge of Barack Obama," is the concluding essay in the LIFE photo-book, *The American Journey of Barack Obama*. The second, "The Meaning of Barack Obama," was published in *Shambhala Sun* and later appeared on Henry Louis Gates Jr's The Root.com. In both these essays I emphasised what I saw as the hallmarks of Obama's campaign: namely, he ran by presenting an image of professional and intellectual excellence, not racial grievances or calcified political ideology. And as we all now know, his personal background is global, stretching from Kansas to Kenya, from Hawaii to Indonesia. He is not simply our 44th president, he is truly a cultural hero in the classic sense of that phrase, with whom millions of people across this planet identify. And his bi-racial background gives us a glimpse of an important demographic of the future. It's way too early to make any predictions about his administration or how successfully it will address so many things that are broken—our economy, our military, our culture, our public schools. But he begins his first term with a tremendous amount of good will, and this is across ethnic or tribal lines, lines Obama seems determined to both honor and at the same time transcend. On a personal note, I have to confess that, like so many others, he is the first president I've truly cared about in my lifetime.

15

The World, the Desert and the Allmuseri God

— Aurélie Bayre

(Avyakta)

> La grandeur de l'homme est toujours de recréer sa vie.
>
> —Simone Weil, *La Pesanteur et la grâce.*[1]

> Quand l'esprit tomba
> Du ventre de sa mère
> Un étrange combat
> L'attendait sur la Terre
>
> Perdu dans la clameur
> Il devint plusieurs
> L'esprit fut l'éclaireur
> De ses membres inférieurs
>
> Commandez, nous obéirons
> Tête - épaules - genoux - pieds
> Ordonnez, nous donnerons
> Nous vous sommes tous liés
>
> Tout le long du voyage
> Tous à l'ouvrage
>
> —Ze Jam Afane, "Le voyage de l'esprit."[2]

Middle Passage describes a political catastrophe, epitomised by *The Republic* sinking into a "chaosmos of roily water and fire"(183). At the same time, the novel dwells into a metaphysical reflexion.

The situation on board *The Republic* could be described as such: there are three levels. On the upper level, the deck, what goes on is pre-political life. This is where we ask, "What kind of government do we want?" Let us now descend one level deeper, into the hold, where the slaves are kept. Now, the question is, "How do we consider other human beings? How do we relate to them?" And, while we're here, let's also visit the secret chamber which holds the mysterious cargo at the stem of the ship. This is where we find the Allmuseri God. There, the question becomes: "What do we think of ourselves? How do we see ourselves? And what is the self, anyway?" As we go from the upper deck to the lower parts of the ship, questions and concerns shift from "the skin of our social life," (Johnson, qtd. in Whalen-Bridge, 88) which can be pre-political, political, anti-political, or even apolitical, to deeper, more fundamental concerns: "How do I relate to other beings? In what way are the people I see as "the Other" really different from me?" Both of these concerns rely on the answer we give to one last question, "Who, or what, am I?"

Let's start with politics. The situation on board is pre-political, and most of the time anti-political, by which I mean that it could lead to politics, but instead gives way to a state that is the opposite of what politics is. Here, I draw on Hannah Arendt's definitions, which can be read in *The Promise of Politics.* She has a very definite and straight-forward answer to the question, "What is politics?" "The meaning of politics is freedom" (Arendt, 108). She sees politics as a very rare moment in history. To the German philosopher, politics can only exist provided that certain freedoms are guaranteed. For politics to appear there must be freedom of speech. In addition to freedom, we also need courage, which is associated with action, and judgment. Moreover, we have to remember that politics is based on the plurality of men. When a government doesn't leave this freedom to the people, when it flouts the people's power of judgment and forgets the plurality of men, it cannot be called political.

What I want to show here is that while overall *The Republic* is a political catastrophe, Rutherford shows all of these political qualities. More importantly, the Allmuseri God suggests a new understanding of plurality, which is no more "*me* versus *thee*,"(140, Johnson's emphasis) a perception incompatible with

Arendt's politics, but becomes "me and thee and thee and thee...(ad lib.)"

By freedom of speech and opinion, Arendt means the ability to speak, which requires the ability to listen. Indeed, freedom of speech and opinion is "the right to hear the opinions of others and to have one's opinion heard"(Arendt, 125). Speech and listening are not to be mistaken with command and submission. Courage is an important political virtue, because the "in-between world... does not owe its creation to production but to human action" (Arendt, 190). Through action we build the world, and courage, according to Arendt, "lies at the root of action"(202). The philosopher also links action to spontaneity, "the freedom that lies in our being able to begin anew"(Arendt, 126). Therefore courage and "freedom to begin anew" are two sides of a same coin.

Arendt defines judgment, "in which political thought is essentially based" (Arendt, 101) as opposed to prejudice. Although she died before she could elaborate her definition of judgment, we understand that she regarded it as a cardinal virtue, of which Eichmann was deprived (qtd. in Taylor, 167). Judgment is the ability to form thoughts that have never been thought before, or the faculty to evaluate a situation without relying on prejudice. Arendt also carefully defines politics as relying upon the plurality of men, as opposed to religion, science and philosophy which only see "Man": "God's creation of the plurality of men is embodied in the absolute difference of all men from one another, which is greater than the relative difference among peoples, nations, or races. But in that case, there is in fact no role for politics. From the very start, politics organises those who are absolutely different with a view to their *relative* equality and in contradistinction to their *relative* differences" (96, Arendt's emphasis).

One cannot account for this absolute difference from one being to another with models such as nation or race. Similarity and difference can always be found between nations and races. Similarity is not to be understood as equality. It is nothing but difference in reverse. As a monozygotic twin, I have a 26-year experience of what Arendt is pointing at. Most people see my twin and I in regards to our relative similarity. The reverse of the relative similarity between us is the relative difference between us two and the rest of the world.

One can see why Arendt distinguished between relative and absolute difference: we could invent another point of reference instead of gemellity, say for example myopia. There, the relative similarity between my sister Lucile and me becomes a relative difference. But in either way, those categories do not tell anything about the absolute difference between Lucile and me, which is as great as the absolute difference between my neighbor and me. Since politics is based on the absolute difference from one individual to another, it considers each of us as unique. Politics makes no assumptions—also called prejudices—such as, "Aurélie is just like Lucile, since they are twins," or, "Aimé Césaire is just like Léopold Cédar Senghor since both are black poets."

In conclusion, Hannah Arendt defines politics as a space which is created by men: it is the space in which speech and deeds contribute to building the "world," man's home on earth. Arendt's world is opposed to the "desert," the desolate place of isolation and force, of "wasteland between men" (Arendt, 190), in which men cannot relate to one another, because they have been deprived of their individuality, their absolute difference. We are in the desert when we lose "the faculty to judge—to suffer and condemn," or, in other words, "the double conjoined faculties of passion and action" (Arendt, 202).

The Republic could be a place for politics, but politics can never be achieved on the ship. The wreckage means that politics is impossible. As a consequence, the world shrinks while "the desert grows" (Nietzsche, 267).

It is when *The Republic* undergoes a crisis that politics could happen. Of course, Falcon's reign in itself is a crisis, because it is anti-political. It allows none of the most basic freedoms, the freedom of speech and the freedom of movement. Instead, it gives way to order and submission. It provokes two mutinies: one superficial, and the other on a deeper level. The former is led by Cringle, and expresses the concerns of the crew members who disagree with the way Falcon manages the ship.

The latter springs from the Allmuseri's refusal to be enslaved. While both movements are motivated by legitimate concerns (Falcon is incompetent and dangerous; it is inhumane to enslave and be enslaved), the double mutiny fails in that it does not result in the openness of the political space, that is, the space between us.

For one thing, Falcon's reign is replaced with that of Diamelo. The two men are similar in that they both rely upon command, submission and coercion. Therefore, their governments are failure in regards to politics. They are anti-political in that they leave no place for speech, listening, interpretation, judgment. Under Falcon's rule, for example, Rutherford is not supposed to speak with the Allmuseri. Under Diamelo's, the Americans must not speak with, or even look at, the Allmuseri women.

Second, the crew mutiny and the slave insurrection conflict each other. The crew fights over the definition of a just government, but it does not ask the fundamental question, "Who can take part in the debate?" The sailors do not question the order which is imposed on everyone on the ship, as they choose to replace Falcon with his second in command, Cringle. Their choice respects the hierarchical order. More importantly, they do not move outside their anti-political box which divides humanity between men and slaves, and sets the slaves out of the crew's world and into Arendtian desert. The crew doesn't ask the vital question of how to enlarge the political space, the world, and this is why they do not expect the slaves' rebellion. Of course, the Allmuseri do ask these questions, and this is why their rebellion, which is more fundamental than the crew's mutiny, turns the situation over. Of all the crew and the slaves, only Rutherford and Ngonyama show interest in understanding what anyone has to say.

Cringle is furious when he understands that Rutherford speaks with the Allmuseri (137). We see there is an unspoken interdiction here. But in the first place, how could Cringle or Falcon, or any of the crew members imagine that Rutherford could speak to the Allmuseri? First, they would have to imagine that he had learned to speak Allmuseri. And, in their eyes, why would he want to do such a thing? The most daring of Rutherford's acts is exactly that he learns to speak Allmuseri. It crosses social and pre-political boundaries as much as, or maybe more than, any of his mischievous deeds as a thief. What seems insane and treacherous to Cringle is in fact the exercise of Rutherford's political freedom and an act of pure courage in Arendt's political terms.

Their political qualities are manifest when Rutherford is beckoned to the forecastle, as the victors are discussing Cringle's fate. While Ngonyama's "plea for sparing Cringle's life [is] *shouted down*" (134, my emphasis), Rutherford asks for the right to have his opinion heard: "*Listen* to me...please!" (Ibid.).

In pleading for Cringle's life, the only man able to steer the ship, Rutherford shows courage, in that he risks his own life, as he understands afterwards: "Now I had endangered my own neck"(135). He realises that speech has become as concrete as a deed, which shows that the situation could switch to politics. It is an evolution he has not mastered yet, since he regrets having spoken up: "Why in heaven's name had I not kept my mouth shut, or choked my luff, as sailors say" (135). Nevertheless, Rutherford's courage reappears later in the novel, after his mystic experience, when he confronts Philippe Zeringue and saves the surviving children (199-204) from "the very Ur-type of Gangster"(13).

Also to be noted is the fact that while Diamelo and Cringle are thinking in terms of relative difference—the Allmuseri and the Americans, the blacks and the whites—Rutherford cuts through and judges from the bare situation: what is at stake is survival. "I'm not on *anybody*'s side! I'm just trying to keep us *alive*!"(137, Johnson's emphasis). Again, the hero shows a political frame of mind. Indeed, while "freedom as the end purpose of politics establishes limits to the realm of politics, the criterion for action within that realm is no longer freedom but competence and efficiency in securing life's necessities" (Arendt, 135).

In spite of Rutherford and Ngonyama's efforts, politics is never achieved on board *The Republic*. Overall, neither the Americans nor the Allmuseri manage to save *The Republic*.

In the end, "the ship goes down because they can't find a way to live together," as the novelist explains (*Passing*, 59). But as the situation worsens, indicating the failure to establish politics, there is still a mystery about the ship that the hero hasn't yet faced: the Allmuseri God. I believe that the God, located at the deepest point of the ship, represents the nature of man, which, Arendt believes, is apolitical (Arendt, 95). While the characters, as a community, cannot reach politics, there is still hope that they can find fulfillment in what the God represents. The quest for politics, the "space between men" fails. What if the Allmuseri God indicated another way to create this space, another way to care for the world?

Charles Johnson shares Arendt's view on the apolitical nature of man when he defines politics as only "the skin of our social life" (Conversation, 88). We can feel it in *Middle Passage*, since what is at stake there is not the question of who will rule whom and how, but, more importantly, how we relate to other beings. How do we learn from one another, and, first, how can we see one another as we see ourselves? To answer these questions, Charles Johnson takes us one step further down, to see the Allmuseri God.

Before answering these questions, I'd like to remind the reader about a piece of advice John Gardner gives to apprentice novelists in his *Art of Fiction*. He discusses the dictum according to which "all expectation raised by the work of fiction must be satisfied, explicitly or implicitly, within the fiction" (Gardner, 3). Taking Homer and Shakespeare as example, he explains that "this aesthetic law is far from absolute" (Gardner, 4). Does Achilles really love Briseus? It is a question the *Iliad* leaves unanswered, because Homer probably thought the matter did not need further explanation. In the same way, Charles Johnson develops the Allmuseri God as an element of fiction in a way that raises questions without answering them. There are two kinds of questions: the first ones are raised by the characters themselves, or by the plot: they are within the fiction. One could consider them trivial, especially since the novelist seems to have decided not to provide clear answers to them. And there are also questions which are, in a way, the skin of fiction itself. Those are the metaphysical questions.

Nevertheless we must begin with the trivial, down-to-earth questions, as they lead the reader to the metaphysical ones: "What is the creature inside the mysterious crate? What does it eat? Where does it go when the ship sinks into the ocean?"

When the narrator first writes about a mysterious cargo, the reader is, like the shipmates, burning with curiosity "What is that thing?" she wonders. A first tentative answer, early in the novel, is that the cargo is a colossus who took the life of five of the men who tried to capture him(53). A colossus being quite an extraordinary being, this marks the moment when the supernatural begins to creep in, but as the reader is provided with detailed descriptions of the Allmuseri tribe, which is another element of the fiction to marvel at, the mysterious cargo tends to stay in the background of the reader's fictional dream. This first answer is complicated later in the novel, after Tommy O'Toole's encounter with the creature. It then appears that the creature is bodiless, as it "[does] not so much occupy a place as it bends space and time around itself like a greatcoat"(68). If we're able to bend space, we can travel in time. Therefore, the Allmuseri God is in time and space more than we can be, since it is now, yesterday, tomorrow, here and there. And as such, it is also out of time and space.

The Allmuseri God dissolves those structures of the mind which we call space and time. In "China," we understood that everything is at the center of the universe, that is that the universe has not one definite center: everything is at the center of the universe, and the center is moving (*Sorcerer*, 87). In *Middle Passage*, we learn that space and time are only structures of the mind, and that the mind can be without those structures. Space and time are limitations, because they create dualities and they erect walls between what is. There is tomorrow, yesterday, and today. I can't have what I had yesterday, and I can't have what I will get tomorrow. I am here, and not there. But those structures let us do things that the Allmuseri God does not have to do, like geometry (101). What is geometry but a way to measure space, to name it, to picture it? The Allmuseri God doesn't have to picture anything—at the very best it *sings* them (69). It does the things themselves. More than that, it *is* those things, all things.

And yet, as the creature first appears to Tommy to be out of space, it seems to be without a body. This impression is immediately contradicted by a clue which indicates an evident bodily existence, since the floor is covered with "dark coils of the creature's defecation"(68). The reader, at this point, is reassured: the creature must be some kind of gigantic animal after all. But aren't those clues of earthbound connection a little unusual? They are "slithering with insects, worms, sluglike beings, that apparently lived inside its bowels"(68). These new details spark off our curiosity again. How could insects live inside the bowel of an animal? Is it some form of life within life, as in a kind of symbiosis?

Our interest about the creature's digestion leads us to another question, raised by Rutherford when Falcon tells him that no one is to feed the new cargo except himself. "Might I ask what it *eats*?"(67, Johnson's emphasis). Again, the immediate answer is not satisfying: "Nothin' from your supplies." We are to understand that the cargo isn't fed with what humans eat. What then? It has to be something on *The Republic*.

After Tommy is taken out of the storeroom, Squibb says the creature "eats people," while Rutherford specifies that it "delight[s] in divesting men of their mind"(167). More precisely, it "eats" dualism. It attracts opposite elements one to the other, and plays with them as if they were magnets: particular and universal, freedom and bondage, body and bodilessness, light and dark. Inside the mysterious crate, for example, is "luminous darkness," and Tommy is "himself chained now yet somehow unchained from all else" (69).

As the God attracts opposite polarities together, it recycles dualism into an endless creation. It plays with dualities, forces them together, creates another thing (n+1), and when some of us elaborate dualities on that new creation, it takes it back and recreates yet another thing (n+2). It never ends.

What does it mean that it "divest[s] men of their mind?" Simply, man's mind is made of dualities and structures such as space and time. As the God suppresses those structures, its visitors find themselves figuratively naked, in a state that reminds infancy or madness. Cringle, recalling the fate of Raphael García is utterly afraid of that nakedness (43). But should we be?

Do we have to fear this nakedness of the mind? Not at all. I connect the Allmuseri God with what Charles Johnson told me when I met him in Seattle last April. He explained the meaning of *Shunyata*. *Shunyata* is the Buddhist notion of emptiness. What shall we hear by emptiness? "It is not a lack," he said, "it's rather like the emptiness of the womb." An empty womb is full of possibilities. It waits and lives its own secret life, nurturing the ground on which sometimes another creation, another form of life, may grow. Thus, it is "a silence where all [is] possibility, perfection, preformed," (168) as perceived by Rutherford.

Here, I have answered only half of the question, "What is the Allmuseri God?" To ask this question is to wonder what it does, and there again, it is not enough to say that it creates without stopping, if we are to give down-to-earth answers to down-to-earth questions. Now, what does the creature do to those who go near it? It mirrors each of its visitors and at the same time completes them: it attacks its captors, and is a "witty conversationalist" (101) with Falcon, himself a casuistical braggart. With Tommy, it takes the boy's appearance, while with Rutherford, it is the hero's father, and each time, visitor and god are "a single thing" (69).

Rutherfords realises *Shunyata*, the absence of "I"—black and white selves thus becoming fictions upon a fiction—"we" emerge, as an infinite plurality of intertwined creations (171). It is only then that we understand why the creature "has a thousand names" (101)—of course! It's everything!—while at the same time "it has no name" (63)—of course! It can't say "I"!

Having understood *Shunyata*, we cannot go any further, and we can now begin our way back upward, towards the world.

What kind a journey can it be? What will it be like to be in the world, from now? I believe Arendt and Charles Johnson provide answers that are quite close one to the other. The German philosopher explains that "[i]f someone wants to see and experience the world as it "really" is, he can do so only by understanding it as something that is shared by many people, lies between them, separates and links them, showing itself differently to each and comprehensible only to the extent that many people can talk about it and exchange their opinions and perspective with one another, over against one another" (Arendt, 128). Being in the world and using one's political faculty, among which freedom of speech and opinion, is an intersubjective activity.

As shown in his interview with Jonathan Little, Charles Johnson's definition of phenomenological intersubjectivity is strikingly reminiscent of Arendt's description of being in the world: "Of course, all science begins that way too, with a first person seeing—the scientist looking into the microscope. It's one person, one consciousness and this object. He has to say to a colleague, "Come here, look at this, do you see that?" Then you have intersubjectivity. If you have three people, it's even better. That's what I believe in far more than objectivity. Intersubjectivity is shared meaning, a shared vision" (*Passing*, 103).

Indeed, Arendt's politics is a delicate work of intersubjectivity, which requires free perception. And what have we gained, from our encounter with the Allmuseri God, but a sharpening of our senses, that enables us to listen to the world, watch its fluidity, instead of hearing the dim of the babbling self, and contemplating the overwhelming walls into which the self tries to solidify?

As we leave the Allmuseri God and start our way back upward, to the upper deck of our ship, we may wonder what there is to do, since there's no more "I" to do something. Intersubjectivity, applied to politics, or art, or any aspect of human life and work, is all there is to do. In fact, it's not so much "something to do" as a "doing," since it, like the Allmuseri God's creation, never stops.

Another way to answer is to quote the end of *Oxherding Tale*: "After the war, Fruity and I turned to the business of rebuilding, with our daughter Anna (all is conserved; all), the world" (*Oxherding*, 176). As "singer, listener and song"(69) are after all but one thing, we are to recreate ourselves over and over. In fact, everything is to be done. This is why, every time I read any of Charles Johnson's novel or short story, I am thrust back into the world with the appetite and energy of a young child.

PS: You may have noticed that I haven't really answered the last of the three logical questions raised by the novel, "where does the Allmuseri God go when the ship sinks into the Atlantic?" Okay, here is the answer if you really want it: "Mu."

Notes

1. "The greatness of man is always to recreate his life." (My translation.)
2. "When the spirit fell from its mother's womb, the Earth welcomed it with a strange struggle. Lost in the clamor, it became many selves. The spirit was the enlightening leader of its lower limbs. Command, and we will obey, head, shoulders, knees and toes. Order, and we will give, we are all intertwined. All along the journey, all are at work." (My translation.)

Works Cited

Arendt, Hannah, and Jerome Kohn. *The Promise of Politics*. New York, Shocken Books, 2005.

Jam Afane, Ze, and Vincent Courtois. Le Voyage de l'esprit. *L'Homme Avion*. Chief Inspector, 2008. CD.

Johnson, Charles. *Oxherding Tale*. Scribner, 1982.

McWilliams, Jim, et al. *Passing the Three Gates: Interviews with Charles Johnson*. Seattle, WA: University of Washington Press, 2004.

_______*Middle Passage*. New York: Scribner, 1990.

_______*The Sorcerer's Apprentice*. New York: Athaneum, 1986.

Nietzsche, Friedrich, and Graham Parkes, trans. *Thus Spoke Zarathustra*. New York: Oxford University Press, 2005.

Taylor, Dianna. "Hannah Arendt on Judgement: Thinking for Politics." *International Journal of Philosophical Studies* 10.2 (2003): 151-169.

Weil, Simone. *La Pesanteur et la grâce*. Paris: Plon, 1988.

Whalen-Bridge, John, et al. "A Conversation with Charles Johnson and Maxine Hong Kingston." *MELUS: The Journal of the Society for the Study of the Multi-Ethnic Literature of the United States* 31.2 (2006): 69-93.

16

Kala Pani (The Black Water)

for Charles Johnson

— Shayla Hawkins

Across the forbidding Kala Pani
comes the winter-haired lion,
the black bodhisattva
who braids riddles of race and reason
with the practiced skill
of a tantuvaaya
at his ancient loom

Across the Kala Pani he comes,
student and master
of word and body and mind,
his being a bastion
of strength and calm,
his eyes quick and encompassing
as a raging sea

Across the Kala Pani
this kalaakara comes,
his labor and life
both the deep, unconquerable
Black Water
and the bridge
for its people to travel
its known and unknown worlds.

17

Holding onto Truth: Gandhi and King Jr.

— Charles Johnson

One of the most intriguing photographs that we have of Martin Luther King Jr. captures him during an apparently peaceful moment when he is far away from the turmoil and police dogs, the jail cells and hostile crowds of his many campaigns for justice and equality. He is shown in what appears to be his office, standing with his arms crossed in front of a portrait of Mohandas Gandhi. The juxtaposition of these two spiritual titans always reminds me that in both King's political and personal life, and at the heart of his belief in a "beloved community," *satyagraha* was not simply a technique to bring about social and political change, but instead was intended to be a way of life, what Gandhi called a pragmatic, on-going "experiment with truth."

King first publicly declared his admiration for the father of modern India during the Montgomery bus boycott when he said, "Christ gave us the goals and Mahatma Gandhi the tactics." The simplicity of this statement conceals its profundity, for methods and techniques like *satyagraha*, far from being neutral tools devoid of cultural or spiritual values, contain within themselves a precise, challenging blueprint for leading the moral life.

It was during his seven-year campaign in South Africa that Gandhi coined the term *satyagraha* by combining the Sanskrit word *sat* (truth) with the verbal root *grah* (to seize, hold, or grasp). "Its root meaning," said Gandhi, "is holding onto truth, hence truth-force. I have also called it love force or soul force."

For Gandhi, who took at age 37 the vows of a *Brahmacharya* (celibacy and self-restraint) and regarded the *Bhagavad Gita* as "an infallible guide of conduct," *satyagraha* must be based upon the yogic value of *ahimsa*, a term familiar to Buddhists as the "nonharming" of sentient beings in either word or deed. It is love in action. If he "holds truth," a *satyagrahi* never seeks to defeat or humiliate his opponent, because he and the other are one. He endeavors to respect and retain him as a friend, and provides him with a way to save face during their encounter, maintain his dignity, and join the ranks of the enlightened.

These principles forged in South Africa, then India and seasoned by Gandhi's study of Jesus, Tolstoy, Thoreau inter alios, were dramatically tested in an American context during King's 14-year career as this nation's most preeminent minister and Socratic gadfly of the state. On the night of January 30, 1956 during the Montgomery bus boycott, King was at a meeting and learned his home had been bombed. He rushed there and, fortunately, found his wife Coretta and their baby Yolanda unharmed. But outside the ruin of his home, an angry, armed black crowd was spoiling for a showdown with white policemen at the scene. The situation was edging toward violence. King raised one hand to quiet the crowd, and said, "I want you to go home and put down your weapons. We cannot solve this problem through retaliatory violence. We must meet violence with nonviolence....We must meet hate with love." According to white policemen there that night, King's calming words in the heat of racial violence saved their lives. Furthermore, they were skillful means (*upaya kaushala*) that brought something uniquely redemptive to the 300-year, bloody struggle for black liberation in America and made the Civil Rights Movement morally superior to those who opposed it.

A second application of *satyagraha* can be seen in the electrifying Birmingham campaign that brought segregation to its knees in Alabama. "We shall wear you down by our capacity to suffer," King proclaimed, again fusing the passion of Christ and the *satyagraha* doctrine that the endurance of suffering, loss of property and even pain inflicted upon ourselves and our loved ones are means to a spiritual end. King and his lieutenants filled the jails with peaceful protesters, adults and children, who defied the unjust (and violent) laws of segregation. Their numbers on the streets reached twenty-five hundred. Racist Police Commissioner Eugene "Bull" Connor responded with fire hoses. He followed that by using police dogs—a show of brutality that in news footage broadcast worldwide sickened America and people of good-will everywhere.

It sickened the firemen, too. On May 5, 1963, hundreds of blacks held a prayer meeting near the city jail. Enraged, Connor shouted, "Dammit! Turn on the hoses!" But his men fell back as if they were mesmerised, some weeping, and they let the protesters continue. This remarkable event proved yet again the power of "soul force" in winning over the hearts and minds of one's opponents. That victory was surely helped by the ten points of the "Commitment Blank," a kind of activist's version of the bodhisattva vows signed by all leaders of the Southern Christian Leadership Conference and their followers during the Birmingham campaign:

Commandments for the Volunteers

I Hereby Pledge Myself—My Person and Body—To The Nonviolent Movement. Therefore I Will Keep The Following Commandments:

1. Meditate daily on the teachings and life of Jesus.
2. Remember always that the nonviolent movement seeks justice and reconciliation—not victory.
3. Walk and talk in the manner of love, for God is love.
4. Pray daily to be used by God in order that all men might be free.
5. Sacrifice personal wishes in order that all men might be free.
6. Observe with both friend and foe the ordinary rules of courtesy.
7. Seek to perform regular service for others and for the world.

8. Refrain from the violence of fist, tongue, or heart.
9. Strive to be in good spiritual and bodily health.
10. Follow the directions of the movement and of the captain on a demonstration.

When practicing "soul force," activists were urged, as this document shows, to work on changes in the world and themselves simultaneously. These "moral experiments," tested in our daily lives as a scientist might approach the proving of a theory, are in perfect accord with *satyagraha's* insistence that it is futile to implement ideas such as nonviolence in the public realm if we fail to work on them in our personal lives. A dharma teacher like mendicant monk Claude AnShin Thomas understands this well when he says, "As a Buddhist, I cannot think myself into a new way of living, I have to live myself into a new way of thinking....We must simply stop the endless wars that wage within" if we hope to end war and violence in society.

His testing of these principles led King to India in 1959, a guest of the Gandhi Peace Foundation, and he returned to America determined to devote one day a week of his unimaginably tight schedule to fasting and meditation. He received fifty assassination threats, the wrath of J. Edgar Hoover's FBI, lived with a $30,000 bounty on his head, was stabbed once in Harlem, and was arrested and jailed again and again. All that only reinforced his conviction, expressed in his Nobel Peace Prize acceptance speech of 1964, that "Civilisation and violence are antithetical concepts." And, of course, King donated the money he received from lectures and speeches to the Movement, his $54,000 for the Nobel distributed evenly among five organisations devoted to civil rights and peace.

As a champion of nonviolence operating on the world stage by the mid-1960s, it was natural for King to become the first prominent American leader to oppose the Vietnam War (My second favorite photo shows King at a 1967 press conference with Thich Nhat Hahn, whom he nominated for a Nobel), and just before his death he was devoting his energies to the challenge of eliminating the suffering caused by poverty.

All these things King achieved in just 39 years before his life was tragically cut short, like Gandhi's, but his powerful legacy endures, reminding us that brotherhood is our goal, love our method, generosity and forgiveness our rule, and that, "Strangely enough, I can never be what I ought to be until you are what you ought to be. You can never be what you ought to be until I am what I ought to be."

18

The Manichean Divide and Ontological Truncation: Charles Johnson on the "Black-as-Body"

— George Yancy

> Negro brought forth biology, penis, strong, athletic, potent, boxer, Joe Louis, Jesse Owens, Senegalese troops, savage, animal, devil, sin.
>
> —*Frantz Fanon*

> ...a white person who is bad is failing to be 'white,' whereas a black person who is good is a surprise, and one who is bad merely fulfills the expectation.
>
> —*Richard Dyer*

Introduction

Philosopher and literary figure Charles Johnson is one of the first American philosophers to give a self-defined, acute, and powerful *phenomenological analysis* of the Black body within the context of American racism. Prior to the recognition of a disciplinary matrix known as Africana philosophy of existence, Johnson explores the phenomenological or *lived* experience of Blackness within a cultural terrain where Black people are ontologically truncated and reduced to what he refers to as the "black-as-body." Johnson engages the Black body at the level of its embodied interiority, an interiority that is constantly threatened by the force of an effective history that is structured by a Manichaean divide, a racial dualism. This racial dualism functions as a metaphysical given; it operates as a "natural" way of dividing the world, a framework within which desires are formed, decisions are made, judgments are devised, perceptions are shaped, and certain bodies are deemed white/Black, normal/deviant, fit/unfit, ethical/unethical, clean/dirty, sexually restrained/sexually uncontrollable.

Functioning as a presumptive metaphysical framework or orientation, such a racial dualism is a site of obfuscation. It is the invisible background against which various bodies emerge within our perceptual field. Indeed, the racial Manichaean divide is *productive* of forms of *racial perception*. It is through the prism of this divide that the Black body and the white body are distorted and rendered one-dimensional. Yet, this dualism is so fixed, so well-orchestrated, that we often show no interest in interrogating the conditions of intelligibility in terms of which our bodies are rendered meaningful (fixed) in racial terms. We do not seek an account of the Black body's and the white body's social ontological arrival.[1] Indeed, a critical genealogical effort to trace the ideological steps leading up to the Black (and white) body's "arrival" is rendered mute, covered over by various myths of origin. With descriptive-phenomenological poignancy, Johnson places the reader at the very core of America's racial dynamics. He focuses on Black *Erlebnis* at the site of racial embodiment, while suspending, in classical phenomenological style, the question of the epistemological or scientific status of race as such. It is what is revealed or unveiled within Johnson's descriptive-phenomenological account that I will delineate. However, Johnson's "Postscript," one that he wrote in 1993 and that appears at the end of "A Phenomenology of the Black Body," also contains very significant, self-referential insights. My sense is that the postscript is a variation on doing phenomenology itself.

The Postscript

Through the disclosure of important autobiographical fragments in the postscript, Johnson invites the reader into the domain of his own *lived*-experience at a particular moment in time and space. Indeed, he invites us, or so I would argue, to tarry there, to ponder the deeper existential and familial space of the genesis of "A Phenomenology of the Black Body." Johnson wrote "A Phenomenology of the Black Body" back in 1975. It was, as he says, "my 'style paper' for the Ph.D. program in philosophy at SUNY-Stony Brook."[2] He then further contextualises the writing process, one that is far from Cartesian intellectual comfort and solipsism. Indeed, Johnson situates the reader within a blues space, a space of struggle and yet transcendence. "If memory serves," Johnson notes, "this was easily one of the hardest years of my life."[3] He was financially broke, living on a teaching assistantship. He adds, "...but that June saw the birth of our son Malik, and the feverish writing of the first draft for *Oxherding Tale*, a novel I would publish seven years later."[4] Johnson shares that he lived in "one of the foulest apartment buildings in Port Jefferson, New York."[5] However, it was precisely within this context, this existential crucible, that he devoured Sartre's *Being and Nothingness*, Heidegger's *Being and Time*, and Merleau-Ponty's *The Phenomenology of Perception*. He says that he read these decisive texts within the time frame of a month. He summarises, "Out of that context of unemployment and impoverishment and general concerns for my son, and fresh from my immersion in these seminal works of the German and French phenomenological movements, this chapter was conjured."[6]

As I read through Johnson's moving postscript narrative, I thought of Richard Wright's *12 Million Black Voices*, where, among other things, Wright describes the horrible conditions of Black people living in apartment buildings filled with putrefaction and profound stink. Johnson's narrative content resonates with Wright's rendering of what it means to be Black in America, particularly in terms of living and inhabiting physical spaces that are constricting in size and debilitating to the spirit. One feels the sense of urgency in Johnson's narrative recollections. After all, he was broke, unemployed, and there was the *stench* of it all, the impoverishment. Focusing on the "kitchenette" in mid-twentieth century Black America, Wright notes, "The kitchenette is our prison, our death sentence without a trial, the new form of mob violence that assaults not only the lone individual, but all of us, in its ceaseless attacks."[7] One might argue that Johnson's *lived* reality was a microcosm of a larger social and political context that impacted millions of Black bodies, a Manichean divide with profound economic and existential differentials. Wright also notes, "The kitchenette, with its filth and foul air, with its one toilet for thirty or more tenants, kills our black babies so fast that in many cities twice as many of them die as white babies."[8] For Johnson, there was the parental challenge that resulted in deep existential angst, questions of security, safety, and protection. In short, *that June saw the birth of Malik.* For Johnson, the birth of Malik signaled a new form of profound *Mitsein* (being-with) that intensely raised his level of responsibility and concern. Wright is well-aware of the danger. He notes, "The kitchenette fills our black boys with longing and restlessness, urging them to run off from home, to join together with other restless black boys in gangs, that brutal form of city courage."[9]

My point is *not* to argue that Wright's observations describe the inevitable fate that Johnson feared for his son. Rather, my point is to draw a "family resemblance" (in a Wittgensteinian sense) between Wright's description of such detrimental physical spaces, on the one hand, and Johnson's description of his own existential predicament, on the other. Johnson's predicament is one filled with a sense of imminent disaster where the juxtaposition of poverty, the birth of a new son, and the effort to be creative, tests the strength of his endurance and sanity. Also, as noted, it was out of this situation that "A Phenomenology of the Black Body" was, as he says, *conjured.* Given the challenging contextual and situational *Umwelt* that Johnson describes, the use of the term "conjured" is apropos. For the term suggests the sense of being "called forth," summoned, as if by magic, within an environing space prone to militate against philosophical creativity and clarity. Johnson telescopes the sheer tension of "doing-philosophy-in-Black" within social and physical spaces that are depressing, angst-ridden, and impoverished. I would argue that "A Phenomenology of the Black Body" is infused and informed by Johnson's attempt to come to terms with his own Black embodiment within a raced and racist *Lebenswelt.*

Hence, the motif that structures the "style paper" is one that runs through the lives of Black people and is implicative of Johnson's *profile* of his own life in 1975. Also, the movement between 1975 and 1993 (or even 2010) reveals a Charles Johnson who is meta-stable, one who is protean and transphenomenal. In short, then, Johnson's postscript exhibits something demonstrable about his phenomenological framework, and perhaps something about a form of *lived-aesthetics* of transformation. The postscript is itself demonstrative of genetic phenomenology. Johnson describes a genetic phenomenological orientation as one that examines "an individual as he (or she) exhibits over time a series of profiles or disclosures of being."[10] As already suggested, Johnson invites us into one of his profiles—living in the midst of poverty, the smell of stench, and the deep parental concern and love for his son—by taking us back to 1975. In stream with genetic phenomenology, Johnson knows that "a life is process, not product (or pregiven meaning). It more resembles the verb, not the noun."[11] By taking us back to 1975, Johnson invites the reader to appreciate a specific disclosure of *his* being, while implicitly arguing for a philosophical anthropology of the human being as *homo absconditus*—as always more than what appears and as always more than what can appear. In this way, Johnson's being (or the meaning of his life and identity) is never exhausted, but an ontological surplus.

As a process, human beings are always ahead of themselves, becoming something more, something different, something that requires new ways of seeing, appreciating, enjoying, and bearing witness. If "consciousness is always transitive,"[12] then it too must be able to appreciate (keep up with) the protean character of and aesthetic beauty of the dynamic and transformative modalities of constant human fruition.[13] Moving the reader through the ever changing profiles of Malcolm X, Johnson shows that the sheer process of becoming El-Hajj Malik El-Shabazz (far from Malcolm Little) signifies a marvelous narrative openness—something to be marveled at, awed by, like a work of art—a meaning that is always already yet to be determined. To be awed, within this context, suggests that the aim/direction of one's "consciousness-of" does not freeze or do violence to the "object" that is at the other end of the pole of consciousness, that in terms of which consciousness aims. Thanks to Spike Lee, Johnson notes, "For the first time in motion-picture history, and perhaps in pop culture, the black male body is experienced as the embodiment of intellectual, political, and spiritual ideals."[14]

Were Johnson to revisit his postscript (perhaps write a "post" to the postscript), where he shows "a gradual accumulation of profiles that expand and qualify our experience of black men," he would end with the current U.S. President Barack Hussein Obama—a Black male who in many ways outstrips America's imaginary that is still unable to incorporate or accommodate such a radically different/new Black profile. To make sense of Obama, many whites in America have collapsed Obama's difference into that of a caricature—the myth of the "exceptional Negro" or in some cases caricatures more sinister like the mythical Black simian/monkey or the stereotyped "Muslim terrorist,"[15] a type of Manchurian candidate just waiting to reveal his true identity. In short, Obama's difference, his alterity, has been reduced to more of the (white) same. Whites are so fixed upon certain meanings of the Black body that only certain profiles are deemed legitimate, only certain meanings come to constitute the dominant (white) narrative vis-à-vis the Black body. It is more than reasonable to conclude with Johnson that "too little has changed in the social world since the essay was first published."[16] In hindsight, writing from the perspective of 1993, Johnson notes, "Looking back across eighteen years at this descriptive analysis, I realise that my hope was to examine the black male body as a cultural object and to inquire into how it has been interpreted, manipulated, and given to us."[17] My sense is that Johnson did just that and did so brilliantly.

The Black-as-Body

I now turn to Johnson's descriptive analysis of the "Black-as-body" (his astute term) which captures the problematic ways in which "it" (the Black body) is given to us. Johnson argues that the specific "issue at stake is how blacks experience their own bodies within a world of racial restriction."[18] The problem, though, transcends the sort of restrictions imposed by racial segregation. Such racial restrictions also have deep existential phenomenological implications.

One defining and central feature of Sartrean existentialist philosophy is the thesis that existence precedes essence. According to Sartre, "It means that, first of all, man exists, turns up, appears on the scene, and, only afterwards, defines himself."[19] In short, for Sartre, there is no pre-given essence that defines human reality. We are thrown forward, always already ahead of ourselves. Yet, when theorised within the context of the racial Manichean divide, Sartre's ontology of the human person, particularly when it comes to the *lived* experiences of Black people, must concede (and be challenged by) the specific *racial* ways in which Black people are perceived as and made to feel like essences. As Frantz Fanon argues, "Jean-Paul Sartre had forgotten that the Negro suffers in his body quite differently from the white man."[20] And as Johnson insightfully observes, "The experience of the black-as-body becomes, not merely a Self-Other conflict, nor simply Hegel's tortuous Master-Slave dialectic, but a variation on both these conditions, intensified by the particularity of the body's appearance as black, as 'stained,' lacking interiority...."[21] As suggested above, the Manichean divide is "a field of diverse yet interchangeable oppositions between white and black, good and evil, superiority and inferiority, civilisation and savagery, intelligence and emotion, rationality and sensuality, self and Other, subject and object."[22] In fact, given the particularity of the body's appearance as Black, or stained, Black people are deemed "sub-Others" in the Sartrean Self-Other conflict, and enslaved "sub-persons" for which the dynamics of the Hegelian dialectics of recognition are occluded *ab initio*.

Charles Johnson opens "A Phenomenology of the Black Body" with a Black folktale that frames a Black male, Willis, within the context of the Manichaean divide. In this case, the Black male is reduced to his genitalia—the mythically enormous Black penis. While the folktale is humorous, Johnson notes, "...we may lose sight of the fact that his [Willis'] triumph is based on cultural assumptions that lock him into the body....”[23] Indeed, Willis’ so-called triumph is what was violently removed within those ethically and sexually perverse spaces of white mob lynchings—that is, spectacles of horror. But it is the phenomenon of being locked into the body that is of phenomenological significance here. As locked, Willis is reduced to his body, a sensuous “thing,” which is *not* ahead of itself as an open possibility, but always already ahead of itself as a *closed essence*. Johnson brilliantly describes such a situation in terms of being “much like a mugger at a boardwalk’s end.”[24] In other words, Willis’ meaning, defined by his “hyper-sexual essence,” is waiting *for him*. Unlike Sartre’s thesis, his Black body, his so-called Black essence, turns up, appears on the scene, already defined. He has become the *Black-as-body*. As a “corrective” to this problem, Johnson does not wish to re-inscribe the perennial mind-body problem of ontological dualism. Rather, Johnson draws from the important work of Maurice Merleau-Ponty’s where the latter argues: “I am my body.” Theorising the body (or, more precisely, embodiment or embodied consciousness), Johnson writes: “It is my point of reference on the universe. I, as subject, am often at ‘one’ with it, yet my relation as a human self to my body is also that of radical otherness. I am my body while I am also not my body (or experience myself as not simply reducible to my body as the empirical object of physics, chemistry, neurology).”[25] Succinctly stated, Johnson writes, “I am conscious of the world through the medium of my body.”[26]

Yet, it is within the context of a racist Manichean divide that Black embodied *consciousness* is rendered null and void. In fact, Black embodied consciousness is “made a problem for itself by ‘stain.’”[27] In terms of Black bodies, stain-discourse, a discourse that signifies an ineradicable mark of shame, is precisely intelligible vis-à-vis the racist Manichean divide. For example, the stain reminds Black people of their so-called consanguineous ties to Noah’s son, Ham. Blacks are both the products and transmitters of this stain. As Johnson notes, “Stain recalls defilement, guilt, sin, corpses that contaminate, menstruating women; and with them come the theological meanings of punishment, ostracism, and the need to be ‘cleansed.’”[28] For example, it is this stain that pre-marks Black men as dangerous, as the always already guilty. As Fred C. Lofton notes:

> Even in what is claimed to be a post-racist America, I am unable to break the mold and loose the shackles. When I am alone in an elevator with a white woman, I am uncomfortably aware she can yell 'rape' and bring my life, with all of the achievements and honors precious to me, to an emasculating conclusion.[29]

Not being able to break the mold or loose the shackles is another way of saying that one is locked into the body, that one is indelibly stained, that one is Black-as-body, and that one's existence is truncated, lopped off, as it were. On the elevator, Loften's Black body comes ready-made, stained by the history of the myth of the Black male rapist. Nathan McCall and William Julius Wilson are also familiar with the racial logic of Blackness qua stain and how that stain functions to elicit white fear. McCall writes:

> The [white] woman in the elevator has that look, that expression that seems to say she knows the myths [to be true]. She suspects what you want, and she seems filled with the wildly absurd terror that, in the brief ride between the twelfth and first floors, this black man may rape her, rob her, and leave her for dead.[30]

Wilson observes:

> I am an internationally known Harvard professor, yet a number of unforgettable experiences remind me that, as a black male in America…, I am also feared. For example, several times over the years I have stepped into the elevator of my condominium dressed in casual clothes and could immediately tell from the body language of the other residents in the elevator that I made them feel uncomfortable. Were they thinking, "What is this black man doing in this expensive condominium? Are we [white folk] in any danger?"[31]

Like Johnson, who describes entering a bar thinking about Boolean expansions, Loften, McCall, and Wilson could have also entered the elevator thinking about Boolean expansions or quantum mechanics or relativity theory. Yet, the whites only need scream "help!" and the mere presence of a Black male body immediately "confirms" the whites' bellowing terror. "Epidermalisation spreads throughout the body like an odor, like an echoing sound."[32] Goodbye, Boolean expansions, quantum mechanics and relativity theory. Loften, McCall, and Wilson are seen. It is a case where their "subjectivity is turned inside out like a shirtcuff."[33] They are familiar with the fact that so many whites fail to see (or can't possibly see) profiles that don't reduce them to the black-as-body. The *noesis*-pole of intentionality, structured through the Manichean divide, "has been conditioned culturally or racially to fix [whites] upon certain 'meanings.'"[34] Within the context of the elevator, Loften, McCall, and Wilson are aware of their fragility vis-à-vis the whites' trepidation. They know that the meaning that they give their lives can be (and is often) stolen/confiscated. Johnson writes, "Our body responds totally to this abrupt epidermalisation; consciousness for the subject is violently emptied of content: one, in fact, draws a 'blank,' though clearly for the white Other my interiority is, if not invisible, a space filled with sensuality, crime, or childlike simplicity."[35] Consciousness, under such circumstances, is "darkened" by one's corporeality. As Johnson describes this, "I feel its sleepy awkwardness, and know myself not as subject but as slumberous, torpid matter."[36]

Merleau-Ponty reminds us that "it is never our objective body that we move, but our phenomenal body."[37] And yet, within the context of the elevator, I would argue that those Black bodies encounter white gazes that fix them as objects, as stagnant. Within such racially inundated spaces, one's body becomes an exterior surface with nothing more to be seen or discovered. The space within the elevator has become mathematically mapped. The Black body is so many measured feet from the white body. The white woman feels slightly safe as long as the Black male body keeps his *distance*. Under such circumstances, the Black body, from the perspective of the Black male, is perhaps experienced as a detached mass, an *objective* body, something that one, unfortunately, lives "in." The white gaze draws the Black body out as an appendage. In short, the body is experienced as if it were an encasement that chokes, that suffocates the soul.

The Black-as-body also disrupts the seamless dialectic that obtains between the body vis-à-vis its surroundings. Johnson writes, "The body extends itself in vehicles, buildings, machines, and clothing."[38] In other words, "the body" moves within *lived* space, responding to the call, as it were, of already meaningful objects. What happens, though, when one becomes an object among other objects? Merleau-Ponty writes:

> Similarly the subject, when put in front of his scissors, needle and familiar tasks, does not need to look for his hands or his fingers, because they are not objects to be discovered in objective space: bones, muscles and nerves, but potentialities already mobilised by perception of scissors or needle, the central end of those 'intentional threads' which link him to the objects given.[39]

Within the context where the Black-as-body is the dominant profile, Johnson writes, "It is intense, as though consciousness has shifted to the skin's seen surfaces."[40] In other words, Black people move and have their being within the context of a world that refuses them a moment free from objective scrutiny—either as scrutinised by themselves or whites. The Black body becomes a *thing*. The Black body is seen as a *thing* in space, something to be policed and controlled, even self-policed. As experienced, the Black body takes on the form of something to be found in space; "it" is *the* threat, *over there*, unmistakably dangerous.

Situated in a world where embodied consciousness has been reduced to the Black-as-body, Black embodied consciousness becomes stultified, experienced *not* as a potentiality vis-à-vis the call of its surroundings. Rather, the Black body, translated as "total physicality,"[41] comes to "see such a call as dubious, even though the 'White Only' signs have been torn down, because there remain strict territorial boundaries, real or imagined, when we experience the searing Sartrean 'look' of the hate-stare, when the world is epidermalised."[42] One's surroundings do not call or invite. One's surroundings do not offer affordances. Rather, one's surroundings are experienced as uncertain, as obstacles, as negations, as occlusions in relationship to the Black body as "stain." Unlike the perception of the scissors or the needle, the Black-as-body does not feel potentiality mobilised through an act of perceiving white bodies. Instead, in the presence of white bodies, Black bodies become ontologically stiff, as if having looked into the eyes of Medusa. Indeed, the Black-as-body as "stain" is ontologically frozen in the face of white gazes that repeatedly install the color-line. Whether on elevators[43] or within other quotidian social spaces, as Johnson writes, "this stain of my skin gives in a sudden stroke of intentionality 'darkness,' 'guilt,' 'evil,' an entire galaxy of meanings."[44] The Black-as-body becomes a quintessential object fit for physics. "We are," as Johnson notes, "reduced to the body as the subject of physics—Brute Power."[45]

In Richard Wright's novella "Big Black Good Man,"[46] he provides a powerful narrative portrayal of white fear and how that fear relates to the Black-as-body. Jim, the Black protagonist, is described by Olaf Jenson, the white man who owns the hotel (in Denmark) where Jim is temporarily staying, as sheer physicality. At various points throughout the text, Jim is ontologically truncated. He is described as a "black looming mountain," as having a "clawlike hand," as having "gorillalike arms," "buffalolike," a "hunk of blackness," a "huge black *thing*," and as "black mass." Jim is also referred to as the "devil of blackness," a "black beast," and a "nameless terror." As we know, Jim is none of these things. Depicted in animalistic terms and racially reified, Jim has become the expulsion, the byproduct, of a racist infused sickness that "originated" with Olaf. Not only is Jim reduced to his body, his surface features, but to the extent that he has any inner life, any subjectivity, "it is the repository for the offscum of racial relations—to black subjectivity is attributed the contents that white consciousness itself fears to contain or confront: bestial, sexuality, uncleanliness, criminality, all the purported 'dark things.'"[47] In other words, Jim is Olaf's creation, a teratological freak of nature. As Ralph Ellison writes, "When they [white folk] approach me they see only my surroundings, themselves, or figments of their imagination—indeed, everything and anything except me."[48]

Similarly, Johnson writes about a white professor who does not "see" him, "Passing, he sees me as he sees the fire extinguisher to my left, that chair outside the door."[49] Johnson is "seen" as part of the environment, something of no particular significance. As *the* Black, another item in space, the experience lacks richness, uniqueness, human recognition. Johnson's body is just *there* like the rising sun, "seldom figured forth save as maid, taxi driver, or janitor."[50] To return to the beginning of "A Phenomenology of the Black Body," Johnson, like Willis in the Black folktale, is locked into his body by his professor, and, perhaps, just for that moment, he undergoes a process of double consciousness. After all, he has glimpsed what his professor has seen—the Black body as "stain." Like Pecola, in Toni Morrison's *The Bluest Eye*, Johnson, in the light of his professor's misrecognition (or non-recognition) temporarily sees himself as a problematic object. Given that his subject status has been called into question, perhaps even nullified, he might feel the desire to take flight.

Johnson, however, is especially cautious here. Flight in the face of corporeal "stain" can function as a flight into bad faith. For Johnson, when it comes to countering white myths, one has to be careful not to reinstate the logic of the Manichean divide. He argues that the option of strategically manipulating whites through pretending that one is precisely what they say (all brute and dumb force) is itself a continuation of the same. For example, while I may use the Manichean divide to my immediate advantage, the binary system remains in place. As another option, one can flee one's Blackness, one's "stain" by hyper-accentuating evidence of one's (white) interiority. Perhaps one speaks German impeccably and does so especially in the presence of whites. The aim here is to negate one's status as African-American/Black, which, as Johnson says, is "a flight from the historical experience of American antebellum slavery in which epidermalisation reaches its acme."[51] On this score, through an act of self-negation, one simply takes sides *against* the "stained" side of the racial divide, while again leaving the Manichean divide in place. Then again, one can introduce a meta-narrative that valorises Blackness, one that construes Blackness as the axiological apex of beauty, civilisation, and being. The dancing Black body, for example, becomes the site of high praise, especially over the stiff and awkward dancing white body. As we all allegedly know, white men can't jump or dance. White bodies, within this reverted symbolic order, are too civilised, too intellectual; there isn't enough emotion, not enough funk and spontaneity in them. Johnson points out that this inversion is deeply a-historical; "it must involve a complete reconstitution of cultural meanings with the black body as its foundation."[52] But to make Blackness the new foundation, the summit of the ontological chain of being, means that the Manichean divide remains unbroken. For Johnson, each approach fails to bridge a false dualism. In fact, one might argue that Johnson sees each variation, each response, as remaining within the logic of whiteness itself.[53]

Perhaps, for Johnson, part of the realisation has to do with what he sees as the perennial human dilemma: "That we are, after all, beings who must fashion moment by moment what meaning our lives will have...."[54] We are, for Johnson, an ontological *process,* each one of us, in a single lifetime, will experience self-contradiction, fear of death, joy unspeakable, trivial-mindedness, tension, self-transformation and continuous growth. We are, as it were, a multitude of expressible and inexpressible *profiles*—always already more than we have been and always already more than we can possibly imagine. This is *not* a condemnation, but something for which, and I am sure that Johnson would agree, we ought to give thanks. It is this thankfulness, for Johnson, that bespeaks an ontology of human openness that militates against a concept of race that reifies and restricts who and what we may become.

Notes

1. For an insightful examination of the concept of "arrival," see Shannon Winnubst's review of Sara Ahmed's *Queer Phenomenology: Orientations, Objects, Others* (Durham and London: Duke University Press, 2006) in the *APA Newsletter on Feminism and Philosophy*, Vol. 07, No. 1, 2007, 20-22.
2. Charles Johnson, "A Phenomenology of the Black Body," in Carol E. Henderson (ed.) *America and the Black Body: Identity Politics in Print and Visual Culture*, Madison: Fairleigh Dickinson University Press, 262.
3. Johnson, "A Phenomenology of the Black Body," 262-263.
4. Ibid., 262.

5. Ibid., 263.
6. Ibid.
7. Richard Wright, *12 Million Black Voices*, New York: Thunder's Mouth Press, 1941, 106.
8. Richard Wright, Ibid., 106.
9. Richard Wright, Ibid., 111.
10. Charles Johnson, "A Phenomenology of the Black Body," op. cit., 264.
11. Ibid.
12. Max Van Manen, *Researching Lived Experience: Human Science for an Action Sensitive Pedagogy*, New York: State University of New York Press, 1990, 9.
13. As will be shown, it is within the Manichean racial divide that raced and racist consciousness fails to bring the Black body forth in all of its complexity because it truncates/reduces the Black body to a limited set of profiles. Thus, the Black body is dehumanised, rendered ontic and static.
14. Charles Johnson, "A Phenomenology of the Black Body," op. cit., 265.
15. Tim Wise, *Between Barack and a Hard Place: Racism and White Denial in the Age of Obama*, San Francisco, CA: City Lights Books, 2009, 72.
16. Charles Johnson, "A Phenomenology of the Black Body," op. cit., 263. "A Phenomenology of the Black Body" was first published in the Winter 1976 issue of *Ju-Ju: Research Papers in Afro-American Studies*.
17. Charles Johnson, "A Phenomenology of the Black Body," op.cit.,263.
18. Charles Johnson, "A Phenomenology of the Black Body," op. cit., 254. The reader should note that Johnson uses Eldridge Cleaver's *Soul on Ice*, particularly the chapter entitled "The Primevil Mitosis," as an important point of embarkation into the philosophical question of experience, Black consciousness, and corporeality. My sense is that he understands Cleaver's text as more politically driven and less philosophical. Yet, Cleaver's text does provide an important description of the various psycho-sexual dynamics and power relations that can emerge within the context of a binary racial system (in this case, Black and white). In this chapter, however, I will not consider Cleaver's work or Johnson's deployment of his work.
19. Jean-Paul Sartre, *Existentialism and Human Emotions*, New York: Philosophical Library, 1957.
20. Frantz Fanon, *Black Skin, White Masks*, (Translated by Charles Lam Markmann) New York: Grove Press, 1967, 138.
21. Charles Johnson, "A Phenomenology of the Black Body," op. cit., 257.

22. Abdul R. JanMohamed, "The Economy of Manichean Allegory: The Function of Racial Difference in Colonialist Literature," Henry Louis Gates, Jr. (ed.) *"Race," Writing, and Difference*, Chicago and London: The University of Chicago Press, 1985, 82.
23. Charles Johnson, "A Phenomenology of the Black Body," op. cit., 254.
24. Ibid., 258.
25. Ibid., 254–255.
26. Ibid., 255.
27. Ibid., 258.
28. Ibid.
29. Fred C. Loften, "Preface" in *Living in Hell: The Dilemma of African-American Survival*, (eds.) Mose Pleasure, Jr., and Fred C. Loften, Grand Rapids, Michigan: Zondervan Publishing House, 1995, 9.
30. Nathan McCall, *What's Going On: Personal Essays*, New York: Random House, 1997, 151.
31. William Julius Wilson, *More Than Just Race: Being Black and Poor in the Inner City*, New York: W. W. Norton & Company, Inc., 2009, 1.
32. Charles Johnson, "A Phenomenology of the Black Body," op. cit., 258.
33. Ibid.
34. Ibid., 255.
35. Ibid., 259.
36. Ibid.
37. M. Merleau-Ponty, *Phenomenology of Perception* (translated from the French by Colin Smith), New York: Routledge, 1962, 106.
38. Charles Johnson, "A Phenomenology of the Black Body," op. cit., 260.
39. M. Merleau-Ponty, *Phenomenology of Perception* (translated from the French by Colin Smith), New York: Routledge, 1962, 106.
40. Charles Johnson, "A Phenomenology of the Black Body," op. cit., 259.
41. Ibid., 260.
42. Ibid.
43. In *Black Bodies, White Gazes: The Continuing Significance of Race* (Lanham, Maryland: Rowman & Littlefield, 2008), I explore multiple ways in which the Black body has been distorted vis-à-vis the white gaze. In fact, in chapter one, "The Elevator Effect: Black Bodies/White Bodies," I give detailed attention to the existential phenomenological dimensions no doubt experienced by many Black male bodies on elevators with white bodies. The primary objective of that chapter was to provide a complex

description of the elevator effect and to provide a lens and a discourse in terms of which Black males might use to make sense of their experiences.

44. Charles Johnson, "A Phenomenology of the Black Body," op. cit., 256–257.
45. Ibid., 259.
46. Richard Wright, "Big Black Good Man," in *Eight Men* (introduction by Paul Gilroy), New York: Harper Perennial, 1940.
47. Charles Johnson, "A Phenomenology of the Black Body," op. cit., 257.
48. Ralph Ellison, *Invisible Man*, New York: Vintage Books, 1995, 3.
49. Charles Johnson, "A Phenomenology of the Black Body," 256.
50. Ibid., 256.
51. Ibid., 261.
52. Ibid., 262.
53. See chapter four, "The Agential Black Body: Resisting the Black Imago in the White Imaginary" in *Black Bodies, White Gazes*. This chapter theorises Black agency and identity vis-à-vis whiteness without committing the flights of failure that Johnson delineates.
54. Charles Johnson, "A Phenomenology of the Black Body," op. cit., 264.

19

Literary Mentors and Friends: An Interview with Charles Johnson

— Zachary Watterson

During the last few years that Dr. Johnson taught at the University of Washington, Seattle, I was lucky enough to study with him in UW's MFA program. I grew up in New York and New Jersey and lived a mostly nomadic life in my twenties; I sold bread, washed dishes, built rock staircases in the Adirondacks, doled medication to schizophrenics in a halfway house, drove a truck and planted trees for a nursery in Albuquerque. When I moved from New Mexico to Seattle in 2005 and took my first workshop with him, he led me to new reckonings with regard to how I was able to perceive the world. His example challenged me to consider the possibility of a morally coherent world, a world where all things are possible, including goodness and virtue. His mentorship has been a gift that I am in no way capable of reciprocating.

I am not alone. Counted among his former students are such authors as Johanna Stoberock, G.W. Hawkes, Kathy Alcala, and David Guterson. He's mentored scores of students, both at the graduate and undergraduate level. And there are dozens—if not hundreds more—whose writing and whose lives he's challenged and inspired by his work, by his thought-provoking example, and by his kindness, compassion and integrity. The following interview took place as a series of email conversations in January and February 2010.

Watterson: Let's begin with mentorship. Who were your first mentors and how did they contribute to your growth?

Johnson: My first mentor was the prolific cartoonist/writer Lawrence Lariar. When I was fifteen I began studying comic art in a correspondence course with Lariar, who published over 100 books, wrote detective fiction under a couple of pseudonyms, was a Disney studio "idea" man, cartoon editor for *Parade* magazine, and editor of *Best Cartoons of the Year.* Some summers when I was in high school I'd travel to New York City to see if I could score some assignments with magazines and publications located there, and I'd visit him at his home on Long Island, where he gave me some of his original work and good, professional advice. Back in Evanston, Illinois, my home town, I began publishing my stories and illustrations when I was 17. And for the next seven years that's what I did when I went away to college, publishing two collections of political cartoons, *Black Humor* (1970) and *Half-Past Nation-Time* (1972) and over 1,000 drawings and illustrations. I also created, hosted and co-produced in 1970 the PBS how-to-draw series, "Charlie's Pad." Last week I was at University of Houston-Victoria, and one of my hosts told me he saw the show in Texas in the early 80s when he was a kid. Each of the fifty-two, fifteen-minute lessons was based on the course I took with Lariar between 1963-65, and we stayed in touch until I moved to Seattle to teach at UW in 1976.

Watterson: Could you talk about how John Gardner's mentorship helped you grow as a writer?

Johnson: When I met Gardner—when I was in my second, final year of a master's-degree program in philosophy and working as a journalist on a small newspaper in Southern Illinois (journalism was my bachelor's degree)—I had already written six novels in a period of two years (the second in that series was an early attempt at doing what later became *Middle Passage*). Prose rhythm and voice were two things Gardner was skillful at doing, so I began my focus on those elements of craft during the nine months I wrote *Faith and the Good Thing* with him looking over my shoulder. We hit off it, I think, because Gardner had an interest in philosophy, and I admired the example he offered as an imaginative fiction writer who was also a scholar of medieval literature, a literary critic, a poet, a musician and composer of librettos, a playwright, and not a bad painter (I have one of his still life oil paintings and two sketches of characters from his novel *Jason and Medeia* in my home.) In his fiction work I saw formal virtuosity, a respect for the moral and spiritual life (at least for Christianity in his case, which I appreciated since I was raised in an African Methodist Episcopal church), and he was as prolific and dedicated to creating as my earlier teacher Lariar. One of the six novels I'd written before meeting Gardner was accepted for publication when I was working on *Faith*, a book that was very much in the style of James Baldwin, which is why I believe the publisher liked it. I asked Gardner if I should publish it because with *Faith* I was finally getting a handle on the original approach to philosophical fiction that I'd been trying to achieve. His advice was, "If you think later you'll have to climb over it, then I'd say, no." So I requested it back from the publisher, and I've always been glad I did. That novel simply wasn't my philosophical vision so, though it was difficult to turn away from a book contract (every young writer wants to get published), I did, and gambled that *Faith* would be published when I finished it, which it was when I was twenty-six.

Gardner's influence helped me understand all of what is at stake when we write. He told me a novel should be as perfect as one can make it before you submit it for publication; he counseled often that, "Any sentence that *can* come out *should* come out." Knowing him ratcheted up my concern with craft—experiments with form as a meditation in itself—and literary aesthetics.

Watterson: As a philosopher and a Buddhist, you must have had spiritual mentors who influenced you. Can you talk about their impact on your literary and spiritual life?

Johnson: I can't say that I've had a particular spiritual mentor. But I am fond of the work of scores of Buddhist writers as well as those who follow a spiritual path in other religious traditions. And I took formal vows, the Ten Precepts (as a layperson or *upasaka*) with my friend, Claude AnShin Thomas, a mendicant monk and author of *At Hell's Gate: A Soldier's Journey from War to Peace*.

Watterson: As you know, the poet and memoirist E. Ethelbert Miller is going to be one of the writers who will appear onstage at this tribute event in Denver in April 2010. Would you reflect on your friendship with him?

Johnson: Poet Miller tells me we first met at a PEN/Faulkner ceremony when my first story collection, *The Sorcerer's Apprentice,* was a nominee in 1986. I like to call him BrerBert and Mr. Wizard because of all the remarkable things he accomplishes as an arts activist. In this country in general, and in Washington D.C. in particular, he is "Mr. 411," the person who you call for an answer to any question about contemporary black writers or black culture. He has a heart as big as all outdoors. He is a relentless advocate for emerging and often forgotten writers or those who have not received the recognition and support they deserve. As a matter of fact, he has lobbied to get jobs for writers. There is simply no one like him.

Watterson: Would you speak about your friendship with the late playwright August Wilson?

Johnson: I recently published a story (or maybe it's really an essay) on the fifteen years August and I had eight to ten-hour dinner conversations about Everything until five in the morning here in Seattle at the Broadway Bar and Grill (in other words, until they had to close and kicked us out.). It's called "Night Hawks," and appears in the summer, 2009 issue of *Kenyon Review*. A slightly shorter version (by 1000 words) was published in the spring 2009 Lincoln Center Theater Review when director Bartlett Sher directed August's play *Joe Turner's Come and Gone*—the same performance that President Obama took First Lady Michelle to see. It took me several years after his death to reach a point, emotionally, where I could bring myself to share in a literary work the wealth of impressions and personal details I'd accumulated in my head about America's most celebrated black playwright. Writing this piece was very hard, because he was my friend and rather like a brother because we were born just three years apart, and grew up in the same cultural and racial worlds of the 50s and 60s. (The latest edition of my novel, *Oxherding Tale*, has a cover that August came up with, and he gets in the book credit for cover design and art.) I recommend that readers of this interview take a look at "Night Hawks" in *Kenyon Review* for the full story of our friendship.

Watterson: I love that essay. I remember a moment when you talk about how August Wilson used to dream that after finishing his ten play cycle he would take a decade out of the spotlight. And how he'd emerge from that long span of seclusion like Eugene O'Neill did after his decade out of the public eye. What is it about the power of silence and isolation that can be so nourishing for one's work?

Johnson: I think every artist needs a quiet place where he can hear himself think without being constantly interrupted by others, by their needs and concerns. This is very much like needing to have a quiet, secluded place for the practice of meditation. Often during my life I've simply had to disengage from the social world in order to finish a project—like the month I spent in January, 1998 writing the twelve stories for Africans in America (later released as my third story collection, *Soulcatcher and Other Stories*). In our society we're constantly bombarded by external stimuli—the phone ringing, the 3,000 product messages we're exposed to daily and, of course, the needs of our spouses, children, family, friends and students. August simply wanted the uninterrupted time to think about and work on a novel he very much wanted to write, to create new plays not related to his ten-play cycle, to spend quality time with his wife and young daughter, and to sit on his porch reading a big stack of books he never had the time to get to since he was producing a play for the cycle every two years or so, seeing it through production, living away from home (Seattle) for months at a time, answering the questions of reporters, and doing public events of one kind or another. One has to "let go" these public exigencies in order to create. August and I talked about this problem—the constant "performance" pressure we lived with—all the time. To be honest, that's one reason I retired from teaching last year after thirty-five years in the classroom. Just a day or two ago I read an interview by actor Linda Hamilton about her years of working with—and being married to—director James Cameron, and one statement she made stuck with me. She said Cameron once said anyone could be a husband or a father, but there were only five people in the world who could do what he does, and he was committed to pursuing that. Is this selfishness on his part? I don't think so. In order to serve the art, which will become a gift to others (and the culture) perhaps for generations, an artist often has to just step away from the quotidian demands of public life and the social world.

Watterson: In "Night Hawks" you talk about how you and August Wilson both had parents who were raised to value good manners, promise-keeping, personal sacrifice, loyalty to their own parents and kin, and a deep-rooted sense of decency. Do you ever find yourself disillusioned by new evidence of a loss of these values?

Johnson: Yes, I'm very saddened by the erosion of those values in contemporary American society. I think about this every day, and this sea change will be dramatised front-and-center in my next novel.

Watterson: There's that moment toward the end of "Night Hawks" when you and August Wilson left the Broadway Grill, where you'd been talking for hours, and went to a nearby IHOP. As you sat at a table, you could feel the tension in the air, and then two guys stomped a third guy's fingers and kicked his face to pulp. When the three of them fled, you looked around and noticed August was gone. His instincts from growing up in the Hill District of Pittsburgh kicked in, and he scrambled to an exit at the back of the restaurant. What advice would you give to writers who in their work want to address the violence they witness?

Johnson: Be honest about it. That scene I described isn't pretty. I just tried in the best journalistic fashion I could muster to put on the page with the greatest granularity of detail I could achieve what was given in perception to August and me in those brief, violent moments, unadulterated and uncensored. Later in this piece I venture an interpretation of what that violence means, or at least what it meant—as I see it—when you view it through the lens of our lives as black American male artists who grew up in the 50s and 60s.

Watterson: In what ways did your friendship with August Wilson, a writer of your generation, anchor you as a writer? Have your friendships with writers significantly contributed to your life as a writer?

Johnson: Except when we're collaborating on projects with others, which I've done a lot of, the activity of writing is lonely, very solitary. That's never bothered me because I was an only child and from kidhood learned to find ways to amuse myself for hours on end with no one else around. Nevertheless, sharing thoughts, feelings and experiences with another artist on a regular basis is refreshing. That person becomes like a mirror. Their experiences and practice can clarify and bring a subtler understanding to our life and creative practice. This is so because regardless of the discipline we're talking about—writing fiction or plays, drawing, acting, etc.—there are commonalities at the core of the creative process and the creative imagination. (I would even extend this to the sciences and philosophy.) The other is always a helpful mirror for understanding ourselves better.

Watterson: When I asked you this question three years ago, you said you wrote at night. Since my wife is pregnant and due in July, this question comes up for me a lot, and so I want to ask you to explain again how you managed to maintain a disciplined writing life while being a husband and father. If you were to write a manifesto on how best to generate new work and also fulfill one's role as a parent, what would it say? Does generosity matter? Is there something powerful about the idea of serving?—serving one's work, serving one's family? Could it be that one's various roles have an underlying unity?

Johnson: Congratulations, Zach, to you and your wife! This is happy news. Regarding your question, I have to confess that in sixty-one years of living I've never taken a vacation. Not once. When not teaching, or doing speaking engagements, all my free time—summers, holidays, weekends, etc.—has been devoted to the dove-tailing creative projects I've had since I was an undergraduate, and to the things I love to study (Sanskrit, the logarithmic progress today of developments in the sciences, Buddhist sutras, and philosophy). Sometimes during the summer, I'd send my wife and kids off for a month of vacation with our relatives in the Midwest or South, and I'd stay in the empty house with the cat or dog, writing novels and screenplays. (They came to understand early on that sometimes Daddy is "here" physically but mentally is living somewhere else for a short period of time until he finishes the project(s) on his desk.) There have been more days than I care to remember when I taught or lectured, here or abroad, without going to bed the night before; nights when I suddenly and involuntarily burst into tears from total fatigue while working at three a.m. on some project with its deadline looming.

My being a Buddhist has always helped. Thirty years of practicing meditation helps. When working, with my full concentration focused on an object (especially an imaginative one—a fiction, a drawing—as it takes shape in the world), I utterly forget myself and any personal concerns I might have at the moment. The illusory "self" disappears and there is only the present moment of doing, being completely absorbed, serving the work, which I know will financially serve my family's needs, and ideally serve in the long run literary culture. It also helps, I guess, that I've been a martial-artist since I was nineteen-years-old and love to work out. My doctor told me last fall that I'm healthier than most men my age and I could live to be 100. In our home gym, I regularly get on the treadmill for 100 minutes, bench-press 240 pounds, review my old Choy Li Fut kung-fu sets (the fighting system friends and I taught for ten years at our studio here in Seattle in the 80s and 90s), do sets of twenty-five push-ups, etc. I like to turn on my I-Pod (filled with hours of soft jazz, anything with a saxophone in it) and sweat. Those hours in the gym are (for me) like a mini-vacation from the demands of the social world. So all these things flow together—mind, body, spirit—and reinforce each other in the realms of family, profession, and personal discipline. It also helps to remember something once said (I believe) by William James: "The essence of genius is knowing what to overlook." I've always ignored everything that doesn't relate directly to my family's well-being and the particular work, creative and intellectual, that I was given to do in this life-time. If something doesn't serve that, then it's not on my radar screen.

Watterson: You addressed slavery in *Middle Passage* and *Oxherding Tale* and its legacy of racism in *Dreamer*. How do you feel about the persistence of racism in our society, and whether or when or how it will ever end?

Johnson: I don't believe what we call "racism" will ever end. Racism is based on our belief in a division between Self and Other, and our tendency to measure ourselves against others (which is a natural thing, like looking at others and wondering, "How well am I doing?"), and to judge them as either better or worse than ourselves. Sad to say, it is also based on fear. This constant measuring of ourselves in a social context is something human beings will always do until they experience—as a Buddhist would say—awakening, which frees us from judging others or ourselves. And, in my humble opinion, it will be a very long time before all the billions of people on this earth awaken.

Watterson: Would you be willing to share some of the lessons you learned from your parents and talk about how they felt about your career?

Johnson: I always told my Dad, who died six years ago at age eighty-one, that he was the one who taught me how to work. Especially how to work unselfishly for the sake of one's family—I remember back in the 60s when there was a time my father worked three jobs a week (construction during the day, as a night watchman in the evening, and helping an elderly white couple fix up their suburban home on the weekends). Seeing him work like that every day taught me that a person with a strong back and a good mind could accomplish anything he (or she) set out to do. My mother, who died in 1981, was the person in my family who gave me an appreciation for books, learning, and the beauty of art. They were always proud of me—their only child—and I never, ever, wanted to do anything with my life that would make them feel ashamed, because of all the sacrifices they made for me.

Watterson: You mentioned earlier that you withdrew a book from publication, a novel that would have been your debut. Can you talk a bit about what you learned from writing six apprentice novels before Faith?

Johnson: Those six "apprentice" novels, as I've always called them, taught me that a person who wishes to be a writer must write all the time. Every day. Even if only in your writer's notebook or journal. They also taught me that 90 per cent of good writing is revision. I'd write three drafts of those first six books, finishing one every ten weeks, but I hadn't learned until I did *Faith* how to revise—that true revision is re-envisioning every sentence and paragraph, deepening and polishing them for music and meaning until no more revision is possible. And so I learned to generate pages. My ratio of throwaway pages to keep pages is often twenty-to-one. For *Faith* (written in nine months), I tossed out 1200 pages; for *Oxherding Tale* (written in five years) I tossed out 2400 pages; for *Middle Passage* (a six-year project), it was 3000 pages; and for *Dreamer*, more than 3,000 over the seven years I worked on that book. However, as Gardner mentioned to me in the early 70s, as the years—and decades—roll by, it becomes possible to write fast and with a high level of craft or professionalism because you no longer make the mistakes you made in your youth. Also because by the time I sit down to do a first draft of something, I've already composed in my head (or sketched out notes for) the opening sentence and thought a great deal about the movements in a piece. In other words, one of my cultivated, literary habits when I think is to revise a thought—playing with diction or word choice, and sentence structure—before I speak or put pen to paper. It's just one of those habits you develop from writing for forty years and teaching for thirty-five

Watterson: You mentioned earlier that your next novel will dramatise the erosion of values in contemporary American society. Can you say more about your inspiration for this novel?

Johnson: My inspiration is the lack of civility and the disinterest in civilised living that I see every day around me in contemporary America, the lowering of personal and professional standards, the selfishness and violence and anger, and the absence of shared values in a country that has been culturally Balkanised for my entire adult life. I've been addressing these matters in my essays and articles for a decade now, especially the essays in *Tricycle*, *Buddhadharma* and *Shambhala Sun*. In the new philosophy book I co-authored with Michael Boylan the first story is my tale, "The Cynic," narrated by Plato, which was originally published in *Boston Review*. He describes the moral collapse of Athens after the Peloponnesian War. What happened to the Athenians is, in my view, very much an analog for what we are seeing in America today. We have our ruthless people like Thrasymachus and Jason in Euripides' *Medea*, our political leaders like the ones described by Thucydides ("Inferior intellects," he wrote, "generally succeeded best"). And we certainly have our teachers at the universities (in the humanities) who are the spitting image of the Sophists.

Watterson: Your book *Philosophy: An Innovative Introduction: Fictive Narrative, Primary Texts, and Responsive Writing*, which you coauthored with Michael Boylan, is coming out this month from Westview Press. From advance praise for the book, I gather it combines writing exercises with short fictions starring Plato, Kant, and Dr. Martin Luther King, Jr. Can you say more about this new book?

Johnson: What I want to say is that from start to finish this is Michael Boylan's book. He was inspired to put it together after reading a few of my short stories that have philosophers as protagonists (Plato, Descartes, the Buddha, Martin Luther King Jr.). But Boylan did *all* the work, *all* the heavy lifting in terms of pedagogy. He wrote six new stories of his own about traditional philosophers, but with my stories and his on Hannah Arendt and Iris Murdoch, he expanded the list of thinkers beyond what is in the usual philosophy textbook to include women and people of color, in the West and East. He wrote the introduction for each section; the study questions for both the stories and classic, primary texts; and provided the glossary at the front of the book and the "philosophy games" at the end. He explains the difference between direct, deductive presentations (philosophy), and indirect argument (fiction), and shows teachers how to get their students to write in both ways with intellectual rigor. Boylan is an outstanding educator. My contribution is minimal compared to his. But I have to add that this new book, my eighteenth, is an addition to my body of work (as well as to Boylan's—he's published over twenty books and ninety articles on philosophy and literature, as well as a novel of his own, *The Extinction of Desire*, for which I wrote an introduction) that makes me enormously happy. It should be very helpful to everyone interested in the relationship between philosophy and literature. Last week the publisher, Westview Press (they are Boylan's regular publisher), sent me a lovely card that said, "We are tremendously proud of this book, as I hope you are, too." Well, I am. And I'm in Michael Boylan's debt forever.

Watterson: Thank you for your time and energy. May your work continue to unfold in ways that surprise and delight you. We look forward to reading more.

Johnson: Thank you, Zach.

20

The Game

— Michael Boylan

It was early in the afternoon one day when Henry came to the park. We were just a bunch of guys engaged in our weekly game. The air was chilly, but not cold. You know, late October before the grip of winter has taken hold: the end of autumn. Each Saturday, after our chores were done—around noon, a few of us from the neighborhood would head over to the park, which lay just across the freeway, to play touch football. Sometimes we'd see some people already there and invite them to play in our game. At other times it would be just the six or seven of us.

But none of us, save Mucho Pani, had ever seen Henry before.

On this particular day Eddie Meyer was already running routes with Billy Washington. Billy is the only black guy in the neighborhood. He teaches up at Jefferson High. Eddie was, I guess you could say, the best friend Billy had in the neighborhood. Eddie didn't have any pretensions. He said what he thought and was not self-conscious about living in the smallest house while having the largest family on the block. He was a foundry worker, I think, and I'm quite sure he never finished high school. Still, there was something dependable about Eddie.

I came down to the park with Lincoln McCrae and Angelito Domingez. We were going via the northern bridge over the freeway. It's only three blocks to the park, but you have to enter it from one of two gates. The rest of the park has a high fence around it for security. The park itself is about two miles around with a lake in the middle. It is pretty nice, I guess, for an urban park. There isn't much violence, and there are often games of baseball in the summer, and soccer and football in the early fall. Lots of kids use our park. Why there's even a group of Latinos (our area has the second highest concentration of Latinos in the city) who play a game that resembles volleyball except they kick a small wicker ball over the net.

On this day there wasn't anyone in the park except Eddie and Billy. We could see them from atop the hill that overlooks the north gate to the park. What an odd combination. Fat, little Eddie was running out for passes while the tall, nearsighted teacher (who never wore his glasses to our games) tossed him arching offerings. I almost laughed aloud except that I didn't know what Lincoln might say. Lincoln was always so involved with things, you know: serious. Lincoln had been a member of the civil rights commission and the ACLU so that I didn't feel comfortable making light around him.

Angelito didn't say much.

I began to wonder if we would have enough for a game. We always required at least three-on-three. It made for a better afternoon. There didn't appear to be any people in the park this afternoon who we could ask to play with us. At that moment we only had five.

"Maybe we won't have a game," I ventured to Lincoln.

"Don't forget Mucho and Tattler. One of them is bound to show. Those two egos couldn't both miss together."

Angelito nodded and so we made our way down the hill. The field on which we played was field number one. It was designed for both soccer and football. On each side were smaller fields which served the same purpose. On Friday afternoons there were always three games going on from two until seven. Our park gets lots of use.

As we made our way down the hill I saw no one. The lowland basin, with its two baseball backstops and five-tiered bleachers, looked as bare as the trees were becoming. There was a 'nippiness' to the air, but it wasn't cold. At least not yet.

"Hi Eddie," I yelled when we got to the bottom of the hill.

"Send one over here," cried Lincoln to Billy Washington who had the ball. Billy sent a wobbling pass to the senior member of our group.

Lincoln muffed it, but laughed it off as he generally did by declaring that it took his forty-five-year-old-bones awhile to warm up. Lincoln was like that. Said that a person should bide his time and wait for the opportunities. Who am I to disagree? Lincoln was a lawyer and I didn't even finish college.

Soon the four of us were tossing around the pigskin (or more precisely *cowskin*) and were feeling the sweat begin to flow when we heard the loud car stereo of Jimmy Tattler. Jimmy, who hated any other appellation, was perhaps the richest among our group. I use the superlative guardedly because though Jimmy certainly wanted us all to believe this about him, I'm not all together sure that this was actually true. What a man wears and what he drives can often be deceiving. Revolving charge plans on credit cards make it easy to become over extended. I never use credit cards.

We were tossing the ball pretty well. It was time to begin the game. But even as we were dividing up, there suddenly appeared, at the top of our natural green amphitheater, the forms of Mucho Pani and another, unknown man. I don't know why, but we all looked up at the same time. They hadn't called attention to themselves. But for some reason we were all transfixed.

"Have you started yet?" yelled Mucho as he glided easily down the hill. And without waiting for a response he added, "We would have been here sooner, but we tried to get through the south gate. It's closed. Some road work, I guess."

Mucho walked with a confident stride of a man who felt he was among friends. I think Mucho always feels he is among friends—wherever he is. Anyway, as the two approached, Angelito turned away and began to pace off the field. We usually do this as a group after the teams are formed, but the rest of us were still standing there and Angelito wanted to get things going.

"Where'd you pick-up that one?" began Jimmy in a needling tone.

I laughed, though no one else did. Jimmy was right that the stranger had a peculiar look about him. He reminded me more of a machine—a computer perhaps—than a being of flesh and bone. Though flesh and bone he had in abundance. He must have outweighed any of the rest of us by forty pounds. I was glad we were playing a friendly game of "touch."

"This is Henry," said Mucho. "He's going to play with us today."

There was a note of authority in Mucho's voice. Mucho was the manager at the supermarket on Capitol Court. He sometimes forgot who he was talking to. I suppose it's easy to mistake your friends for a couple of stock boys.

Everyone except Lincoln and I walked away to help Angelito. It was up to the four of us to choose teams.

I suggested that Eddie, Billy, Lincoln and I stand Angelito, Jimmy, Mucho and Henry. The others agreed except Henry. He scowled.

The first two possessions went all right except that Henry didn't seem to be doing much. He appeared to be studying us. At the time I thought he was trying to get the hang of our style of football. I wouldn't find out until later that I was totally wrong.

The score was one touchdown to none when we had the ball about midfield with a good chance to increase our lead. It was then that Henry declared sharply, "Rule change!"

"What's the matter?" asked Lincoln.

"The defense should be able to use their hands," was his mechanical reply.

"There's nothing against that," said Lincoln, "provided that you don't grab someone and that it doesn't get too rough."

Henry muttered something and the game went on. We had driven down near to the other team's goal when Billy Washington went out for a pass and Lincoln threw him a perfect strike. Billy had it for a touchdown when suddenly

Henry sent his hands, as though propelled by pistons, into Billy's back. The play should have been over. Billy was unprepared for the blow and was thrown to the ground.

All of us were stunned except Tattler and Pani who chuckled at Billy's misfortune. I think Tattler is a closet racist.

"What you think you're doing?" cried Billy as he pugnaciously arose. "The play was over. You don't hit a man after he has made a touchdown."

"All I did was 'two-hand-touch.'"

"It was pretty hard for two hand touch. Besides, that was a late hit."

Henry didn't respond but walked down to the other end of the field with his team for the kick-off. Billy was muttering to himself. I was in some confusion. Billy never played roughly at all. He was a finesse player depending upon speed and agility. To change the style of our game would not be to his advantage. But there was more to it. This outsider was coming in and trying to run our game for us. I resented this. I also resented Mucho for bringing us this bore. He made Mucho seem like a decent kind of guy. Still, no one wanted to make a big thing of it, so we went on.

In the next series the other team had gotten halfway down the field when Henry picked up the snap himself and ran right over Lincoln and Billy. Lincoln was knocked over by Henry's shoulder hitting his ribs. Billy had taken the full brunt of Henry head-on.

Billy lay flat on his back. The soft-spoken schoolteacher looked hurt. A bunch of us ran to his aid. But Henry kept us away.

"I'll see to this," he said in a flat voice. There wasn't any great loudness to his speech, but somehow it seemed to carry great authority.

Henry helped Billy to his feet. He only had the wind knocked out of him. None of us did anything. All we did was stand there and watch.

"Billy better play on my team for awhile," he concluded.

This seemed like a logical arrangement so we left it at that. We got Jimmy Tattler in the exchange. In the next play Henry gave Billy the ball. The nearsighted schoolteacher followed Henry's block which flattened me and Jimmy.

I felt something hot and flowing. I had a nosebleed.

"I think this is getting a little rough," said Jimmy.

Billy, who had just made a touchdown, said, "How does it feel being on the other side of it? You seemed to think it was pretty funny when I got it."

"Get screwed, sambo," said Jimmy quietly, but so that Billy could hear.

Henry didn't say anything. He gathered his men and kicked off. The kick was right to Jimmy who got it and was instantly flattened by Billy.

"What in the name of shit are you doing?" yelled Jimmy as he got up hot and ready to punch Washington. "You nearly ripped my $300 Carabinni body suit."

Billy's eyes flashed. He wouldn't have minded laying into Jimmy right there. Then Henry intervened.

"Rule change," proclaimed Henry. "From now on tackling is allowed."

"Just a minute," Lincoln put in. "We play touch here. We've never played tackle."

Henry stepped up to the lawyer. "We're playing tackle now."

"I'm not. I'm leaving." Lincoln turned around to go when Henry stretched out his left arm and grabbed Lincoln by the shoulder and turned him around. The lawyer's eyes showed a fear which I had never seen. He had faced many important cases and had stood up to all odds, but now the threat was physically immediate.

"Let me go. I don't want to play anymore."

"You have to play. The game depends upon your presence." Henry's voice seemed almost to echo. There was a quality to it which reminded you of a loudspeaker system sending out its message to some crowd.

Then Eddie Meyer stepped forward. "You can't do this. If Lincoln wants to go, then so be it. I've had enough of this myself. This isn't football; it's butcher ball." Eddie stood up to Henry. There were two of them in front of this man and his dictatorial output. If only we had all taken that opportunity to rush him just then. We had our chance, but we muffed it. We just watched—myself included.

Henry wheeled and stared at Eddie a moment and then, with a terrible swing, he knocked Eddie's head at the temple with such a force that the stocky foundry worker fell to the ground. Eddie didn't get up. I rushed to Eddie's aid, but Henry told me to get back in my place.

Why hadn't we done something? Even then the six of us could have subdued him. But even Lincoln seemed impressed with what Henry could do if he wanted to. Henry could kill, and none of us wanted to be next.

"The game goes on. We play tackle."

None of us wanted to continue. Even Mucho seemed to lose that air of self-confidence he always tries to affect. But continue we did.

It was with a different feeling that we resumed. Henry was now making more and more changes in the rules. Lincoln whispered to me that we should watch for our chance to jump Henry and so effect our escape.

This seemed like a good idea, but I could not help going over in my mind the fact that we had had the opportunity to jump Henry and we hadn't taken it.

Henry was now making up all the plays. He assigned Mucho and Angelito to tackle Lincoln. When the lawyer had taken several jarring tackles he began to send sharp punches to the bodies of his hunters. After this had occurred three times Angelito sent a fierce blow to Lincoln's jaw. The lawyer went reeling. Angelito didn't stop there. He tackled the former civil rights activist attorney, and pushed Lincoln's face into the dirt. Lincoln fought back.

Jimmy yelled to Lincoln, "Take care of that wet-back, Link. It's time we got the garbage out of here anyway." As he said this he looked back to Billy who responded by putting the salesman and his designer athletic costume down to the ground. Mucho went in to help Jimmy against Billy. I didn't like to see two against one so I got in to help Billy.

I'm not sure how long we were on the ground, but it wasn't long. Soon Henry stopped it. We had fought with passion, but for some reason we did not turn our violence against Henry. He had intervened. We obeyed.

The game must proceed," he said.

We stopped fighting. Billy had a puffy ear and a cut over his left eye. Jimmy was suffering from abdominal pains. Mucho seemed pretty good except for shoulder stiffness. My nose was bleeding again. This time it was broken.

The teams were rearranged again. Lincoln, now without two teeth, was playing alongside Angelito. None of us seemed to be same. We just kept doing what Henry said.

I looked around hoping someone would come and rescue us. The park is normally very busy. But today it was completely vacant. I hoped someone would come and stop Henry. If only we had acted earlier when we had had the chance.

Now Henry ran every play. We did what he told us to do. I kept waiting, as Lincoln had suggested earlier. But now, none of us were allowed to talk to each other so that organisation would be difficult. The only one we could talk to was Henry. I felt he could be stopped, but I couldn't do it alone. I needed help. But how could I get it when everyone was so badly divided? No one was himself anymore.

If only someone would come. We continued with the game. Each of us waited—waited for a way out. In the center of the field was the body of Eddie. It was getting stiff by now. Strange, we all seemed to ignore it. We shut it out. We played the game. We waited, and we played the game.

21

Kamadhatu, A Modern Sutra

for Martin Hughes

— Charles Johnson

The body is the Bodhi Tree;
The mind is like a bright mirror standing.
Take care to wipe it all the time.
And allow no dust to cling.

—*Shen-hsiu*

Thus have I heard:

Not far from Osaka, deep in the forest, there is a 1400-year-old Buddhist temple called Anraku-ji, which in Japanese means "peaceful, at ease." But the young priest who took over the care and upkeep of Anraku-ji not long ago, Toshiro Ogama was his name, felt neither truly peaceful or at ease, and having said something as puzzling as that, it is now necessary, of course, to tell you why.

When Toshiro Ogama was fifteen, both his parents were killed in an automobile accident in Kyoto. An only child, he was suddenly an orphan. His parents' funeral, conducted by a priest in the Pure Land tradition, and their cremation were engraved into the emulsion of his memory. At the crematorium, they were incinerated at 800 degrees centigrade. Their bodies burned steadily for two hours. They had a thirty minute cooling-down period. Finally, their bones were crushed and mixed with ashes—all total his parents each weighed two pounds at the end—and they were given back to Toshiro in two white urns. Those containers, which he kept and placed beside the altar at Anraku-ji, led him all his adult life to listen attentively whenever he heard the Buddhist Dharma or teachings. And what more? Well, he was painfully shy and, like the English scientist Henry Cavendish, he could barely speak to one person, never to two at once since four eyes looking at him made Toshiro stammer. At eighteen, he entered Shogen-ji Monastery and devoted four years to rigorous training, living on a prison diet of cheap rice and boiled potatoes in bland soup. He later passed his examinations at Komazawa University, where many Soto Zen monks have studied, but after this Toshiro decided he did not want to teach or try to work his way up through the politically treacherous Buddhist hierarchy and rigid, religious pecking-order in Japan, which was brutally competitive, and had corrupted the Sangha or community of spiritual seekers by the greed and hypocrisy of the world—or at least this was what Toshiro told himself since he was unable to speak to anyone about his real Zen fears, and why he sometimes felt like a failure, an outright fraud. Knowing he didn't have the family connections or the constitution to rise very high in the religious power structure, Toshiro chose instead to take a free-lance job translating best-selling American books for Hayakawa Shobo, a publishing company in Tokyo, and he looked around for an abandoned temple that he might repair, manage, and perhaps turn into his own private sanctuary from suffering and all the unpredictable messiness of the social world. Across Japan, there are thousands of these empty, wooden buildings falling into disrepair, full of termites and rats, with tubers growing through the floorboards, as if each was a vivid illustration of how everything on this planet was so provisional, with things arising and being unraveled in a fortnight, a fact that Toshiro meditated on deeply, day and night, since the death of his parents.

So when he was granted permission to move into Anraku-ji, the young priest felt, at least for his first year there, a contentment much like that described by Thoreau at Walden Pond. He had no wealthy parishioners or temple supporters paying his salary. Whatever he did at the temple was voluntary, with no strings attached, paid for by his translation work, and done for its own rewards. With great care, he spent a year remodeling Anraku-ji's small main hall and adjoining house, quietly chanting to himself as he worked. He pruned branches, sawed tree limbs and raked leaves. He trimmed bushes, did weeding and trans-planting, and drifted off to sleep to the sound of crickets, bullfrogs, and an owl that each night soothed him like music. Sometimes he talked to himself as he worked, which was a great embarrassment when he caught himself doing that, so he kept a cat to have something to talk to and cover up his habit. He was alone at Anraku-ji, but not lonely, and he decided a man could do far worse than this.

Thus things stood when one afternoon a pilgrim from America arrived unannounced on the steps of his temple. This did not please Toshiro at all because, traditionally, the Japanese do not like surprises. She was a bubbly, effervescent black American about forty-years-old, with an up-tilted nose, a smile that lit up her eyes behind her gold-framed, oval glasses, and long chestnut hair penned behind her neck by a plastic comb. At first, Toshiro felt ambushed by her beauty. Then he had the uncanny feeling he should know her, but he wasn't sure why. In Japanese, he said, "*Konnichiwa*," and when she didn't answer, he said in English, "Are you lost?"

That question made her lips lift in a smile. "Spiritually, I guess I am. Aren't we *all* lost? Are you Toshiro Ogama-san?"

"Yes."

"And are you accepting students? My name is Cynthia Tucker. You're translating one of my books for Hayakawa Shobo. I would have called first, but you don't have a phone listed. I'm in Japan for a month and a half, lecturing for the State Department and—well, since I'm *here,* and have a little unscheduled time, I was hoping to meet you, and discuss any problems you might have with American words in my book, and maybe get your help with my practice of meditation." Now she laughed, taking off her glasses. "Roshi, I think I need a *lot* of help."

"I...I'm not a teacher," said Toshiro.

"But you *are* the abbot of this beautiful temple, aren't you?"

"Yes..."

"Well, if it's all right, I'd love to stay a few days and—"

"Stay?" His voice slipped a scale.

"Yes, visit with you for awhile and ask a few questions." He was amused Tucker said this while standing under the sign posted at every Zen temple and monastery, which read, *Look*

Under Your Feet (for the answers), but this pilgrim did not, of course, read Japanese. "I can make myself useful," she said. "And I won't be a bother. Maybe I can help you in some way, too."

As she spoke, and as he studied her more closely—her flower-patterned blouse, sandals and white slacks, how early afternoon sunlight was like liquid copper in her hair, Toshiro slowly realised that among the five books he was leisurely translating for Hayakawa Shobo there *was* one by a Dr. Cynthia Tucker, a Sanskrit scholar in the Asian Languages and Literature Department at the University of Washington. Her author's bio and American newspaper interviews with her told him she'd survived colon cancer, two divorces, had no children, taught courses in Eastern philosophy, and described herself whimsically as a Baptist-Buddhist. Her book, *The Power of a Quiet Mind,* was a hefty, 300-page volume devoted to interpreting the Dharma in terms that addressed the trials and tribulations of black Americans. Toshiro was only two chapters into his translation, but he'd found her work electrifying—even culturally necessary. Her prose was incandescent, shimmering with the Right Thought of all buddhas in the ten directions, but placed within a twenty-first century black American context. Toshiro also found this ironic. In Japan, the old ways and old wisdom had become antique after World War II. The traditions of Soto and Rinzai Zen held little interest for this younger, business-minded generation of Japanese who seemed quite satisfied pursuing the goods of the world and being salary-men. But the Americans? Since the 1960s, they had become passionate about the Dharma, even when they got it wrong—as Kerouac and Ginsberg did—and he often suspected that much of the continuation of Asian spiritual traditions might fall to them, the *gaijin* of North America who had grown weary of materialism. As much as he valued his privacy at the temple, he saw how impolite it would be to turn this very distinguished visitor away. He wasn't happy about the prospect of having to be entertaining, but it couldn't be helped. If he didn't, her publisher—his boss—would not be pleased. Even so, he had always been awkward around people and felt afraid of this situation.

The young priest brought his palms together in the gesture of gratitude and veneration, called *gasshó,* and made a quick bow.

"Forgive me for not recognising you at first. I think your book—and *you*—are wonderful, and you *can* help me with some of the words. But I don't think you should stay for too long. One day only. I don't see people often, and I'm not such a good teacher of the Buddhadharma. Really, I don't know anything."

"Oh, that's hard to believe." The corners of her eyes crinkled as she smiled. "I've read that all beings are potential Buddhas. Anyone or anything can bring us to a sudden awakening—the timbre of a bell, an autumn rose, the extinguishing of a candle. Anything!"

Toshiro's eyes slipped out of focus when she said that. She really knew her stuff, and that made his heart give a very slight jump. How would she judge him if she knew the depths of his own failure? The priest invited the pilgrim inside, offering her a cup of rice wine and a plate of rice crackers. He showed her around the temple, the two of them sometimes walking out of step in their stocking feet and bumping each other as they conversed for half the afternoon about English grammar, with Tucker sometimes placing her hand gently on his shoulder, and peppering him with questions that made Toshiro's stomach chew itself—questions like, "What time do you get up? How often do you shave your head? Is your tongue on the roof of your mouth when you meditate? Do you eat meat, Roshi? Why are Zen priests in Japan allowed to get married, but not those in China?" Toshiro noticed his palms were getting wet, and wiped them on his shirt, but his arm still tingled with pleasure where she had touched him. He excused himself, saying he needed to work awhile on the stone garden he was creating. He repeated his apology, "I am the poorest of practitioners. You must ask someone else these questions. And not stay more than one night. People in the village will talk if a woman sleeps at the temple. And *don't* call me Roshi."

"I understand, I'll leave." Tucker put back her head and he could feel the smile on her face going frozen. "But Ogama-san, since I've come all this way across the Pacific ocean, please give me something to do for the temple. I insist. I want to serve. I could make a donation, but college professors don't earn very much. I'd prefer to work. I could help you in your garden."

Not wanting that, and because the words left his mouth before his brain could catch them, he told Tucker that cleaning out one of the small storage rooms at the hinder part of the main hall, which contained items left over by the temple's last abbot fifty years ago, was a chore he'd been putting off since he moved into Anraku-ji. He gave her a broom, a mop and a pail, then Toshiro, his stomach tied up in knots, hurried outside.

For the rest of the afternoon, he pottered about in the stone garden, but he was in fact hiding from her, and wondering what terrible karma had brought this always questioning American to Anraku-ji. He was certain she would discover that, as a Zen priest, he was a living lie. He knew all the texts, all the traditional rituals, everything about ceremonial training and temple management, but he had never to his knowledge directly experienced nirvana. He feared he would never grasp *satori* during his lifetime. It would take a thousand rebirths for the doors of Dharma to crack open even a little for one as stalled on the Path by sorrow as Toshiro Ogama. In Japanese, there was a word for people like him: *Nise bozo*. It meant "imitation priest." And that was surely what Cynthia Tucker would judge him to be if he let her get too close, or linger too long on the temple grounds. If he was to save face, the only solution, as far as he could see, was to demand that she leave immediately.

At twilight, Toshiro tramped back to the main hall, intending to do just that. But what happened next, he had not expected. He found his visitor standing outside the storeroom, her hair lightly powdered with fine, gray dust, and heaped up around her in crates and cardboard boxes were treasures he never knew the temple contained. She had unearthed Buddhist prayers, *gatha*, written a hundred years before in delicate calligraphy on rice paper thin as theater-scrim, and wall-hangings elaborately painted on silk (These were called *kakemono*) that whispered of people who had passed through the temple long before he was born—past lives that were all the more precious because they were ephemeral, a flicker-flash of beauty against the backdrop of eternity. There were also large, pewter-gray tin canisters of film, a battered canvas screen, and a movie projector from the 1950s, which Tucker was cleaning with a moistened strip of cloth. When Toshiro stepped closer, she looked up, smiling, and said:

> "When I was a little girl, my parents had a creaky, old projector kind of like this one. I think I can get it working, if you'd like to watch whatever is in those tin containers."
>
> "*Yes,*" said Toshiro, "I *do*." He picked up one of the canisters and read the yellowed label on top. "I can't believe this. These are like—how do you say?—home movies made here by my predecessor half a century ago."

Toshiro stepped aside as Tucker carried the screen and projector into the ceremony room. He plopped down on a cushion, watching her carefully thread film through sprocket wheels, test the shutter and lamp, then she placed the blank screen, discolored by age, fifteen feet away next to the altar. She clicked off the lights. She threw the switch, and the old, obsolete projector began to whir. There was no sound, only the flicker of images on the *tabula rasa* of the screen, slowly at first, each frame discrete and separated by spaces of white, as if the pictures were individual thoughts, complete in themselves, with no connection to the others—like *his* thoughts before he had his first cup of tea in the morning. Time felt suspended. But as the projector whirred on in the silent temple, the frames came faster, chasing each other, surging forward, creating a linear, continuous motion that brought a sensuously rich world to life before Toshiro's eyes. He realised he was watching a funeral in this very ceremony room taped at Anraku-ji probably during the period of the Korean War. He felt displaced, not in space, but in time. On the screen, an elderly woman lay in state, surrounded by four grieving relatives, and long-stemmed white chrysanthemums. A thin blanket covered the old woman's shriveled body from her neck to her ankles. Someone had placed a small, white handkerchief over her face, and as a young man seated beside her, perhaps her eldest son, suddenly lifted the cloth and kissed her cold forehead, Toshiro felt his own face stretch and his back shiver, the experience of ruin and abandonment that overcame him during his own parents' funeral welling up inside him once again. In spite of himself, he surrendered his personal anguish, his pain—the powerful energy of his emotions—over to the people at this funeral, and this transference thickened the screen so thoroughly that the young priest's nose clogged with tears and mucus, his eyes burned with tears, but even as he sobbed uncontrollably, he knew himself to be locked in a cycle of emotion (his own) which these fleeting, black-and-white images borrowed, intensified, and gave back to him in a magic show produced by the mind, a dreamland spun from accelerated imagery. After a second, he realised this—yes, *this*—was what the sutras meant by *kamadhatu,* by the realm of illusion, by Samsara. All at once, the ribbon of film in the projector broke, returning the screen to an expanse of emptiness completely untouched by the death and misery projected upon it. For these last few moments he had experienced, not the world, but the workings of his own nervous system. And this was truly all he had *ever* known. He himself had been supplying the grief and satisfaction all along, from within. Yet his original mind, like the screen, remained Lotus flower pure and in a state of grace. At that moment, Toshiro Ogama understood. He knew. He saw clearly into his own self-nature, and forever lost the sense of twoness.

Outside a breeze wuthered through yew trees and set chimes on the porch to ringing. Inside, the temple seemed to breathe, a gentle straining of wood on wood, then relaxation. Tucker clicked the lights on in the ceremony room. She saw tears streaming from Toshiro's eyes, and took a step toward him. "Ogama-san? Are you alright? I didn't know this would upset you so."

He rubbed his red eyes and stood up, self-emptied. "Neither did I. Thank you for working the projector."

She gave him a fast, curious look, and then moved to where her black, leather briefcase rested in a corner of the room. "I guess I'll be going now."

"Why?" said Toshiro. "In that film, I saw how once Anraku-ji was thriving with parishioners. There was a Sangha here of all sentient beings, and with no religious officials in sight. It should be that way again. Later this week I want to invite the villagers down the road to visit. Would you join my temple as its first member?"

The pilgrim did not speak, for words can be like a spider's-web. She simply bowed, pressing both brown palms together in *gasshó*—one palm symbolising Samsara, the other Nirvana—in a gesture of unity that perfectly mirrored Toshiro's own.

22

Charles Johnson: Philosopher, Writer and Friend

— Richard E. Hart

Charles Johnson and I first crossed paths in the fall of 1973, when we were both in our mid-twenties. Obviously, a lot of water and years have passed under the bridge since then, nearly forty years to be sure, a fact that both of us I believe find rather astonishing, perhaps unbelievable. That fall we were brand new, probably a bit anxious and wet behind the ears, Ph.D. students in Philosophy at the State University of New York at Stony Brook (now known as Stony Brook University). If memory serves, we were two of nine new entrants to thc program that year. As many of us "old-timers" label it, that was a "golden time" for graduate philosophy study at Stony Brook. The Ph.D. program was but a couple years old, the inevitable rough edges were still being worked out, obviously no degrees had yet been awarded, but a sort of intellectual electricity was in the air. The Philosophy Department was uniquely strong in continental and American systematic philosophy. The Ph.D. program was innovative for its time, emphasising and requiring study of different styles of philosophy and, of critical importance to the two of us, interdisciplinary pursuits. In those days it was near impossible to be taken seriously as a philosopher if your goal was to merge philosophy with other fields of enquiry or creativity. But to its credit philosophy at Stony Brook enthusiastically reached out to and meaningfully intersected with other disciplines—physics, the social sciences, visual arts, and literature, among others.

Indeed, it was a rather heady and exhilarating time at Stony Brook. We all felt part of something really unique and special in philosophy. Of course, typically, it was, also, a very poor time for us graduate students.

As ironic as it may sound, I can recall with some fondness how Chuck and his wife (and within a year or so new son) and my wife and I pretty much subsisted on paltry graduate student stipends (especially considering living costs on Long Island, New York) supplemented by spouse minimum wage jobs. Chuck's little sports car of sorts seemed to always be in the shop, and our one car was scarcely better. We shared a lot of rides in the early morning and late afternoon between home and campus. We did well to make the rent for the converted North shore summer cottages we occupied during the school year. I can recall one spell where Chuck was without wheels for a fairly long period. Every day I would pick him up at some ungodly early hour in the morning so that my wife could drop us off at campus and then commute away to her dreary job. So early that we were usually without coffee or breakfast, and he and I would typically have to pool whatever change we had to get some scrambled eggs and coffee at the unoccupied student union. When his son was born there were times when I would lend him a buck or two (if I had it) for the purchase of milk. So those days for us were both lean and highly spirited.

I think Chuck and I had a couple of seminars together our first year, and got to know each other a bit. But in our second year we both were given sections of our own undergraduate courses to teach. This is when things really took off. Why? Because we were given an office to share. Actually, three of us doctoral students occupied one rather small office (Room 158) on the first floor of the Old Physics (renamed by us students, Metaphysics) building. The third occupant was a fascinating fellow from either Greece or Turkey (can't quite recall) who already held a Ph.D. in physics, was an avowed Marxist, and came to Stony Brook to pursue philosophy of science and add another doctorate to his arsenal. Chuck was then a smoker, the physicist drank coffee endlessly (as did Chuck) and read every newspaper he could find every morning, and I sat quietly munching on my bag lunch of peanut butter and raisins. But the animated chatter in that small room, the energy and free flow of ideas, made us wonder at times how the room kept from detaching and floating off into space.

During the first year I had no clue that Chuck was a writer or accomplished cartoonist. Or that he had hosted his own campus TV show while at Southern Illinois University. Prior to Room 158 we would sometimes talk about philosophy and literature, and it was abundantly clear that we both had an abiding interest in what was then called the "interface" between the two domains. But little did we know (I suspect) that such would end up being the focus of our respective careers. We didn't even have careers yet. Things accelerated rapidly once we all moved into Room 158. There, for hours on end, Chuck and I would find ourselves embroiled in debates about virtually every possible angle of the relation between literary art and philosophy. Are they really sister disciplines? Did Plato have it right about the poets? How could a work of fiction actually "do philosophy?" Is there such a category of philosophical fiction, and, if so, who belongs in it? How does phenomenology/existentialism relate to novels and short stories? Did Sartre accurately define what literature is? This went on and on, day after day, sometimes extending into the evenings or weekends. We took Independent Studies together on Sartre, and struggled to decipher what he was doing in *What is Literature?* or *Saint Genet.* We each taught some literary texts in our introductory philosophy courses, and would talk about how we dealt with the texts and the students' reactions. We ended up co-founding something we called the Graduate Colloquia on Philosophy and Humanities, where grad students and faculty could present works in progress on interdisciplinary topics. He always had me reading things. I had him reading things. Every day it seemed one of us would have a new author or book or critical review that needed to be examined.

One day around 1974 (perhaps in fall or winter) out of the blue he told me that his first novel was going to be published by Viking. It was to be called *Faith and the Good Thing*. I recall being utterly flabbergasted. I had met a few authors before, principally scholars, but could it be that this fellow who had rapidly become my best of friends was actually a novelist? Amazing! Well, the book came out, met with some good and encouraging reviews, and, looking back, one can surely say that from that point on Chuck was off to the races. The proprietor of the Corner Bookshop just off campus got wind of the novel and offered to host a book party. I well recall the excitement of our small, familiar group of Stony Brookers toasting Chuck, and wishing him well on future endeavors. Chuck then told me about the six prior drafts of the novel that had ended up in the trash. He told me about working with his mentor, the then celebrated author John Gardner, while both were at SIU. A couple of years later, Gardner was to publish his highly controversial, *On Moral Fiction*. Since the topic of morality in fiction was a favorite of ours, Gardner's book kept Chuck and I engrossed in a running dialogue that extends to this very day. Somewhere around 1975 or so Chuck invited me to accompany him into New York City for a visit with John Gardner and his family. What an experience that proved to be—a sleepless, wine inspired night filled with endless ruminations about Nietzsche and Aristotle and Sartre and then current novels, and God only knows what else. My head was both literally and figuratively spinning. I felt as though I had, if only for a moment, hit the big leagues.

The Stony Brook days were wondrous, largely because of the incredibly interesting and intelligent and worldly graduate students. They were an endless source of inspiration, provocation and good humor. Need I say, we all rather enjoyed some good partying together. But I believe what happened in those few years for Chuck and me was just something unspeakably special. To this day, I have no idea why I should have been so fortunate to accidentally come across a guy in grad school who would end up so profoundly affecting the remainder of my life. To this very moment, his conversations, his novels and stories, his essays on black literature, on Buddhism and writing, his letters and e-mails, continue to challenge me to explore ever deeper into the world of philosophical literature.

Our Stony Brook days together would surely come to an end, a little earlier perhaps than I would have preferred. Following publication of *Faith*, and the favorable attention it received, I recall him telling me one day that he was going into NYC for an interview with a professor from the English Department at the University of Washington. He had been solicited for the interview. Well, the interview went well and he was given an offer. Frankly, he needed the money and was up for the challenge, even if it meant taking up residence in a department other than philosophy. It seemed to me that in a virtual heartbeat he was packing up his most essential belongings in the little car, sending off his wife, Joan, and son, Malik, to hometown Chicago for a temporary respite, while he embarked adventurously on the drive from one end of the continent to the other. By now, everyone knows that he made a really big splash at UW, that, in legendary style, he was (and is) the hardest working creative writing teacher who ever entered a classroom, and that his writing life simply mushroomed triumphantly after landing in Seattle. Over the past 35 years, he has no doubt spent many a sleepless night in Seattle churning out stories, novels, screenplays, critical studies, essay collections, reviews, cartoons and more, work that has earned him more accolades than I could begin to list. But readers know all about this. So, in short, my pal, Chuck, went off to become a National Book Award winning novelist and endowed professor on the West coast, and I remained on Long Island all these many years, holding down the Eastern coast I suppose. I ended up doing the adjunct faculty route for a number of years while completing the dissertation, and then went on to a stint in academic administration before in 1986 taking up my post as a philosophy professor at a small private college in northern New Jersey.

When I landed my full-time teaching position 25 years ago, among the first things I did was introduce an introductory course on philosophy in literature. Over the years I have taught it more times than anyone can remember. While I always change up the reading lists, one thing remains constant. There is always a novel or story collection by Chuck Johnson included. In the fall of 1986 our course was the first at any college or university to read and study the stories in *The Sorcerer's Apprentice*. Chuck wrote a lovely letter to my students, thanking them for taking his work seriously and exploring the philosophy in the stories. The students were just bowled over. Later on I enjoyed a long stint of lecturing in an interdisciplinary core course called the Sophomore Core. Every student at the college had to complete the course, the generic theme of which was (and is) social responsibility. For a couple of years I used selected stories from *Soulcatcher and other Stories* to help frame my lectures. So, for a period of a few years every student at my college would have read some of Charles Johnson.

Over the past decade or so I have several times taught special topics, honors seminar on literature and philosophy. There we have read *Dreamer* and *Dr. King's Refrigerator and Other Bedtime Stories*. Unlike some other authors I've used, I can say with total candor that I've never had a bad teaching experience with Johnson's work. Students have always warmed to his fiction. Presently, I am using a brand new introductory text in philosophy, put together by Chuck and Michael Boylan called appropriately enough, *Philosophy: An Innovative Introduction*. It blends short stories about certain philosophers with excerpts from the philosophers' writings.

In 1999 I was named to an endowed professorship in applied ethics. Funding for the position makes possible visits to campus from distinguished scholars and artists. Chuck was the first to deliver the annual Holley lecture on ethics. He gave a splendid, incisive talk on ethics and literature. I realise now, thinking back, how hard we worked him during his three-day visit. He spoke to the Sophomore Core, met with a group of writing students, conducted an informal discussion with faculty and staff, delivered a formal lecture, and sat with incredible patience to sign books from students and others in the college community. The line seemed to wrap around the block. His visit was one of the most inspiring moments in the recent history of our college.

Over the years we've participated in conferences together, and shared our work with each other, sometimes prior to presentation or publication. I've had the pleasure of introducing him as keynote speaker. Some years back the International Association for Philosophy and Literature wanted to have a special session on the work of Charles Johnson and asked me to organise a panel. It was so well received that yet another Johnson panel was convened for the following years' annual meeting, this time organised by someone else and including me as a presenter. It would be impossible to recall all the things we have done over the years—things talked about, projects contemplated, gifts exchanged, family moments shared. Regrettably, I inevitably leave out so much.

But probably the greatest, most steady impact Chuck has had on me, both personally and professionally, has been manifest in the letters and e-mails we regularly exchange. I have hundreds of his letters scattered throughout my files. We used to call our mailings to each other—copies of articles, newspaper clippings, bibliographies, critical reviews, books, etc.— "care packages." Every time I received one I knew that the rest of my day would be absorbed in delving into all the incredible items he had gotten excited about and just had to send along. His messages have always been both personal—concern for family, health, our careers, aging, and the like—and intellectually stimulating. It feels as though the conversation begun back in Room 158 in the mid-70's has never played out. The great adventures of ideas (as Whitehead once said), the explorations about teaching, the ruminating on the plight of the humanities, the never settled wonderment about literature and philosophy, this is the stuff of 40 years of continuous dialogue, perhaps in a grand Socratic tradition. In a word, no one in my life and experience—no one I've read, met or spoken to—has had more of an impact on my understanding of philosophical literature and its possibilities than my friend Chuck Johnson.

As one last instance, for the past twenty years I have been studying, teaching and writing about the great American author, John Steinbeck. I've published a dozen or so articles and reviews, spoken at Steinbeck conferences both at home and abroad, serve on editorial boards for Steinbeck scholarship, and at present am at work on a Steinbeck book. Frankly, I don't think any of this would have come to be without the influence of Chuck Johnson on my thinking, my sensibility, my perception and dreams of what could be seen in literary art. And I'm not sure he is much of a Steinbeck fan. Philosophy can operate fruitfully out of the box. No one has more ably proven this point, with total imagination and distinction, than Chuck Johnson.

Let no one doubt for a second—Chuck Johnson is a fine philosopher. His philosophic comprehension and novel insight is both expansive and subtle. His thought is forever exploratory and synthesizing. He knows the continental tradition, particularly phenomenology, like the back of his hand. I've probably learned more about Husserl from him than from any other single person. He is a serious student of Descartes. He has expert knowledge of Sartre, Camus and Merleau-Ponty. He knows well the history and traditions of Western philosophy (he can quote Heraclitus or Empedocles with understanding all day long), but he is, at the same time, that rare philosopher who is equally accomplished in mastery of Eastern thought, particularly Buddhism. And, as everyone who has read him knows, he is a masterful writer of philosophical fiction, quite possibly the best we have in America today. A challenge to any possible skeptic—do a serious read and re-read of any handful of Johnson stories, think about them deeply, and then, after careful reflection, tell us who does it better? Who has a richer, more complex network of ideas and concepts and arguments permeating every page of the text? Who does a better job of making his reader think about the toughest, perennial questions of life and its meaning, of history and culture, of moral responsibility and the value of human experience? Johnson is a thoroughly inimitable artist, scholar, philosopher, illustrator, and, yes, person. A faithful Buddhist, martial arts expert, student and teacher of meditation, African-American man of letters, sophisticated philosophic intellect and creator of the most refined and challenging philosophical literary art our country has likely ever known. All this in one human being—it's not likely we'll ever see anything like this rare specimen again any time soon. But beyond all of this, Chuck is a great and loyal and trusted friend. Notwithstanding the efforts of American philosopher, Josiah Royce, loyalty is a trait of character much forgotten in today's world, but down deep we all know just how much it means. Without it friendship is hollow and one-directional. I could never, ever, say enough about this truly original and fine man of character and accomplishment. I have been the beneficiary of so much from him, so much that he will never know and that I couldn't begin to describe. I've been blessed, shall I say, to have grown up with, indeed, grown old with, this amazing philosopher and writer and dearest of friends.

23

Contemplations

— Robert E. Abrams

I

He sits by this quiet water
Where white birds peck.

II

Here at midday the mountains
Are only a distant mirage.

No dust is stirred by the wind down this quiet road.

In this stillness
The trees
Are gently diminishing
Tree by tree
Toward the mountains,

The fields ripple like time
Far away from the eye,

The white birds pecking in the water
Grow deep
And unreal.

III

He enters the distances
Of this landscape
Like a stranger

Sitting quietly by this water
Where white birds peck.

IV

He neglects the invitation of the road.

24

The Elusive Art of "Mindfulness"

— Charles Johnson

> As a student wrote: If one is trying to do something really well, one becomes, first of all, interested in it, and later absorbed in it, which means that one forgets oneself in concentrating on what one is doing. But when one forgets oneself, oneself ceases to exist, since oneself is the only thing which causes one to exist.
>
> —Christmas Humphreys, *Concentration and Meditation*

For more than twenty years I've kept this intriguing statement about the relationship between self and work pasted to the writing desk in my study to remind me—as a Buddhist and creator, husband and father, teacher and citizen—that concentration (*dharana*) not only is traditionally the first stage in the ancient practice of formal meditation (*dhyana*), but also expresses itself in the one-pointedness of mind required for the doing well of *any* worldly activity, including the lifelong labor of writing. In fact, as someone who has been publishing stories for thirty-eight years, practicing meditation for twenty-three, and studying Eastern philosophy for thirty-two, I cannot help but marvel sometime at the striking analogues between meditation and moments of intense creative inspiration, and how both overlap in my life and literary offerings.

Yet it matters not at all if the activity we're talking about is writing a novel, preparing dinner, teaching a class, serving tea, or simply walking, the spiritual point is everywhere and always the same; any action is performed best and most beautifully, especially unpleasant tasks, when the actor practices what Buddhists call "mindfulness"; when he is wholly and selflessly aware of every nuance in the activity and immersed in it; when he gets the gossamer-thin illusion of the self out of the way and, in a delightful modulation of consciousness and temporality, experiences only the *here* and the *now*, with no concern at all for the unrecoverable past or a future that never comes.

But, sadly, for most Americans, that kind of concentration and nonattachment (*vairagya*) is elusive, particularly in a TV-oriented and movie-drenched carnival culture that produces a short attention span in a population relentlessly bombarded by trivial distractions and weighted down by ego baggage—elusive, that is until one learns to carefully observe the behavior of the mind and make it one's servant.

No one knows better than those who regularly practice some form of meditation that we are seldom, if ever, the complete master of our mind's operations, thoughts, and cravings. For that reason, early in the canonical Buddhist text *The Dhammapada*, we find this observation:

> Hard to hold down,
> Nimble,
> alighting wherever it likes:
> the mind.
> Its taming is good.
> The mind well-tamed
> brings ease.

At first glance, one thinks: What a preposterous challenge! You might as well try to tame the wind. In *Raja-Yoga*, the nineteenth-century philosopher-teacher Vivekananda employed a popular, East Indian metaphor for the mind's contumacy, one found sprinkled throughout Hindu and Buddhist literature, to describe this every quotidian dilemma:

> There was a monkey, restless by its own nature, as all monkeys are. As if that were not enough, someone made him drink freely of wine, so that the monkey became still more restless. Then a scorpion stung him. When a man is

> stung by a scorpion, he jumps about for a whole day; so the poor monkey found his condition worse than ever. To complete his misery a demon entered into him. What language can describe the uncontrollable restlessness of that monkey? The human mind is like that monkey, incessantly active by its own nature; then it becomes drunk with the wine of desire, thus increasing its turbulence. After desire takes possession comes the sting of the scorpion of jealousy of the success of others, and last of all the demon of pride enters the mind, making it think itself of all importance. How hard to control such a mind.

Vivekananda's humorous yet horrifyingly recognisable "monkey mind" is, obviously—*unclear*. (As cartoonist David Bergman put it, "A mind is a terrible thing to watch.") It is a mind clouded by its passions and self-doubts, deluded by its own ideas, its distorted perceptions, its belief in an enduring personal identity, and its countless presuppositions and highly provisional explanations about the world and others. Such an undisciplined, chaotic mind will perpetually be in a state of suffering and turmoil and cause pain to all in its vicinity until it is quieted, then tamed by the meditation practices (*abhyasa*) outlined in the magnificent *Mahasatipatthana Sutra* (Great Mindfulness Discourse), where one learns to "abide contemplating feelings as feelings...mind as mind...[and] mind-objects as mind-objects."

There are, of course, numerous meditation traditions, but common to them all are exercises that provide a practitioner with but a single object for the mind's attention (*ekagrata*). For beginners, the simplest exercise is offered by the body itself: one's own breath. Try, if you can, to observe for fifteen minutes *only* the rising-falling movement of your abdomen as you breathe. Soon enough, after a few seconds, as you attempt to focus on each inhalation and exhalation, you discover your mind drifting away from the breath—into memories, imaginings, daydreams, and perceptions of physical discomfort (an itch, a stiff back, and so on) as you try to sit perfectly still. (Another cartoonist, Franks Modell, captures this wonderfully when he asks, "It's ten o'clock. Do you know where your mind is?")

In Vipassana "insight meditation," for example, you do not ignore these fugitive wanderings of the mind, its tendency to go AWOL at the first opportunity, but instead carefully observe and identify each erumpent mental act as it appears, like clouds passing across the sky or waves on water—"reflecting," "planning," "feeling pain," "feeling pleasure," "feeling lazy," "feeling bored," "hearing a sound nearby"—and then you let them go, making no effort to hold on as you turn back to your breathing.

◆◆◆◆

Over time this deceptively simple yet daunting exercise of just quietly tracking the labile mind's movements reveals, first, that each evanescent eruption of desire or emotion, each "imagining" or "feeling lazy," melts away like a mirage after it is vetted once or twice. Each is impermanent, with its own "arising and falling away" trajectory and, at bottom, is empty (*shunyata*). Second, one realises the unicity of what we call subject and object (the phenomenologist Edmund Husserl's terms were *noesis* and *noema*), which arise simultaneously in each flicker-flash instant of perception; they are ontologically twinned and inseparable, nondualistic, the one incapable of existing without the other. Put another way, the subject does not exist independent of an object, as David Hume noted two and a half centuries ago in his *Treatise of Human Nature*, where he pointed out, "For my part, when I enter most intimately into what I call *myself*, I always stumble on some particular perception or other, of heat or cold, light or shade, love or hatred, pain or pleasure, and can never observe anything but the perception."

From this elementary task of holding the mind to one's breathing, the beginner advances to attempting the same uninterrupted awareness not only when quietly sitting, but when engaged in other activities. The point of such concentration, which eventually flows seamlessly into meditation, is to attend with all one's heart and mind to the business at hand. Different schools of meditation employ range of phenomenal "objects"—some physical, some mental—to achieve both that end and the spiritual goal of satori, or *moksha* (enlightenment). One might contemplate a symbolic image such as mandala; a mental or physical picture of a beloved saint or savior, as practitioners of *bhakti* (devotion) prefer; or the visualisations characteristic of tantric yoga. Or one might repeat a single sound, or *mantra*, over and over, like the *Namu-myohorenge-kyo* of the Nichiren Buddhists.

◆◆◆◆

Clearly, spiritual practice is nothing if it is not about attention. (The Sanskrit word for attention, *ekagrata*, can be translated as "one," *eka* and "to seize," *grah*.) The same is true of reading and writing. Like a memory, a mathematical entity (numbers), or the visualisations in tantra, the aesthetic object experienced in any literary work is ontologically, as Jean-Paul Sartre points out in *What Is Literature?*, transcendent.

Open any novel. What is there? Black marks—signs—on white paper. First they are silent. They are lifeless, lacking signification until the consciousness of the reader imbues them with meaning, allowing a fictitious character like the nameless protagonist of Ralph Ellison's *Invisible Man*, say, to emerge powerfully from the monotonous rows of ebony type. This magical act is, of course, achieved through a concentration, as one reads, and an act of self-surrender that allows an entire fictional world to appear, redivivus, in the reader's mind: "a vivid and continuous dream," as the novelist John Gardner once called it. As readers, our focused awareness invests the cold signs on the pages of *Invisible Man* with *our* emotions, *our* understanding of oppression and fear. Then, in what is almost an act of thaumaturgy, the electrifying figures and situations Ellison has created reward us richly by returning our subjective feelings to us transformed, refined, and alchemised by language into a new vision with the capacity to change our lives forever.

That same *ekagrata* is at work on the writer's side of the creative equation, too, for the sustained and continuous fictional "dream" that the reader discovers was initially experienced by the author, who, to create an imaginary world, first had to visualise with vivid specificity each and every one of the thousands of details in his novel or short story.

For example, if a dramatic scene is richly evoked, placing us so thoroughly within its ambience that we forget the room we're sitting in or fail to hear the telephone ring; if in it we can "see" the *haecceitas* ("thisness") of every carefully described object on the fictional stage; if our senses imaginatively respond to, say, the quality of late-afternoon light as it falls upon the characters, and to imagery for evoking smells, sounds, and taste; if each revealing, moment-by-moment action, feeling, utterance, pause, and sigh of the characters is microscopically tracked and reverentially inhabit *all* the players at *every* moment in that scene; if every significant nuance of that scene is present with almost a palpable feel on the page, then it is because the radical attentiveness to detail, *here* and *now* in the mind's eye, demanded of the writer (who, knowing no division of creative labor, must in a single work of fiction play each principal role, be the set designer, director, costumer, hairstylist, makeup artist, lighting technician, prop master, casting director, dialogue and sound editor, location manager, and postproduction editor) is a species of the *ekagrata* (attention) practiced in meditation.

No story or novel I've been privileged to write came to me "whole." Rather, what I was initially given was a situation, dilemma, or character that intrigued me and caught my attention throughout the day, so that my curiosity compelled me to sit down to explore it further. What was—and always is—required for the seed of the story to flower was *greater* attention to all the prismatic possibilities of the imagined object, the story, plus the tossing aside of my own presuppositions concerning what the tale and its characters *should* be (I like to call this "beginner's mind"), until over time I've managed to strip away the interesting but inappropriate details and plot misdirections that do not lead to a complete, coherent, and consistent vision—never willing or forcing the fiction into existence, mind you, but instead scrupulously watching its manifestations from one draft to the next, then nurturing the moments that brought me the greatest sense of discovery. (My ratio of throwaway to keep pages is usually 20 to 1). In other words, when I'm writing well, I am merely the servant of the story, its midwife.

And always this process, at least for me, involves letting go of the numerous ideas that arise during intense periods of creativity (ideas I might love and feel attached to) if they do not contribute to what John Barth once called a story's "ground situation"; and yes, like a *bhikshu* (Buddhist monk) dutifully counting his breaths or contemplating impermanence or compassion, I must repeatedly return my wandering mind again and again and yet again to the original spark for the tale: an especially demanding task for philosophical novels such as *Oxherding Tale, Middle Passage*, and *Dreamer*, which had five- and six-year gestation periods.

Yet for all its surface and subtle similarities to meditation, the sustained periods of *ekagrata* required for crafting finely wrought fiction do not in themselves lead to spiritual liberation. So much more is required for that. However, I'd like to believe that for a few literary artists, a lifetime spent harnessing the mind to the labor of creating transcendent objects can prepare them for the first, tentative steps on the Way. And I'm convinced, as I am of nothing else, that when mindfulness—so reverential toward all being—is brought to any task, irrespective of how humble, it transforms work into an opportunity to practice a form of worship that, as *The Dhammapada* puts it, "brings ease."

25

Cartoons, the Dharma and Kung Fu: Conversation with Charles Johnson

— Chris Thomson

A longtime participant in Humanities Washington's Bedtime Stories, Charles Johnson took time to answer a few questions about writing and philosophy as well as cartoons and martial arts.

Thomson: You have written for Bedtime Stories each year since its inception; why is this event so important to you?

Johnson: I've been publishing short stories since 1965 when I was 17-years-old so I love this genre. Unlike, say, a novel, a modern short story (its creation is usually attributed to Edgar Allen Poe) can't tolerate waste, padding, or what the French call *remplissage*. It must have a plot, be economical and efficient, and deliver to the reader a memorable emotional experience. As a philosopher, I naturally feel it should be thought-provoking and transform our perceptions.

Those are a few reasons I love working in this form, and each year for 11 years now Humanities Washington has given me the freedom to create a new story on any subject I wish as long as it connects with that year's theme. This is the kind of challenge every artist enjoys, like jazz musicians invited to improvise a particular musical theme.

Thomson: Who are some of your favorite authors that you've shared the stage with over the years? What draws you to their works?

Johnson: I've had the pleasure of reading with many, many people in the last decade. Some were my former students such as David Guterson (and his sister), and Dan Orozco. Other were famous and well-established writers like August Wilson, Steve Barnes, his wife Tananarive Due, and David Shields. In the case of Bedtime Stories, what drew me with interest to their reading was my curiosity about how they would handle a specific theme for that evening.

Thomson: August Wilson, a close friend of yours and gifted playwright, was another early champion of Bedtime Stories.... What led him to support Humanities Washington in this way?

Johnson: I invited him to participate and he did so eagerly whenever he was in town. I think he enjoyed the event for the creative challenge it presents to all of us.

Thomson: When did you realise that you wanted to be a writer?

Johnson: I never wanted to be a writer. During my late childhood and teens all I wanted to do was draw and become a professional cartoonist and illustrator, which I was almost exclusively from 1965 to 1972. (My bachelor's degree is in journalism so I worked a lot for newspapers in Illinois.) Then when I was 18 and discovered philosophy that became my second passion. (My master's degree and doctorate are in those fields.) Unlike many people I know, who say they wanted to be a writer since they were five-years-old, the so-called "writer's life" as I understood it in the '60s and '70s never appealed to me. But ideas for novels started coming to me in late 1969, things I felt would enrich American literature, and so I had to write them. I still never call myself a writer without wincing—I usually just say I'm an artist, one who works on literary art or visual art or martial arts.

Thomson: What were a few of the ideas that compelled you to sit down and start writing?

Johnson: I wrote six novels in two years (between 1970 and 1972) before writing and publishing my seventh book, *Faith and the Good Thing* in 1974. In other words, I wrote one book every 10-week academic quarter, 10 pages a day five days a week. I always refer to these novels as my "apprentice" work before I met and studied with novelist John Gardner in the fall of 1972. The first of these early novels was based on my experiences in a martial arts school in Chicago in 1967 and how they related to Buddhism—I later returned to that subject in two short stories, "China" (1981) and "Kwoon" (1991).

Thomson: Why writing?

Johnson: A work of literature is, first and foremost, a performance of language. It can achieve things that only language—not drawing or film or sculpture—can achieve. And language, of course, is intimately associated with consciousness, *i.e.,* the grammar and processes of thought itself.

Thomson: How does writing compare with drawing cartoons?

Johnson: As I mentioned, I can do things with language and literary forms that I can't do with drawing, and vice versa. Both are necessary for me as a means of self-expression and for exploring the world around me. Ideally, both spring from the always bubbling pool of our imagination.

Thomson: Do you still draw cartoons?

Johnson: I still draw whenever I can for publication. Although I once completed five drawings a day back in the early '70s when I was in graduate school (and that's how I earned our weekly grocery money when my wife and I were first married), these days I prefer to spend about eight hours on each drawing, trying different sketches and compositions, doing research, then spending the time inking with soft jazz playing in the background. During that process, I'm in heaven—the concentration called for is very much like the concentration required for formal Buddhist meditation.

Thomson: You've often said that much of your writing explores philosophy and spirituality. What captivates you about these two areas?

Johnson: Philosophy (the name of which means "the love of wisdom") is the oldest intellectual discipline in the West, and from it springs physics, ethics, psychology, sociology, theology, economics, epistemology, all the disciplines that eventually separated from it to stand as fields on their own. The study of philosophy is, therefore, the study of intellectual history. It puts one in touch with all fields of inquiry and, therefore, enables a writer to write about any subject under the sun (and beyond the sun). And once upon a time, our spiritual life was not separate from our intellectual life. For that reason, I see life as a whole—mind, body, spirit as a single phenomenon.

Thomson: Who are some of the key thinkers and spiritual leaders that have inspired you personally?

Johnson: Plato, Marcus Aurelius, Hegel, Kant, Husserl, Merleau-Ponty, Jean-Paul Sartre, Heidegger, Shakyamuni Buddha, Jesus, Gandhi, Martin Luther King Jr., Dogen, Nagarjuna. All the philosophers in the book I co-authored this year with Michael Boylan, *Philosophy: An Innovative Introduction.*

Thomson: What can we learn from these teachers?

Johnson: The depths of the human intellect and spirit, *i.e.,* our own possibilities. And how to think well. Remember: Writing well is always the same thing as thinking well.

Thomson: Why, at this point in history, are philosophy, writing, and the other humanities fields so critical?

Johnson: Just now it is my feeling that the humanities are bruised and battered after 40 years of what some call the Culture Wars. It isn't enough to say we "need" the humanities because we ARE the humanities. They are gifts to us from our predecessors, ancestors and contemporaries. They represent the imagination, the innovative, and ask us to think deeply—as the greatest philosophers and artists have always asked us for the last 2,500 years—about our experience, and to think beyond the various intellectually lazy forms of ideology circulating in America today. For the ancient Greeks, "the unexamined life is not worth living." The humanities, and especially real art, help us to critically examine our lives, live more fully, and appreciate the mystery of the world around us and the possibilities for Goodness, Truth, and Beauty within ourselves. Each year Bedtime Stories is a robust celebration of that time-honored mission of the humanities.

Thomson: If all of Washington State could only read one book on Buddhism, which one?

Johnson: I would recommend *The Lotus Sutra* and, if not that, *The Dhammapada,* both classic sutras. Beginners might also try my friend Gary Gach's *The Complete Idiot's Guide to Understanding Buddhism*, which is very entertaining and informative.

Thomson: In addition to a writer-philosopher, I hear you are also a martial arts expert. What's the scoop?

Johnson: I started training in the martial arts in Chicago when I was 19-years-old. That basement school, very rough, was called Chi Tao Chuan of the Monastery. Over the years, I studied three karate and three kung-fu systems, finally devoting myself to one—Choy Li Fut as taught by grandmaster Doc Fai Wong of San Francisco—in 1981. For a decade my Seattle friends in this system and I taught that martial art at various locations around the city. Retired from teaching now, I love having the opportunity to work on my Choy Li Fut empty hand and traditional weapons sets (sword and staff) as well as Tai Chi Chuan every day, to weight-lift three days a week (bench-press at 260 lbs this week), and sweat on the treadmill for 100 minutes three times a week.

Thomson: What do you see as the connections between martial arts and Eastern religion?

Johnson: Historically (and in terms of legend), martial arts entered Chinese Buddhism when the patriarch Bodhidharma traveled from China to India. He found the monks at one monastery in such poor health that they couldn't practice meditation long enough to achieve awakening, and so he studied the various forms animals used for fighting, developed combat exercises from them, then taught those exercises to the monks. Not only did their health improve, but the monks at Shaolin monastery (legend says) became as enthusiastic about martial arts practice as Dharma practice. I understand why. Mind, body, and spirit are one. We need to regularly discipline all three to make progress in life.

Thomson: Do you have any killer moves?

Johnson: I know how to kill—numerous ways to do that—but, as a Buddhist, I took formal vows (the 10 Precepts) not to kill or harm any other sentient being. I try to live by the

Bodhissatva vow of devoting myself to helping other sentient beings achieve happiness and avoid suffering.

Thomson: What can you tell us about your piece for this year's Bedtime Stories?

Johnson: Well, I'm going to try to stay on-point with the theme of "night flight." I have an idea I'm playing with, one inspired by a recent, powerful and memorable poem, "The Ear Is An Organ Made For Love," written by my friend Ethelbert Miller and a spiritually unsettling experience I had here in my neighborhood of Wedgwood just a week or so ago.

Thomson: This sounds interesting ....Tell us more!

Johnson: I'm still working on this so it's better if I don't give too much away. It's still in a delicate state of incubation.

26

The Black American Narrative Continued

— John B. Parks

The literary accomplishments and productivity of Charles R. Johnson are impressive. He has built a formidable reputation as a literary artist and, as he told Nancy Pearl in a recent interview at the University Book Store in Seattle, he is prolific writing six novels in two years at 10 pages a day. Johnson, a philosopher, the 1998 MacArthur Fellow, and the S. Wilson and Grace M. Pollock Endowed Professor Emeritus of English at the University of Washington holds, among others, the 1990 National Book Award which he describes as his most prized as he is the first African American, since Ralph Ellison in 1953, to have received it. In a recent interview with friend, Poet and literary activist E. Ethelbert Miller, Johnson explained that he employs philosophy through language for "self expression and exploring the world...to critically examine our lives, live more fully and appreciate the mystery of the world around us and the possibilities for Goodness, Truth, and Beauty within ourselves." This also describes Johnson's personal epistemological mission. He told Miller that his adolescent phenomenological quest led him to philosophy, and ultimately Buddhism and Kung Fu which has influenced his literary career.

As a revisionist historian I approach historical phenomena with the same epistemological humility that Johnson uses as a Buddhist and a philosopher. Yet my approach begins with asking how do we know what we know and why? It is a question formed and informed by my experience growing up in the late 1960s and 70s in a culture of constant public defiance of authority, particularly the American government. Somehow a message in either a TV commercial or one of the many anti-Vietnam demonstrations captured my imagination and was emblazoned on my mind: "Question Authority!" And somehow this influenced my interest in historical inquiry. This fit quite well with my personal epistemological quest to find the answers to my own questions about human and spiritual phenomena. It wasn't until college that I discovered the fifteenth century Italian humanist Lorenzo Valla. Valla employed textual criticism to deconstruct the authenticity of the Donation of Constantine. Valla proved that it was a fake. Valla's scholarship confirmed the legitimacy of questioning everything to find the truth, whatever or wherever it may be. Historical inquiry in and of itself was for me my epistemological mission. Though separated by time and proximity Lorenzo Valla, myself, and Charles Johnson all have epistemological missions that we explore in our work. We want to know what there is to know, and how one knows. But what we know is limited to our experiences and is always changing. Recognising this is what Johnson calls epistemological humility. Our experiences quite naturally lead us to craft literature out of language not only to record our thoughts, but to convey them to others, what Johnson calls "epistemological missions." Homer's *Iliad*, Herodotus' *Histories*, the *Bible*, the *Koran*, oral traditions, national histories, Hitler's *Mein Kampf*, J.D. Griffith's *Birth of a Nation* and the slave narratives all have epistemological missions.

Let's take an example of James Albert Ukawsaw Gronniosaw's slave narrative which for our purposes is more relevant here. James Albert Ukawsaw Gronniosaw, an enslaved African, who's *Narrative*, published in 1770, described his childhood as being frequently "lost in the wonder of the works of the Creation" and wanting "to be informed of things that no person could tell me." This was Gronniosaw's personal epistemological and phenomenological quest, but it was narrated reflecting a Eurocentric-Christian, and particularly Calvinist, world view which prided itself on the conversion and saving the souls of Africans and their enslaved descendants who were "born under every outward disadvantage and in regions of the grossest darkness and ignorance." Gronniosaw found the answers to his quest in the Western hegemonic expectation of submissiveness to white men while learning to wait "patiently for his (God's) gracious call...(to) deliver us out of the evils of this present world...to the Everlasting Glories of the world to come."

The antithesis to the view of Christianity in Gronniosaw's *Narrative* is Frederick Douglass' repudiation of it in his *Narrative*. "I love the pure, peaceful and impartiality of Christ," Douglass says, but I "hate the corrupt, slaveholding, women-whipping, cradle plundering, partial and hypocritical Christianity of this land." In the centuries long advancement toward racial equality Gronniosaw's *Narrative* would not be the model of emancipation black people would employ because the "Everlasting Glories of the world to come" did not address the "evils of this present world." There is a tension between Gronniosaw's *Narrative* which advertises racial and religious submission and Douglass' which forces the reader to acknowledge and question social and religious hypocrisy and provide a motivation for a more immediate response to social inequity.

Johnson's article "The End of the Black American Narrative" (2008) was one of many that expressed optimism and predictions about race and race relations in America during the presidential campaign of Barack Obama. The black American narrative is what Johnson calls "a very old narrative," used as a tool to interpret all that has happened to black people in America. He goes on to define what a good story is and that the black American narrative contains all of the narrative virtues of a good story: coherence, consistency, and completeness, a dramatic narrative with emotional power, a conflict that we care about, and a dilemma to emotionally identify with. For Johnson this story "has an epistemological mission" to explain the human experience and that the "unique black American narrative emphasizes the experience of victimisation...." It is commonly accepted to begin the black American narrative with the arrival of the first 20 Africans in 1619 in Jamestown because it characterises the circumstances of African migration to and their lives as enslaved persons in

North America. It serves as an iconic sound bite to summarise the status of Africans from that point forward, but consider another starting point 106 years earlier when 30 Africans accompanied Balboa in 1513 to North America. Preciseness of language and accuracy of fact is critical to the epistemological process because it demonstrates that Africans had a broader experience beyond enslavement. I believe the point Johnson was trying make in "The End of The Black American Narrative" is that Barack Obama's presidential campaign is the antithesis of black American victimisation. This too, like the first 20 Africans in 1619 in Jamestown, is an iconic sound bite, and a point of departure from the black American narrative of victimisation.

Johnson, however, did not claim that racism was over. Instead he pointed out that because of the economic and social advancements in the post-Civil Rights era, black America deserves if not demands a new individualised and not a group narrative about itself. This, Johnson asserts, is the fulfillment of W.E.B. Du Bois' vision of "a world where men know, where men create, where they realise themselves and where they enjoy life. It is that sort of world we want to create for ourselves and for all America." Johnson's vision of the black American narrative is a literary one comprising fully the elements of literary fiction. This is not to say that Johnson wishes to create a fictive reality of black America. To the contrary, Johnson is arguing for a new narrative, but a literary one and not a historical one. To suggest an individualised rather than a group narrative may be possible in a literary narrative, but not a historical narrative. The critical difference between a literary narrative and the historical one is the arrangement of language, but no less critical to what Johnson referred, to in the Miller interview, as "a performance of language...and the process of thought itself." But would the epistemological missions be the same?

In "Criteria of Negro Art" Du Bois asked "What do we want? What is the thing we are after?" This question is important to Johnson in part because he says "our unique destiny as a people...[is] tied inextricably to a profound and lifelong meditation on what it means to be free." Aside from the materi?l and tangible objectives of modern life Du Bois was really asking his audience to acknowledge the shortcomings and submission to material possessions and to question whether political legal and economic equality is enough. Johnson seems to suggest that what Du Bois is really asking is to see beyond ideological constraints of their circumstances and transcend the limitations of racialised identity and definition. Could this be the epistemological mission that the literary or historical black American narratives share?

The racialised identity of black Americans was shaped by a racial ideology, a DNA component of the European hegemonic narrative, which claims, in part through negative stereotypes, that black people are inferior and therefore unqualified for any consideration of equality. It is very much an accusation that black people have been proving erroneous for hundreds of years, but won't go away easily in the court of public opinion. Black people had to be race conscious so as not to give the impression that the stereotypes were true. Being a credit to the race was a credo of many generations of blacks and Johnson was no stranger to this. "There was always a weight that you carried as a black person," he said at the 2004 American Literature Association conference in San Francisco. "The moment I stepped outside my door, I knew I represented my people in what I did and what I didn't do." Since the emergence of the Black Arts Movement and the corporate transmogrification and propagation, Hip-Hop culture "being a credit to the race," much like the Buffalo of the Great Plains once were, is nearly extinct. But Obama's campaign message of "Hope," "Change" and "Yes We Can," his nomination and inauguration address echoed the "content of character" portion of Dr. Martin Luther King, Jr.'s I have a Dream speech which embodied, symbolised, represented and personified the "being a credit to the race" credo while tangentially hinting at Du Bois' penetrating questions, "What do we want?" and "What is the thing we are after?"

Despite the 2010 report by "The Council of the Great City Schools"—which identifies an increase in the achievement gap between black students and white students and a larger number of young black men in prison than in college—it would seem that as America's first African American president gave his inauguration address in frigid January weather, black America (and some would say America) had, borrowing from the last line in Johnson's *Middle Passage*, "crossed the Flood, and countless seas of suffering," giving rise to the conclusion that American racism had gone by the way of the Dodo Bird. Yet during the campaign, Obama distinguished himself from his former minister Rev. Jeremiah Wright by denouncing his public and controversial criticisms of America. Obama's nomination depended on it. This made white America more accepting of Obama and illustrated the strength of American racial undercurrents.

"Language," Johnson explained in Miller's interview, "is intimately associated with consciousness, the grammar and the process of though itself." As a historian I use language to identify and describe historical phenomena. The epistemological mission in connection with language and the precise use of language is essential not only to the presentation, but also to a fidelity to the habit of not distorting or misrepresenting facts. This brings us to the language used to describe slavery and it parallels the point Johnson made in his black American narrative article about the scholarship of Holly Jackson who discovered that writer Kelley-Hawkins was not black. Jackson's scholarship had revealed a distortion of the facts on which five decades of scholarship was based. Of slavery in America an even longer period of scholarship is based on a distortion of the facts. Slavery, at least in English and American law was not legal. This is a legal fact, but we are not encouraged to employ an epistemological approach to the subject. Slavery was false imprisonment, and it was based, in part, on the legal fiction that all Africans were slaves before they were transported to the Americas; a legal fiction being something that is assumed to be true, but is not. We are not taught to understand chattel slavery as false imprisonment and that it was based solely on prejudice and not law. Nor are we taught that enslaved persons had no legal obligation to be slaves. False imprisonment never was legal at any time in our jurisprudential history. These legal facts have no chance of liberation in the literary promotion of the black American narrative as victimisation. To discover them requires what Jackson employed while researching Kelley-Hawkins, revisionism and textual analysis, a skill that I am particularly indebted to Lorenzo Valla for.

Understanding slavery as false imprisonment doesn't change the phenomena of slavery, but the language, if we care, is critical for understanding that phenomena. The black American narrative is not one of victimisation. Obama's campaign, nomination and inauguration are a continuation of that narrative. The black American narrative whether literary or historical, can have an overarching epistemological mission which emphasizes triumph over adversity. We can conveniently start with what Johnson calls black America's "quest for freedom" that "runs threadlike from the colonial era through the post-Civil Rights era" and to Obama's presidency. To borrow a few words from Obama's inauguration speech the black American narrative underscores the fact that as black people we "pick ourselves up, dust ourselves off and begin again the remaking of America."

27

Breathing Room

—Julia A. Galbus

In 2003, I taught a short story by Charles Johnson called "China" in an upper-level course on contemporary fiction. I knew the plot and the characters would be foreign to my students: a middle-aged couple find themselves out of shape but comfortable enough, until the husband sees a movie about martial arts, and decides, slowly, to take up meditation and sparring. He buys magazines, takes lessons, acquires new friends. His wife becomes nervous, first, for his ailing heart, and then, for their relationship, which had been familiar and safe. What if he didn't love her any more? Was his new pursuit a sign of a larger problem? The predictable plot would have been a break-up of the marriage, or a failure to reach an ambitious goal, or an argument over the martial arts as a form of fighting for no real purpose. But what I found surprising in Johnson's story was that the husband did not leave. He didn't fall out of love with his wife, didn't threaten her to get back in shape herself, didn't disappear. He invited her, repeatedly, to watch a match, and when she finally found the courage to attend (courage because she was afraid of what she might see, what might happen to him, how he had changed), she found herself proud of him, proud that he did what he needed to do, and relieved. At the end, she was able to see that it was never about her and never about leaving her.

It was the first story I'd read that demonstrated how one person could change drastically and voluntarily over the course of a long relationship without having to break up, even if the other person appeared to stay the same. Love didn't demand sameness; it could make room for uncomfortable growth. I needed to show that possibility to my students, many of whom were struggling with their first serious relationships. Meditation and martial arts were a means to change, but it was as much the openness, diligence and patience that I wanted to display. The pace of the story seemed to mark, accurately, the time over which such a transformation might reasonably take place. Rather than being instant, it was plodding, methodical. His practice took work. And the quieter revelation was the wife's transformation. In allowing her husband to pursue his goal, in permitting herself to face her own fear of what she might discover, she makes room for her own growth: her realisation that she is proud of what her husband accomplished.

Most people fear change because it makes us uncomfortable. In the early stages of a romantic relationship, we understand, intellectually, that both of us will age, but there is often a tendency to think that we won't change fundamentally. I sometimes tease my students about this hidden belief. Why is it, I ask, that we insist that we have grown up a bit since we were 17, but when we meet our partners, we harbor that wish that the other person will not change. We assume not only that someone else's change is negative, but also that we are capable of preventing it.

In 2003, Johnson published "A Boot Camp for Creative Writing" in *The Chronicle of Higher Education.* There he explained his method of teaching creative writing with rigor. He tackled the assumption that creative writing courses often lacked intellectual substance. Then he listed how, systematically, he had infused his own courses with demanding imaginative exercises that taught students how to work with a variety of forms, and how to develop careful, thorough critical skills. Johnson reminded his readers how seriously one could handle a writing class, revealing the details of his goals and his assignments. When describing the writing process, the form becomes a conduit for experimentation, a literal and literary container for writing, but also a shape to be assumed and then discarded. When teaching his students, he said, "I also urge them to experiment with the wealth of literary forms that are our global inheritance as writers" ("Boot Camp"). He lists examples of narrative strategies, voices and linguistic patterns that he requires his students to attempt. I had moved from Johnson's fictional world, to his teaching mind, and found myself admiring both.

To me, the most provocative facet of Johnson's career is his spiritual depth. His Buddhist practice informs everything from his intellectual understanding to his work ethic. His idea of "form" is Eastern. The small word carries an enormous metaphysical and literary legacy that pivots depending on the context. Form is metaphysical. With that usage, we dive into a more complex situation. The bulk of Western metaphysics is largely derived from categories created by Plato and Aristotle to discern the connection between matter and form. Within an Aristotelean framework, we abstract the form of a thing from examples, like scientists trying to decipher traits similar objects have in common that are essential to their type. With a Platonic perspective, we examine how specific examples imitate an unreachable ideal. In either perspective, the "form" in question is static and finished. Johnson finds them both limiting and inaccurate, although they dominate the Western mindset so consistently that they are nearly invisible: In the U.S., we like to think that what is most real does not change.

Johnson prefers phenomenology and the Buddhist sense of flux: "Even though we can say that each person has a 'separate' history, the dharma teaches—as does quantum mechanics—that we are really a process, not a product: We are each an 'individuality' ever arising and passing away... with no 'essence' or 'substance' discernible in the concatenation of causes and conditions that create our being instant by instant" ("Dharma"). The sense of constant movement and impermanence that is fundamental to Buddhism "offers an entirely different way of interpreting reality." A form might describe a pattern of behavior, but it doesn't dictate reality. Johnson continues,

> In the West, desire is something that happens to us which we simply react to. But in Buddhism, there is a critique of desire and how it happens in consciousness, and that

> analysis is wonderful. Everything that we are, it is said in the Dhammanpad, is the result of what we have thought. From thought comes desire. From desire comes will. From will comes our deeds. And from deeds come our destiny. There's a tremendous sophistication and interconnectedness in the interpretation of all life (Miller).

The chain of causation constructs an individual response to situations, giving us choice. And where a traditional Ecclesiastical sense divides time into compartments so that there is room for everything we must do, this alternative metaphysics incorporates all action into the spiritual practice.

Johnson's teaching, his martial arts, and writing, his speaking, and even his communication with students and scholars and writers are all a continuous unfolding of his spiritual practice. He explains, "Buddhist meditation is... a paying of extraordinarily close attention to every nuance of our experience ("Dharma"). In a life fundamentally informed by the Buddhadharma, the antidote to routine is "vigilant mindfulness." A person tries to stay open to what is happening in all its complexity, no matter what is going on. Mindfulness when teaching or writing, interpreting or sparring, is the means to staying engaged. We learn to be completely present without the distraction of expectations or preconceptions.

Form can be frozen and inert, something seemingly permanent to be avoided. In an interview with Nicholas O'Conell, Johnson says that the great fight in life is to keep "a *form* of idea or situation from enslaving you. It's to keep your mind open and your eyes open and your life open, *to find new ways of not being limited...*" (21, emphasis mine). That means writing stories in new forms. However, it also includes spending time in the formlessness of *vipassana*. We realise, when we sit, that forms can capture us under the guise of habits and preferences, as well as in cultural norms.

When I consider the work of Charles Johnson, both in terms of the breadth of media and genre, but also in the way he maintains a life informed by a consistent philosophical and spiritual practice, I encounter a unique model of maintaining agility. He seeks flexibility literally, intellectually, philosophically and personally.

Within a Buddhist framework, there's a way in which Charles Johnson doesn't exist, at least not as a stable, unchanging entity. Every person is in flux, something antithetical to Western identity, which implies *identical.* That is, we think someone is who he is because of the ways he stays the same over time. Since Johnson has changed over the course of his life, both intentionally and in ways he could not have anticipated, and since he indefatigably seeks to elude forms which have become static, what his life yields both as an example, but also in its particularity, is breathing room. He invites us to catch our breath and watch it. He reminds us to take time to consider what is worth doing, to set priorities, but also to explore the present moment. He balances tremendous, mindful productivity with practice. Johnson gives us breathing room by not being himself, but by simply being.

Works Cited

Johnson, Charles. "A Boot Camp for Creative Writing." *Chronicle of Higher Education* 50.10 (2003): B7.

_______ "China." In *The Sorcerer's Apprentice.* NY: Atheneum, 1986. 61-96.

_______. "The Dharma of Social Transformation." *Tricycle*, 16.2 Winter 2006.

Miller, E. Ethelbert. "Interview with Charles Johnson." *Dialogue*, April 30, 1999.

O'Connell, Nicholas. "An Interview with Charles Johnson," reprinted in *Passing the Three Gates: Interviews with Charles Johnson*, edited by Jim McWilliams. Seattle: University of Washington Press, 2004. 16-33.

28

Remembering Charles Johnson

— **Sunita Rani Ghosh**

When I muse over my eight-month long stay in America during 2003-04, I recall with pleasure the things that impressed me about the world's most powerful democracy: The respect for the rule of law, the esteem shown in general for the quality of human life, the sprawling immensity of modern infrastructure, magnificent and huge university campuses, rich and high-tech libraries, respect for privacy, dignity of labor, high sense of responsibility of all citizens, commitment to one's work and so on and so forth. Yet, if I were to remember an event or association that left deep imprints on my consciousness, I will unhesitatingly mention our meeting with Charles Johnson, fondly known as "Chuck" to his dear friends.

Since the day we arrived in Seattle till the day we took our return flight to India, he was our guardian angel who took every pains to ensure we were comfortable in every aspect of our stay in the U.S. Unmindful of his star-status, he would readily drive us over to every place we could think of in Seattle–be it the book stores, the Pike market, the stores in downtown, the University of Washington campuses and the like. He described the Pike market as a cool vibrant farmer's market, a place where we found a variety of vegetables, seafood, fruits, flowers and many other things. We visited this unique market several times in his august company. He would constantly look for nooks and corners where we could get to see things that we might want to buy to take back home.

Back home we were often warned that America is an insular society where mortal millions "live alone." One really has to meet a person like Chuck to see how stereotyped such generalisation can be. He seemed to be doing everything with so much of care and concern that one gets to see rarely even in a strong familial relationship. Once we expressed our wish to attend one of his classes where he taught creative writing. I recall his class where, unlike traditional classes in India, students were allowed to have snacks with tea, coffee and soft drinks but they were mature enough not to go beyond limits. We enjoyed wonderful interaction in his creative writing class. Students were curious to know his reactions on their respective assignments. His one-time student David Guterson fondly told us how as a teacher Chuck tries hard to bring out excellence in his students. We often proudly cite the great tradition of *gurukul* in India. Being in Chuck's class made us realise that good teachers are cherished with respect and affection everywhere in this wide world.

What specially endeared us to Chuck was his magical power of touching human feelings. He always enjoyed making others feel important. Extremely familiar with Indian culture, he has great love for Sanskrit literature. We enjoyed a lavish Indian dinner at his house. The food was arranged by Chuck from an Indian restaurant that claims to be the most authentic Indian restaurant at Seattle. We spent hours at his place. We felt literally at home in an American house. Both of us were surprised to see that he had decorated his personal gym with colorful charts filled with famous Sanskrit quotes written in devnagri script. He brought a scanned copy of my article in Hindi just to confirm his familiarity with devanagri.

Once we accompanied Chuck to Bainbridge Island where David Guterson had invited him to deliver a talk. There we realised his wonderful skill in the art of oratory. It was a rare experience to listen to Chuck and to see how a receptive audience had been engrossed in exchanging ideas or asking questions. It was a delight to see him overwhelming everyone present with his striking authenticity. He has the innate gift of feeling the pulse of the audience and transforming them with his thoughts and ideas.

It was largely on account of Chuck's graciousness that we got a chance to meet August Wilson, the legendary African American playwright. We were among the very few lucky people who had the opportunity to meet him in person. August Wilson had invited us all to dinner where we chatted on till midnight though I was more preoccupied as a photographer capturing those memorable moments.

Talking to Chuck always made us aware of not merely sharing views and ideas but sharing cultures. With remarkable ease and humility he transcends all kinds of man-made barriers of class, color, caste, race and nationalities to embrace the world we inhabit.

May his tribe increase!

29

He Giveth of Himself Endlessly

— John Whalen-Bridge

> ...the sage accumulates nothing but the more he does for others the greater his Existence, the more he gives to others the greater his abundance.
>
> — Lao-tzu's Taoteching, trans.
> *Red Pine (Bill Porter)*

I have a friend, an eminent Victorianist, who insists she never again, ever, write about a living writer. Some permissions battle held up a book over a year. For her, writers not only have to be dead, they have to be out-of-copyright dead. I have to say that working with living writers has been quite a joy, but then I'm spoiled. I have written about Charles Johnson, who has been incredibly generous.

My correspondence with Charles Johnson, who goes by Chuck, began in the late 1990s. I wrote to him about the reference to "Guido the Angelic" on the first page of *Dreamer*, saying I'd looked and looked but couldn't work out who that was. No, it should have been Guigo II (1114-1180), the Carthusian mystic, that Martin Luther King was thinking of in that passage. Some writers might be irked if your first message to them was to notice a typo on the first page of his most recent book, but not Chuck. He praised me for catching this, and we became good friends.

He is, as many know, a lightning-quick email respondent, and one wonders when he sleeps. I can't think of how many questions about his work he has answered, how many times he has put me in touch with his other friends who share interests, or how many times he has sent drafts of work in progress. Most writers keep their cards close to the chest about work in progress, but not Chuck. He relishes feedback, and he acknowledges his interlocutors in his writing to an unprecedented degree.

In 2000 Chuck put me in touch with some of his graduate school mates, Robert Bunch, Michael Boylan, and Richard Hart. The previous year they had put together a panel on Johnson's *Dreamer* for the International Association of Philosophy and Literature conference, and they were going to do it again in 2000. This time the conference was going to convene in Atlanta, an ideal place to get together and think about Martin Luther King, Jr. We talked about so many things. Summer jobs during college? Chuck's father, in the ultimate "keep it real" move, made him work as a garbage man. Several of us were martial arts practitioners. Did Chuck's school do much sparring? "We fought all f...king night!" Philosophy, literature, contemporary American culture—anyone who has had a dinner with Chuck knows how thrilling it is.

Some of us Johnson scholars decided to form the "Charles Johnson Society" at the ALA back around 2003. I suppose it's not surprising that Chuck supported this idea, but the way in which he has supported the society is amazing. I was not able to attend the launch of the society at the East Coast ALA in 2003 because SARS closed down the Singapore airport, but for the 2004 meeting Chuck and Maxine Hong Kingston both read at the ALA for free. The ALA does not have the budget to pay for writers of their caliber, and when I explained this to them, they both came to the conference. I suppose they are used to getting thousands of dollars for talks and readings, but so supportive are these two that they came just to help. Members of the Charles Johnson Society interviewed the two of them together in my hotel room, and a good time was had by all. In a reunion of sorts both came, again gratis, in 2010. When Gary Storhoff and I told him about our "Buddhism and American

Culture" series, he was again wonderfully generous and wrote us a brilliant afterword.

He's always writing an introduction or a preface or a talk, and I've heard him described as America's hardest working writer. He's incredibly generous, encouraging, and friendly.

30

Narrative of Color in Black and White: Conversation with Charles Johnson

— Nibir K. Ghosh

This interview was conducted in Seattle during meetings with Johnson in the academic year 2003-2004. He was extremely generous with his time and shared his thoughts freely.

Ghosh: In a long journey that has seen you excel in diverse roles: cartoonist, novelist, teacher, scholar, orator, philosopher—with awards and accolades standing out as significant landmarks—how does it really feel to end up being so famous?

Johnson: I don't really think about being famous. I don't think about it at all. I still have an image of myself as a younger writer. I am always surprised, humbled, and shocked when I learn that anyone has read something I've written. An author really never knows who is reading him (or her), or if they're reading one's work at all. If you are an actor on stage, you see the audience, you hear their applause but as a writer you don't. You may get the sales figures but you don't sometimes know who is reading your books until they tell you. And I've never been the kind of artist who is comfortable chasing publicity—I just try to let my creations speak for themselves.

Ghosh: The range and versatility of your creative output is overwhelming. Do you approach your writing as a kind of mission?

Johnson: Every true artist's goal is, I believe, to produce so many works in his (or her) lifetime, that one's creations ultimately become inescapable in the culture (or at least for serious readers). For artists of color, who are so often marginalised by society, this approach is especially important insofar as the ability to produce in numerous forms means they become technicians of form and language, able to handle any assignment, and therefore are better able to support their families and loved ones.

Ghosh: You mention that initially you had no intention of becoming a novelist? What drew you to the world of fiction?

Johnson: I wrote stories for fun from High School but I didn't consider myself to be a writer. I was a cartoonist and journalist. Then one day, I think 1970 it was, a novel idea occurred to me and just kept occurring to me when I was alone. To give that idea concrete shape and form I wrote six books in two years. I call those books my apprentice novels.

Ghosh: Did these six 'apprentice' novels have anything in common?

Johnson: No. The first one was about Martial Arts, based very much on the school I went in Chicago. The second one was an early version of *Middle Passage* but told from the white ship captain's point of view. It wasn't very good. The third one was kind of autobiographical about a young black man. The fourth, fifth, and sixth were part of a trilogy. I wanted to write a thousand pages trilogy centered around a musician's life and I got about 980 or something.

Ghosh: Were these novels published?

Johnson: No. F*aith and the Good Thing* is my first published novel. I hadn't arrived really at my vision and voice until I wrote *Faith*. Even there it wasn't completely where I wanted it to be. That moment came with *Oxherding Tale.*

Ghosh: What are the major influences that may have contributed to shaping your sensibility as a writer?

Johnson: John Gardner was a wonderful teacher and my mentor. He literally brought me into the book world because I was not a student of English or literature. I was in philosophy. John was a major influence in that respect. Gardner was an incredibly hard-working man himself. He was remarkably productive and prolific. My father gave me a very strong work ethic by and through his example and, of course, my great uncle Will, whom I glorify in "An American Milk Bottle," inspired me a great deal by giving me a clear sense of what it meant to be a grown man in the world with a grown man's responsibility and a grown man's capacity for work. My mother encouraged my passion for reading. She was in three book clubs. Our house was full of books. There was always something interesting to read.

Ghosh: To which African American writers would you give the credit of charting the path of self-reliance in black literature and art?

Johnson: I can easily recall the names of Jean Toomer, Richard Wright, and Ralph Ellison as very distinctive, uniquely black American writers who came out of the soil of American experience to shape the future course of a truly autonomous African American fiction. In the realm of poetry the name of Langston Hughes comes to me uppermost.

Ghosh: In this context, how would you visualise the role of the Harlem Renaissance?

Johnson: The Harlem Renaissance provided a decisive break with the nineteenth century and its images of African American tribes. For the very first time we have a Northern urban black experience as opposed to that of the Southern black. We have the concept of the "New Negro" as spoken up by Alain Locke. With the publication in 1923 of Jean Toomer's *Cane*, the Harlem Renaissance reached new heights of Negro eloquence. I must argue, as some people do, that the explosions of creativity of the 1960s in America was really a continuation of the Harlem Renaissance. Right now, I think not only Americans in general but also black Americans in particular are in a period of transition. This is indeed a significant moment of cultural transition in the early part of the twenty-first century.

Ghosh: Reading Morrison and Walker after Wright, Ellison and Baldwin appears to be sort of an anticlimax. Does the power of expressing the racial viewpoint (as is evident from the works of this male triangle of influence) seem to be on the wane in the hands of Walker and Morrison ?

Johnson: I suspect that if Morrison and Walker are read in light of the protest tradition, a problem arises because they are writing in the post-Civil Rights period, after the Jim Crow world of Wright, Ellison and Baldwin legally ended in America.

Ghosh: Is it true that your novel *Faith And The Good Thing* (1974), published the same year as Baldwin's *If Beale Street Could Talk,* got better reviews, a fact that had upset Baldwin?

Johnson: Baldwin did mention it to a friend of mine that he didn't like my novel because it wasn't "political." That hurt since I admired Baldwin, but I saw clearly our aesthetic and intellectual approaches were miles and miles apart.

Ghosh: Have you never felt tempted by the idea of using "words as weapons" in the manner of Richard Wright? Would you refer to *Native Son* as "narrow complaint"?

Johnson: Wright's *Native Son* is a segregation-era novel and, therefore, is a powerful indictment of America's version of apartheid, as is Sinclair Lewis's *Kingsblood Royal.* That period of Jim Crow segregation, as you know, ended in the 1960s. So, no, I don't feel the need (at least at the moment) to use "words as weapons." As a phenomenologist, I use words to achieve *aletheia,* or the disclosure of phenomena. As a Buddhist, I use them to heal, not tear things apart. *Native Son* is a fine example of the American novel in the naturalistic tradition, like Dreiser's *An American Tragedy*, but as a fiction it has a few intellectual and artistic flaws. The criminal and cowardly thug Bigger Thomas cannot be said to "represent" black America—for example, Wright refers in the novel to another black man who worked for the Dalton family and kept improving his life, unlike Bigger who accidentally murders Mary Dalton. Also, in Book Two, "Flight," members of the black community are infuriated that Bigger's immature, foolish actions have brought a police search down upon their neighborhoods. Once again, this is a segregation-era novel and must be understood in terms of the historical moment that produced it.

Ghosh: How would you react to a critical statement like "Ellison saw Bigger as the product of the so-called scientific perceptions of the sociologist; Baldwin saw Bigger as the product of white liberal thought. For both, Bigger Thomas was the white man's attempt to understand the African American from a vantage point outside of him—the result is a superficial and dehumanised picture, an abstraction"?

Johnson: When Ellison said in his 1953 acceptance speech for the National Book Award that writers need to "leave sociology to the scientists," he was making a reference to the *way* Bigger Thomas (and other characters in black fiction or fiction about blacks) were conceived prior to 1952 (and we can say have been conceived since then). Those characters (and Bigger) are constructed less from life, with all its complexity and ambiguity, than from someone's *idea* of what a black person is or should be, and usually that person is not black, i.e., they are constructing these ideas from outside the richness of the black experience, based on their racial and sociological presuppositions and prejudices. Baldwin is making the same complaint, one that I've raised in numerous books and essays ("Philosophy and Black Fiction," "Whole Sight," my introduction for Stowe's *Uncle Tom's Cabin*, and in *Being and Race*, etc.).

And the problem of black characterisations (the racial Other) that Ellison and Baldwin are pointing to *remains* a problem today—in American fiction and film. The black characters we get in art are, simply, detotalised abstractions most of the time. Ellison's achievement in *Invisible Man* was the creation of a protagonist rich in his humanity, in the folklore, music, and literary culture of African Americans, as well as the cultures of the West, which is something no white writer can do from "the outside" when creating a black protagonist, and which Wright himself did not achieve. As Ellison said in a letter to Albert Murray, Wright was unable to conceive a fictional character as complex as *himself* (for Richard Wright was, of course, an extremely complex man, though he seldom portrayed his own creations that way—his Cross Damon in *The Outsider* is an advance in this respect over Bigger Thomas).

Ghosh: Since the whole discourse around African American writing is steeped in power issues, isn't it almost imperative for an African American writer of fiction to blend art with politics in order to make it more purposeful?

Johnson: It is not that I am unmindful of the obstacles, traps and racial minefields faced by black men in a society that has long demonised them as violent, criminal, stupid, bestial, lazy and irresponsible. But please bear in mind that when you say politics will make art more "purposeful," what you're doing is *limiting* the possibilities of art to a simple utilitarian function, making it no more than a tool. That's the philistine's understanding of art. Creative expression never needs to justify itself to philistines, who from time out of mind have never seen art as "serious." To put this bluntly, art and its processes have always been incomprehensible to philistines and ideologues on the right and left.

Ghosh: Do you see the basic concerns of the African American writers in terms of Michael Foucault's idea of protest being a powerful undercurrent of any literature or art produced by the "wretched of the earth"?

Johnson: as a storyteller for the last 38 years, I have to say that, no, I don't believe Foucault and the privileging of power relations is the best way to thematise black American literature either creatively or critically. (I dare not speak of Dalit literature since I know so little about it.) The problem with first interpreting black American life in terms of victimisation and oppression, then applying that explanatory model to either the analysis of texts or to young writers as a recommendation for how and what they should create, is that this approach limits, narrows and places into a kind of critical Procrustean bed all the vast experiences that black Americans have and represent. Indeed, such a reduction denies the richness of black humanity, which is so capacious that it outstrips our perception—and certainly outstrips all our political and sociological explanatory models *for* black lives in which we find a surplus of meaning (as Merleau-Ponty might put it). As a writer and critic, I've fought all my life against conceptualisations that deny or are blind to that richness. Yes, indeed, we can thematise the "political" in any phenomenon, but that is but one order of meaning, one I do not privilege above the spiritual, the artistic, or the philosophical, despite the fact that I dutifully studied my Marx and did a master's thesis on the influence of that thinker's materialism and Freud on the psychology of Wilhelm Reich in the 1930s.

To ask that an artist have "the right politics" worries me more than a little since, in America, I've seen many artists with the right political views, but who were artistically shoddy and downright mediocre as thinkers. Example: the great writer Sinclair Lewis is truly right on race matters in *Kingsblood Royal* (1947), but that novel, dashed off in a few months, is more political manifesto than art, more an enraged essay (weakly dramatised) than a powerful performance we can admire for its artistry. We can say the same about Richard Wright's *The Outsider*, and all James Baldwin's novels except for his first one, *Go Tell It On The Mountain*, which is worth talking about (he wrote at least 10 outstanding essays that will endure, but even he admitted that as a novelist he failed). It is important, I believe, that we demand the highest artistic and intellectual standards from our creators—the right politics is no substitute for that, though we hope, of course, that our finest craftsmen *do* place themselves on the right side of politics and history, i.e., the side of compassion and justice for all.

Ghosh: You strongly feel that since the 1970s, the writers of color—who for centuries were marginalised or simply ignored—have irreversibly transformed the social world as it is portrayed in American fiction. What "transformation" of the social world do you have in mind?

Johnson: Writers of color have brought a realism and complexity in their depictions of the racial *Other* to American literature, and by doing so buried many vicious stereotypes created by whites during the last 200 years, that is, made those images unacceptable and expanded our awareness of diversity and meaning *within,* say, the African American community.

Ghosh: Do the tragic events of 9/11 call for the need for any reorientation on the part of an average African American citizen?

Johnson: I think that now, at the dawn of twenty-first century, and especially after 9/11, we are aware that living in a parochial, limited cultural fishbowl is a liability and places on us limits that we can no longer afford.

Ghosh: Why?

Johnson: Because the cultural and racial *Other* is our mirror, and a source of knowledge crucial for our understanding. Today, none of us can afford to be locked culturally in ourselves. Like all minorities, or refugees, we must all begin to live on the "edge" where one can see numerous perspectives at once; we must develop a cultural double consciousness or a cultural poly-consciousness that recognises the racial *Other* as ourselves. Indeed, America in the year 2004 is what writer Jorge Luis Borges would call an *aleph*, which he defines as a point where all points converge, all angles and viewpoints can be viewed simultaneously, yet each remains distinct.

Ghosh: You do state that "if black America has a defining essence (eidos) or meaning that runs threadlike from the colonial era through the post-Civil Rights period, it must be the quest for freedom"[*Turning the Wheel: Essays on Buddhism and Writing* 2003]. Does this quest manifest itself in your writings?

Johnson: Yes, this particular, eidetic sense of our collective meaning, arising out of historical conditions, and the way the Founding Fathers' ideal of freedom was inscribed with a special meaning in the souls of black folk, has shaped almost every story, essay, novel, drawing, teleplay, and critical article I've composed for the last three and a half decades....My sense of black life in a predominantly white, very Eurocentric society was that our unique destiny as a people, our duty to our predecessors who sacrificed so much and for so long, and our dreams of a life of dignity and happiness for our children were tied inextricably to a profound and life-long meditation on what it means to be free. Truly free.

Ghosh: According to you, the greatest challenge before the African American writer is to create and sustain a "black culture that nurtures a passion for knowledge for its own sake" [*Turning the Wheel: Essays on Buddhism and Writing* 2003]. Would you consider the emergence of the Hip Hop generation to be an integral part of this culture?

Johnson: I have not reached any conclusions yet about the significance of Hip Hop.

Ghosh: What, then, would you consider to be your own contribution to the development and growth of the African American fiction?

Johnson: Am I a twentieth-century writer or a twenty-first century writer?

Ghosh: Perhaps a writer who excels in both.

Johnson: I would like to think about my own work as whether it was exploratory—both aesthetically and in terms of ideas and cultural experience. I would like to think what my work does is open up the novel to the philosophical and also to multicultural perspectives that were perhaps not hitherto there in African American literature in so vivid a manner before *Oxherding Tale, Middle Passage, Turning the Wheel* or something like that.

Ghosh: How would you outline what one may call your theory of art or *Ars Poetica?*

Johnson: As a Ph.D. in philosophy (and as a Buddhist), it is natural, I think, that my intellectual, artistic, and spiritual interests focus on that place where fiction and philosophy—both Western and Eastern—meet. But I discovered that such a project demanded more than novels. In order for this body of work to be complete it also required creating short fiction in many forms: works of aesthetics; articles and essays ranging over American history, culture, and literature; screen-and-teleplays; vigorous book reviewing of the work of my contemporaries; teaching and, yes, even cartoons that addressed all the above subjects.

Therefore, I see my body of work as being like a mansion with many rooms. Inside this imaginative "house" are rooms you can wander through or dwell in for awhile. One has novels. Another has short fiction. A third has more than 250 interviews from radio, television, newspapers, and scholarly journals. In the fourth you'll find screenplays. A fifth has philosophical essays such as "Reading the Eightfold Path." A sub-room of that has essays on many subjects—on Indonesia, how to draw political cartoons, the history of black cartoonists, an overview of black literature since the Harlem Renaissance, film critiques, critical appreciations of writers such as Ralph Waldo Emerson, Jean Toomer, Harriet Beecher Stowe, and Ralph Ellison. Yet another room is devoted to book reviews from every major newspaper in America (and a few in England), which I hope serve as position papers on the nature of literary art. Other rooms have editorial and panel cartoons, comic strips, texts for studio photo books, and many public addresses and lectures.

On and on through this house, from the basement to the attic, you'll find prose and visual art in numerous aesthetic forms (the slave narrative, the sea adventure story, the folktale, and political novel). You find television dramas on Booker T. Washington's youth, the black cowboy Charlie Smith, and the Tuskegee Airmen in one room. There is fiction on the martial arts, affirmative action, "exchange value," Dr. Martin Luther King's refrigerator, and a future in which the government taxes people's dreams as well as traditional fables and parables in a sub-room of the bigger room devoted to short stories. This is my conception of what total body of work should be, one that is evolved over a lifetime, is generous in form and content, and offers a variety of different aesthetic experiences.

Ghosh: In your "Afterword" to *Being and Race*, you have stated: "I see taking form on the horizon of contemporary practice, a fiction of increasing artistic generosity, one that enables us as a people—as a culture—to move from narrow complaint to broad celebration." Could you elaborate the term "broad celebration"?

Johnson: I haven't thought about the phrase in quite some time now. But I still stand by it. A literary work of art, in my view, is a gift to the reader—the finest gift an author can compose. I believe it should be generous, creating an entire multi-dimensional fictional "world" for the reader to experience, one so rich that that world can be revisited over and over, and with each re-reading across decades the reader discovers something new, i.e., grows with the text.

In addition to the above, a fine work of art (for me) is a celebration of so many things—the endless possibilities of language, of thought, of spirited storytelling, of human behavior and its possibilities, and the galaxy of fictional forms we inherit from our predecessors from all over the world. In *Being and Race* I argued against the limitations imposed on black literary art by (1) those who feel it should only be "protest fiction," and (2) those people in the Black Arts Movement who had a very narrow notion of what it means to be "black" and naively rejected anything cultural they defined as "non-black." As I saw it then (and now), their artistic products and theorising about black art worked in the opposite direction of generosity and expansiveness, creating fictional worlds one-dimensional, unimaginative and impoverished—spiritually, artistically, philosophically, and even in terms of fidelity to the complexity of the historical record.

Ghosh: Could you cite some examples of artistic works which embody the idea of "broad celebration"?

Johnson: Ralph Ellison's *Invisible Man* is a pretty good example of "broad celebration." I hope my novels and stories are, too.

Ghosh: Isn't your notion of the philosophical novel antithetical to the idea of protest fiction? As an enlightened member of the African American community, with four centuries of slavery embedded in your consciousness, do you visualise the danger of not placing yourself in the unenviable position of "unacknowledged legislators" to espouse racial issues which do cry for attention ?

Johnson: No. First of all, I'm not a politician or an "unacknowledged legislator"—I am, simply and humbly, an artist, philosopher, and educator. Secondly, as a scholar I know quite a bit about 400 years of slavery, but that's not all I know, nor do I live in the past, which is unrecoverable, as every Buddhist will tell you. The only things I feel the need to protest are human ignorance and stupidity (of which racism is a part), delusion and selfishness. In that sense, I don't think my aesthetic position is antithetical to the so-called "protest novel."

Ghosh: You mention in the "Preface" to *Turning the Wheel* that you consider the Buddhist Dharma as the most revolutionary and civilised of possible human choices, as the logical extension of King's dream of the "beloved community," and Du Bois' "vision of what the world could be if it was really a beautiful world." How were you initially drawn to the philosophy of Buddhism? What attracted you most about this "way of life" philosophy?

Johnson: As I have stated in the *Preface* you have alluded to, Buddhism, for me, has always been a refuge, as it was intended to be: a place to continually refresh my spirit, stay centered and at peace, which enabled me to work joyfully and without attachment even in the midst of turmoil swirling round me on all sides, through "good" times and "bad." So I am thankful for the perennial wisdom in its two-millennium-old sutras; the phenomenological insights of Shakyamuni himself into the nature of suffering, craving and dualism; the astonishing beauty of Sanskrit, which I've been privileged to study now for four years; and the methods of different forms of meditational practice, the benefits of which fill whole libraries.

Ghosh: It appears that many African writers and intellectuals have also been attracted, especially in recent times, by the Buddhadharma. Is it a reaction of sorts against their disillusionment with Judea-Christian beliefs?

Johnson: That's one of the reasons. Christianity is a metaphysically dualistic religion that partitions the world of experience into "good" and "evil," heaven and hell, God and the Devil, and at its center it has the concept of original sin, which is nowhere to be found in the Buddhadharma, a radically nondualistic approach to life.

Ghosh: Does Buddhism have any mass appeal in America where the African American populace is concerned? Do ordinary African-American citizens with a relatively poor economic base take to this philosophy with the same kind of enthusiasm that is seen in the case of the elites?

Johnson: The answers, I think, are in my essay, "A Sangha By Another Name," in *Turning the Wheel.* One addresses the popularity in America of Soka Gakkai (Nichiren Buddhism) among blacks and Hispanics, who make up 30 per cent of its 150,000 membership, specifically in the cities. My sister-in-law, who grew up poor in a Chicago housing project, practices Soka Gakkai (and teaches yoga), and in the essay I quote her and one of her friends on why they chose this practice. Also, during my recent book tour I encountered many black Americans (primarily women) in Maryland, Seattle, Santa Cruz, Pasadena and other places who are Dharma followers and not among an elite. I think people often forget that it's only about 25 per cent to 30 per cent of black Americans who can be classified as poor or financially trapped in the inner city.

Ghosh: By the way, has the charm of Buddhism anything to do with peoples' disappointment with established orthodox religion which is often a tool for exploitation in the hands of those who wield both power and influence.

Johnson: Here in America, I rather *do* suspect that many Buddhist converts left their original, family religions because those faiths have become so intertwined with right-wing politics...or, for that matter, left-wing politics. Such converts would probably say they find, in their family's churches or temples, no spiritual nourishment whatsoever, only speeches delivered from the pulpit on transitory, political questions. For the approximately two million Buddhists in America, the Eightfold Path is a map for the Way. But, like any map, it merely sketches the terrain the *bodhisattavas* have traversed for two and a half millennia, leaving open for each follower of the Dharma an adventure of discovery and service: a genuinely creative journey through the mystery of being, which with each step leads to ineffable joy.

Ghosh: How does this adventure of discovery and service stimulate your creative writing, especially fiction?

Johnson: I cannot help but marvel sometimes at the striking analogues between meditation and moments of intense creative inspiration, and how both overlap in my life and literary offerings.

Ghosh: Well, how do you reconcile your intense commitment, as you say, to the cause of your community with the philosophy of Buddhism which points towards spiritual liberation?

Johnson: I have long viewed the sphere of politics—and especially racial politics—to be the perfect illustration of *samsara*, or what the two-thousand-year-old sutra *The Perfection of Wisdom calls Kamadhatu*: "the realism of desirc," characterised by dualism and the hunger for power. For all my aversion to the polarising dimensions of politics, I cannot forget Benjamin Franklin's haunting statement that "democracy is an invitation to struggle," which in the context of Dharma means struggle in the politicised realm of *samsara*. A Buddhist, I believe, struggles to alleviate the suffering of all sentient beings and turn the Wheel of Dharma. Buddhism and politics need not be antithetical, as demonstrated by legendary King Ashoka, a lay follower of Buddhism who ruled the Mauryan kingdom in North India from 272-236 B.C., and in his edicts embraced generosity, compassion, refraining from killing, love of truth, inner insight, and harmonious relations with neighboring states.

Ghosh: Can one categorise all your novels—*Oxherding Tale, Middle Passage, and Dreamer*—as philosophical novels? Does the compelling presence of philosophy interfere with the free flow of creative imagination which the creation of a novel demands?

Johnson: We shouldn't practice what I call creative and intellectual apartheid by placing the "creative imagination" in one box and "philosophy" in another. Doesn't Plato choose a *dramatic* form—the dialogue—as the vehicle for his philosophy? Would you call Jean-Paul Sartre (a true polymath: a philosopher, novelist and playwright), Camus, or Santayana *un*creative? Ideas do not begin in some abstract realm floating high above human experience. Rather, they originate in the historical muck and mud of our daily experience, cloaked in the immediate particulars of this world, and only later do we abstract them for the purpose of study and reflection. What a philosophical novelist does—what I do—is simply return those ideas to the palpable world of experience from which they first sprang. That way, I hope, readers *experience* the ideas viscerally, with flesh put back on their abstract bones.

Ghosh: In all humility you always speak of your idols, mentors and teachers—The Buddha, John Gardner, Ralph

Ellison, Thich Nhat Hanh and others—with enormous esteem and reverence and attribute your success as a writer to such collective influence. (You happily dedicated your acceptance speech for the National Book Award in Fiction to Ralph Ellison.) At the same time, you also feel that it is incumbent upon the creative writer to find, cultivate, and sustain his individual voice and vision. Taken together, would you consider this approach to be in consonance with T.S. Eliot's stance in "Tradition and the Individual Talent"?

Johnson: Yes, it is much like Eliot's position in that essay. As Buddhists are fond of saying, there is no independent origination—all things are dependent on other things. This is true in the world of art and philosophy as well: *pratitya samutpada* means, in the context of literature, that we are nourished by the contributions of our literary predecessors and contemporaries. Yet, as Buddhists also say, each achieves awakening (or one's own literary creations) through his own individual effort.

Ghosh: As an ardent champion of Buddhism involved in the writing of fiction, how would you react to Herman Hesse's *Siddhartha*?

Johnson: I love that book. I first read it as an undergraduate. It was very popular in the 1960s. I can say lots of things about that book: its simplicity, the remarkable achievement that Hesse, a German in the 1920s, made in terms of accuracy by portraying something of the Buddhist spirit. It is simple and so elegant, just like poetry.

Ghosh: Can *Siddhartha* be seen as a novel depicting the essential philosophy of Buddhism?

Johnson: It is true that people criticise the book—the Buddhists do—because they feel that Siddhartha of the novel is too individualistic and that he is too Western in many ways and that's the criticism that one could levy. I think there is a kind of romanticism in Hesse's version of Buddhism, the romanticism of the individual. You cannot simply leap to the transcendent, so we have to have the real world, the world of *samsara*. I would not, somehow, trust the novel in terms of Buddhist teachings. I would say: "go to the sutras."

Nevertheless, I find the book to be a challenging and in many ways an inspiring document.

Ghosh: One does see in most of your fictional work strong undercurrents of humor. As a teenager your ambition was to become a professional cartoonist. Did you think cartoons would be a suitable medium for protest of any kind? Does the form still attract you? Do you consider humor an appropriate tool of protest against oppression?

Johnson: The history of comic art is filled with protest drawings. The first cartoon published in America by Benjamin Franklin depicts a snake with the caption, "Don't Tread on Me" in protest of King George. Thomas Nast, as you know, brought down the corruption of Tammany Hall. Humor is, yes, always an appropriate tool against oppression—and all forms of human silliness.

Ghosh: In *Black Men Speaking* you limit your discussion to the predicament of the African American male. In *Being and Race* you refer rather cursorily to the fiction of Alice Walker and Toni Morrison. Is it indicative of any gender bias?

Johnson: I have no gender biases. Two of the most important people in my life are my wife and daughter. And I feel black women are perfectly capable of speaking for themselves. They don't need me to speak for them.

Ghosh: Who are your favorite contemporary African American writers?

Johnson: Tough question. I like smart writers who have tons of skill, imagination, and formal virtuosity. I like writers who display what Northrop Frye called an "educated imagination." Thus, I admire James Alan McPherson, Octavia Butler, Gerald Early, Albert Murray, Jewell Parker Rhodes. Those are a few. Just a few of many.

Ghosh: You have been professionally associated with the Creative Writing Program at the University of Washington for the last twenty-eight years. How have you felt as a teacher engaged in teaching creative writing? American universities abound in such courses. Do you really believe creative writing can be taught?

Johnson: Obviously, I know that creative writing can be taught—I've been training writers for twenty-seven years. However, what cannot be taught is talent and imagination. Those things the student must have before he even enters the classroom. More than anything else, I want our students to become technicians of literary form and language. And I want them to see that writing well is the same thing as thinking well. A writing workshop, like everything else, must evolve. If it is to truly help apprentice writers, it must deliver *techne*. Yet, in the end, the galaxy of techniques and strategies we teachers provide our students—all that theory and practice—must serve spirited storytelling.

Ghosh: Do you have any regrets of not being trained in such creative writing programs?

Johnson: Absolutely none.

Ghosh: Your *Photobiography of Martin Luther King, Jr.*, and your unforgettable *Dreamer* bear testimony to your intense admiration for this great leader. What attracted you to King's personality and philosophy?

Johnson: Well, what attracted me was the same thing that attracted a generation of Americans in the 1950s and 60s—King's great humanity, his vision of agape, his profound understanding of integration and the interconnectedness of all things, and his remarkable personal sacrifices aimed at realising the "beloved community."

Ghosh: Your purpose in writing *Dreamer* must have been to celebrate the life and glory of Martin Luther King Jr. But the novel is also about Chaym Smith who, I presume, is only a fictional creation since history holds no evidence to the fact of King having a double of any kind. Doesn't this fictional character, endowed with all the sins of the evil one, strike a discordant note to the structure of the novel? Perhaps, a biographical novel based on the life of King would have been a greater tribute to the glorious leader?

Johnson: I don't write biography; I write imaginative, philosophical fiction that is frequently anchored in massive historical research. *Dreamer* delivers more details about King's life than any other novel, yes, but it is also an exploration of inequality, of the Cain and Abel story and, like Conrad's *The Secret Sharer,* it is a probing of the phenomenon of *doppleganger.*

Ghosh: Thrice, I guess, for one reason or the other, your proposed visit to India did not ultimately materialise. I have heard David Guterson, your former student at the Creative Writing Program and author of the best selling novel *Snow Falling on Cedars*, state that "once Johnson goes to India he would never want to return." What is it that holds your fascination for India?

Johnson: I often dream, naturally, of India—its beauty, antiquity, breath-taking art and remarkable people, the peace I feel instantly when my mind drifts to the Buddhist Dharma or Hinduism, that great democracy of Being. I have nurtured my life's long devotion to Buddhism by learning Sanskrit, not at a University but instead by studying the holy texts of Hinduism and *Advaita Vedanta* in the original *Devanagari* script. I am amazed by its astounding diversity where so many cultures converge in a spirit of oneness and harmony.

Ghosh: As one of the most persuasive contemporary voices engaged in confronting the ambivalence of the "American Dilemma," what impression of America would you like to share with the younger generation, both black and white?

Johnson: I would unhesitatingly say that in America *our passions define our possibilities*. Despite the ambivalence of the so-called American Dilemma, there is no denying that America was founded on principles, ideals, and documents *(The Declaration of Independence* and *The Constitution)* that forced it to be forever self-correcting. In this country no individual or group, white or black, could tell me *not to dream.*

31

Poems in Honor of Charles Johnson

— David Ray

A War-Hater Looks at the Eclipse, 2010

Red moon revealed —
and you exclaiming wonder!
But why be surprised, my friend —
the earth has been painted
bloody red many a time for thousands
of human years — and all you
and thousands of others have required
any night has been to open your eyes
and scan with your scope the wounded
moon — the lovely fields of the battle zones.

The Red Moon

"What's God trying to tell you?"
asked a Quaker friend
when I mentioned the blood—
red moon over Miami,
over Tucson, over half the earth,
heading for the other side
where it is tinted with even more
scarlet, as if in order to be fair
Death has moved from one hemi-
spherical breast to the other,
biting deeper than vampires. And
therefore I suggest in a prayer
that a fresh and virginal moon be sent
to replace the tortured old whore
who once was the loved and beloved
of poets — before the advent of warriors.

Desolation

"Where are the good minds of past days, the unshorn?"
—William Carlos Williams, "The Clouds"

Dr. William Carlos Williams was convinced
that nature in its dark and desolate winter
sometimes equals the stupidity of man.

But surely he was mistaken, although in his
time too, men opted to override all sense
common and otherwise in order to indulge

their aggression, carry on with their wars.
What matter their rhetoric, whether pious
or arrogant? In retrospect few fail to condemn

what came out of the mouth of some proved
monster who for years was adored by millions.
But what are we to make of the propaganda?

Words are worn thin in many an ashen mouth.
But would Dr. Williams, restless ghost, not offer
a prescription for peace even in this desolate winter?

Little Emilie

Not even Emily with each session's labor
in the little room at the top of the stairs,
the result stitched with thread like a chapbook
and placed in the bureau drawer,
could advance in her lifetime the cause
she termed *Immortality,* and despite efforts
at avoiding self-pity she could not help
but think of herself as poor little Emilie
and cry out for rescue from oblivion
to the distinguished editor of *The Atlantic,*
Thomas Wentworth Higginson, no lover
or wise mentor as foolish critics have claimed,
and being a distinguished, stiff-collared man
of his times, he would not offer the empowerment
she craved. But neither he nor others could
with their judgments prevent the inevitable,
as if her poems themselves cried out for *Immortality.*

32

Philosophy Matters—Review of *Charles Johnson: The Novelist as Philosopher*

— Ashraf H.A. Rushdy

Marc C. Conner and William R. Nash, Eds. *Charles Johnson: The Novelist as Philosopher*. Jackson: University Press of Mississippi, 2007. 199 + xxxvii pp. $50.00 hardcover.

The contributors to this very fine volume of critical essays on Charles Johnson represent the "novelist as philosopher" in two ways. First, Johnson is seen as holding particular philosophical positions within established systems of thought and belief—European phenomenology, American pragmatism, Buddhist meditation, existential Christianity. And, second, Johnson is seen as a writer who produces philosophical fiction—that is, tales and novels that raise and explore topics and ideas originating from and usually reserved for a different kind of non-fictional discourse.

Six of the essays focus on one of Johnson's key fictional works while teasing out the philosophical implications in the work or demonstrating the ways that the particular work aids us in our fuller understanding of Johnson's ecumenical philosophical vision. Two of the essays are on stories collected in *The Sorcerer's Apprentice*, one on *Oxherding Tale*, one on *Middle Passage*, two on *Dreamer*. Of the remaining three essays, two find Johnson to be indebted to and a practitioner of American pragmatism and the third discovers an "ontological program" in Johnson's latest collection of essays, *Turning the Wheel.*

The two essays on stories from *The Sorcerer's Apprentice* examine the relationship between two important philosophical concepts: pedagogy and power. In his capacious reading of several scenes of apparently failed pedagogy in *The Sorcercer's Apprentice*, Herman Beavers argues that Johnson is making a political statement about the difficulty of disrupting relations established in conditions of hegemony. In this statement, Beavers finds an optimism that earlier critics had denied in their reading of the short stories. In her essay on "Alethia," Linda Selzer adds one more to her series of unfailingly enlightening readings of Johnson's short stories. Positing Max Scheler's nonformalist phenomenology as an implicit critique of formalist Kantian ethics, Selzer shows how Johnson gives us a philosophy professor whose alienation is as much from the prospects of love as it is from the African American community he has fled and whose vibrant culture the student Wendy Barnes represents. The student, as Selzer argues, is the embodiment of all the things the professor has eschewed and craves, including, ultimately, "*alethia* itself."

It is a shame that there is only one essay on *Oxherding Tale* in the volume, especially given how Johnson has repeatedly, and rightly, commented on its being his most challenging and "spirit-stretching creative chore," his "platform book," a novel that, as he puts it, inhabits the "space where fiction and philosophy meet."[1] Gena Chandler's informative essay on "decomposition and art" in *Oxherding Tale* discerns the deeper meaning behind the not readily apparent connection between Johnson's aesthetic vision and some of the graphic scenes of physical disintegration in the novel (Andrew's skinning the deer, the dissolution of Minty).[2] Her commentary on embodiment and art is an important analysis of Johnson's ideas about aesthetics, form, and organic processes of creation.

Marc Conner's essay on *Middle Passage* as a "metaphysical romance" offers a perfect example of how we can develop richer readings of Johnson's writings by attending to the ways that philosophy matters in the work. Here Conner compellingly shows how Johnson is more interested in telling the story of the trans-Atlantic crossing by experimenting with philosophical concepts and concerns, even more than with formal techniques.

The two essays on *Dreamer* both challenge orthodoxies in Johnson criticism. John Whalen-Bridge's thoughtful essay makes the claim that there is something akin to an "invisible feminism" in Johnson's work; it is a welcome addition to the literature on Johnson's representation of gender. Marc Conner's ambitious and insightful essay claims that the novel is simultaneously Johnson's most searching exploration of Christian theology and his most self-conscious critique of the limits of philosophy itself.

William Nash's elegant essay on *Turning the Wheel* makes a remarkable case for reading the volume of essays as an extension of the vision that Johnson expresses in his novels, and particularly as an expression of the delimited "accessibility of the interbeing ideal," which the novels, Nash claims, consistently undo by offering a counterclaim to that ideal.

William Gleason's and Gary Storhoff's essays on Johnson's pragmatism differ in their emphases, but both make a persuasive case for Johnson's relationship to a philosophical school of American origin (as opposed to Franco-German or Indian-Tibetan). While Gleason gauges Johnson's indebtedness to pragmatism through a reading of a series of relatively understudied texts—Johnson's popular book reviews, his evolving commentary on Ralph Ellison, and two scenes of instruction in *Soulcatcher* and *Dreamer*—Storhoff looks at the full range of Johnson's oeuvre to discern the ways that his pragmatism "undergirds" his Buddhism and is displayed as an ethical practice in all his works.

It is hardly surprising that the first "themed" anthology of criticism on Johnson should deal with philosophy, the discipline of his postgraduate training as well as the field where his imagination most happily roams. For decades, Johnson has been an advocate for and producer of "philosophical fiction." In those acts of advocacy and in his own practice in the publication of three collections of short stories and four novels, Johnson has raised some important questions about the purpose of and possibilities in philosophical fiction. The questions that seem most compelling are also the ones where philosophy is in a tense dialectic with other forms of knowledge and action. A brief look at two of those tensions will suffice.

The first is the age-old question of the relationship of philosophy to politics. The modern belief is still accurately captured in Marx's eleventh thesis on Feuerbach, that the "philosophers have only *interpreted* the world," while "the point is to *change* it."[3] Over the course of his career, and the course of his evolution from Marxism to Buddhism, Johnson has provided some subtle and important meditations on the question of the connection between those who interpret and those who change the world, those who represent and try to understand human endeavors and those who try to transform human institutions. The range of his opinions on this topic—and, more importantly, the trajectory of them—are too grand a subject for the scope of this review, but the comments and fruitful disagreements about these ideas in *Charles Johnson: The Novelist as Philosopher* will certainly be an invaluable aid to those who are interested in those subjects.

The second is what might be characterised as a tension between the philosopher's task and the religious sensibility, between the ability to make fine distinctions that matter and the synthetic or ecumenical ability to find profound connections beneath apparent differences. In *Oxherding Tale*, the dialectic is cast as the difference between George Hawkins, Andrew's father, whose inheritance to his son is the perceptual slavery of "seeing distinctions," and Reb, Andrew's mentor, whose literal and psychological liberation comes from his capacious, embracing vision.[4] Johnson has, I think, been much more sympathetic to the religious sensibility, and become even more so in his most recently published novels and essays. The contributors to this volume have demonstrated both the range of philosophical and religious wisdom traditions on which Johnson draws and his own impetus in seeing what he calls the "mutual relatedness and mutual connectedness" beneath the surface disagreements of seemingly disparate ideas and systems of thought.[5]

The editors of *Charles Johnson: The Novelist as Philosopher* are to be congratulated for producing a robust and engaging book that places all of us who work on Johnson in their debt.

Notes

1. Charles Johnson, "Introduction," *Oxherding Tale* (1983; New York: Plume Books, 1995), pp. xix, xviii.
2. There is a telling scene in the novel when Andrew asks his wife whether she knows what Beethoven is now doing. To her response—"Beethoven? He died over thirty years ago!"—Andrew responds: "Yes, I know. He's de-composing." Johnson, *Oxherding Tale*, p. 125.
3. Karl Marx, "Concerning Feuerbach," in *Karl Marx: Early Writings*, Trans. Rodney Livingstone and Gregor Benton (New York: Random House, 1975), p. 423.
4. Johnson, *Oxherding Tale*, p. 172.
5. Johnson, in Linda Davies, "Charles Johnson: Interview," in Jim McWilliams, Ed., *Passing the Three Gates: Interviews with Charles Johnson* (Seattle and London: University of Washington Press, 2004), p. 147.

33

Contextualising Charles Johnson—Review of *Charles Johnson in Context*

— Marc C. Conner

Linda Furgerson Selzer. *Charles Johnson in Context.* Amherst: University of Massachusetts Press, 2009. xi + 306 pp. £28.50 paperback.

The scholarly work produced on the novelist, short-story writer, philosopher, and cultural theorist Charles Johnson has become increasingly sophisticated and penetrating in the past decade. The first book-length study of Johnson's work, Jonathan Little's *Charles Johnson's Spiritual Imagination* (Missouri, 1997), set forth several fundamental readings of and approaches to Johnson; then Will Nash's astute *Charles Johnson's Fiction* (Illinois, 2003) studied Johnson's political and literary influences in keen detail; Rudolph Byrd's *Charles Johnson's Novels: Writing the American Palimpsest* (Indiana, 2005) explored Johnson's work as offering heteroglossic readings of American culture; Gary Storhoff's *Understanding Charles Johnson* (South Carolina, 2005) delved deeply into the Buddhist elements in Johnson's work; and finally Marc Conner and Nash's edited volume, *Charles Johnson: The Novelist as Philosopher* (Mississippi, 2007), brought together a number of scholars in assessing Johnson's work from the multiple perspectives of philosophy, Johnson's original discipline. Over this ten-year span, the general terrain of Johnson scholarship has been marked, and the main issues and concepts have been pursued to some degree of completion. The time has come for studies of Johnson that build upon these fine works and pursue

Johnson's writings further, examining Johnson in combination with other late 20th-century American writers, or in conversation with his historical time and place, or focusing on his development of particular ideas and concepts. Linda Selzer has accomplished precisely this in her superb study, *Charles Johnson in Context*. Moving from the work that has come before her (and to which she herself contributed), Selzer explores Johnson's writing from within three major intellectual contexts, producing an interpretation of Johnson's work and importance that is impressive in its depth and intellectual power.

Selzer engages Johnson through three major lenses of interpretation, focusing on the contexts of black philosophers, black Buddhists, and the "new" black intellectuals. By bringing these crucial contexts into relief, Selzer is able to tie Johnson's artistic achievements to the larger projects of those working to reform the practice of American academic philosophy in the post-World War II era, those seeking to translate an ancient religious practice into an African American idiom, and those attempting to redefine cosmopolitan thought in order to make it a more effective tool for social justice. Johnson's participation in all three of these endeavors deepens the historical import, social consequence, and conceptual depth of his art. Selzer's ambitious intellectual approach accomplishes a double aim, both increasing our understanding of the influence on Johnson of these contexts, and at the same time showing how "Johnson's characteristic fusion of literature, Buddhism, and philosophy...vigorously participates in, advances, and helps to define larger directions in American intellectual life"(2). The result is a series of strong readings of Johnson's fiction, which further illuminate Johnson's own time and intellectual history.

Selzer examines Johnson's own biography, as a young black philosophy student in the late 1960s, as part of a larger movement in which black intellectuals moved increasingly into both the public sphere and the academic profession as philosophers. Such figures as Cornel West, Henry Louis Gates, Jr., Stephen Carter, Johnson, and several others have revised American cosmopolitan thought. Selzer reads Johnson's National Book Award-winning novel, *Middle Passage* (1990), against the background of a rise of black intellectuals who opposed the increasing specialisation and narrowness of traditional academia in favor of "organic" intellectual work and the effort "to articulate a cosmopolitanism that maintains an interplay between universals and particulars"(162, 167). Such efforts harmonise with much of Johnson's thought and work: "Johnson frequently enunciates a position that resonates with attempts to articulate a cosmopolitanism that reclaims the normative force of the universal while recognising multiple, overlapping allegiances"(169). Selzer acknowledges the ways in which *Middle Passage*'s setting—a raucous slave-ship crossing the Atlantic in the 1830s—hardly seems propitious to cosmopolitan thought; yet she illustrates the ways in which Johnson infuses this setting with complex intellectual figures of diverse backgrounds who articulate a range of philosophical, political, and cultural positions, all of which find purchase in the cultural debates of the late 20th century raging all about Johnson. The resulting narrative represents "Johnson's own contribution to the recent efforts by intellectuals, both black and white, to probe the dangers and the democratic potential of cosmopolitanism," and even, through Johnson's multiple narrative strategies, "requires its readers to perform their own acts of cosmopolitan competence" (209).

Selzer also analyses Johnson's specific work as a black philosopher alongside the emergence of other black philosophers in the late 20th century, and the ways in which this phenomenon altered the very discipline and profession of philosophy. In particular, Johnson and other black philosophers have worked to emphasize the social and ethical import of philosophy, to sustain conversations with Marxism and existentialism that academic, analytic Anglo-American philosophy eschewed during this same time, and to engage with non-academic forms of writing, including fiction and memoir. Selzer states, "the factors that have forged a relationship between philosophy and African American literature historically—the reliance by black thinkers on nonacademic forms of writing; the need to recuperate perspectives that have been habitually repressed; the continuing efforts of black philosophers to infuse abstract arguments with narratological, phenomenological, and social immediacy—provide important critical contexts for understanding Charles Johnson's fiction" (19).

Selzer goes on to demonstrate the presence in Johnson's fiction of these specific philosophical positions, in such works as his early short story "Alethia," published in the collection of fiction *The Sorcerer's Apprentice* in 1986, and in a prolonged and extraordinarily insightful reading of Johnson's first novel, *Faith and the Good Thing* (1974). In this chapter-long assessment, Selzer shows the novel's engagement with Marxist thought, then its ultimate movement away from such a theory towards the phenomenology that Johnson himself came to embrace after an early flirtation with Marxism and Black Power. Throughout these discussions, Selzer's complex understanding of philosophy is matched by her subtle and sensitive awareness of African-American culture, enabling her to match Johnson's shifting fictional moves with her own intellectual work.

Selzer examines Johnson's very serious immersion in Buddhism, and places his work among "contemporary black Buddhists [who] are also engaged in a larger revisionist task: the translation of an ancient Eastern religion into a contemporary African-American idiom"(5). This confluence of Buddhism and black America forms the central approach of her chapter devoted to Johnson's self-proclaimed "platform novel," *Oxherding Tale* (1982). Here Selzer argues that, although Johnson had been interested in Eastern thought since his teens, and although his personal commitment to Buddhism increased in the 1990s, culminating in his 2007 taking of formal Buddhist vows, nevertheless *Oxherding Tale* represents a signal achievement in his approach to Buddhism. Here, she argues, "the tension between private enlightenment and civic engagement in Johnson's fiction is therefore most pronounced... [as] he first turns from a neo-Marxist economy of productive subjectivity to a Mahayana Buddhist conception of enlightenment that posits civic engagement largely in altruistic rather than activist terms"(107). Selzer examines the trajectory of black dharma in the United States, placing Johnson within and also showing his decisive influence on this context, and deftly negotiating the tensions within the African-American community, particularly the traditional black Christian church, over the increasing presence of black Buddhism (113-115). The insightful reading Selzer generates of *Oxherding Tale* brings together a range of concepts, including Johnson's commitment to "engaged" Buddhism, his grappling with the legacy of slavery and the Civil War, his effort to balance both individual story and "vast cosmic operations," and his masterful ability to present such complexity through a variety of characters, voices, and narrative styles (156). This last gift may well be what sets Johnson most apart from other late 20th-century writers, particularly within the African-American tradition.

In her final chapter, Selzer turns to Johnson's most recent (and perhaps most ambitious) novel, *Dreamer* (1998), and here her analysis is, to my mind, most penetrating. We might think that Selzer overemphasizes Johnson's commitment to and interest in Marxist thought, and that in places her argument could be more attentive to the religious elements of Johnson's work; yet this is part of the problem of academic discourse today, which has few registers beyond the Marxist to discuss social commitment and a concern for justice; and which has even fewer ways to talk about the religious life in any serious or committed way. Yet the figure of Martin Luther King, Jr. offers the very means, even the very terms, for such a discussion of both the socially committed and the religiously committed life. This is the very reason Johnson is so drawn to King, both in *Dreamer* and in a range of excellent short stories and luminous essays that deal with King's legacy and thought. Selzer views Johnson's fascination with King—itself part of "a newly invigorated debate that unfolded among public intellectuals beginning in the 1990s over [King's] legacy"(211)—as both the culmination and the extension of his interest in black philosophy, black Buddhism, and a revised cosmopolitanism. For Johnson, she argues, sees in King "'one of America's greatest moral and political philosophers'"; he also views him as "an inspiration for the development of an engaged Buddhist practice"; and "as a leading cosmopolitan intellectual"—thereby "embodying in a single figure the black philosopher, religious leader, and cosmopolitan intellectual." Through his focus on King and King's legacy, Johnson "develops a particular resolution to the tension between private conversion and civic action that is evident from the first in his fiction" (211-212).

Selzer thus reads Johnson's career as one of steady development and progression, from early Marxist influence to his late immersion in Buddhist thought, and emphasizes throughout Johnson's interest in and influence by black cosmopolitan intellectual activity. Her readings of his work are rich, and her overarching emphasis on the intellectual "context" to his work provides a compelling view of not just Johnson's career, but the larger intellectual currents through which he has moved in the last four decades. The result is a very learned study, one that contributes not just to our understanding of one of the most important American writers of this age, but also to several major strands of intellectual history that—if the recent presidential election is any evidence—have become decisive for our time.

34

Middle Passages: Charles Johnson and the Raft of Dhamma— Review of *Middle Passage*

—Qiana J. Whitted

> I have taught the Dhamma compared to a raft, for the purpose of crossing over, not for the purpose of holding onto.
>
> —*Alagaddupama Sutta*

At the start of Charles Johnson's novel, *Middle Passage*, a former antebellum slave named Rutherford Calhoun considers the expansive view from a New Orleans pier and wonders if "the analogue for life was water, the formless, omnific sea." To my mind, this fictional character's observations about the cleansing spray of light, wind, and mist also recall the longings of Frederick Douglass's 1845 autobiography in which he writes of standing on the edge of the Chesapeake Bay, alone "in the deep stillness of a summer's Sabbath" to contemplate the sails of ships gliding into the ocean. In these meditative moments, Douglass regards himself not as cargo, the way his owners do, but as a kindred vessel: "You are loosed from your moorings, and are free; I am fast in my chains, and am a slave!" He goes on to lament, "alas! betwixt me and you, the turbid waters roll. Go on, go on. O that I could also go! Could I but swim! If I could fly!" Douglass's counterpart in *Middle Passage* does not see himself as part of this moving multitude of ships, at least not at first; Rutherford, though manumitted, is still a petty thief – hedonistic, self-grasping, and bound to a desire to steal the experiences of others. Over time, though, he will come to follow

Douglass's lead, moving in and through the turbid waters that signify "countless seas of suffering."

Rutherford's transformational—and transnational—journey in this award-winning novel conveys a sense of interconnectedness that Johnson values as a black Buddhist practitioner. What's more, in all of his fiction, essays, and scholarly writings, Johnson models a way of thinking about Buddhism that posits the philosophical and spiritual complexities of African-American narrative as a vehicle for exploring ultimate truths. In his 2003 collection, *Turning the Wheel: Essays on Buddhism and Writing*, Johnson notes an increasing number of black American writers and scholars who are known for engaging in some form of Buddhist practice: Thulani Davis, Jan Willis, Angel Kyoto Williams, Alice Walker, bell hooks, Steven Barnes and others. Jean Toomer emerges as a literary ancestor of sorts, one whose wide philosophical interests set him apart from other New Negro writers of the 1930s. Johnson even cites fellow travelers in the entertainment industry including Tina Turner and Herbie Hancock.

Yet when Johnson uses terms such as "radical, emancipatory, nonessentialistic, and empathetic" to characterize the Dhamma, or when he refers to issues of race "as foremost among samsaric illusions," he is not necessarily speaking for a community of black Buddhists, but to advance an understanding of Western Buddhism that is mindful of African-American suffering. *Turning the Wheel* enthusiastically underscores points of convergence between Buddhist teachings and African-American creative and intellectual thought, placing the voices of Shantideva and Thich Nhat Hanh in conversation with Martin Luther King, Jr's aspirations for "beloved community," the sounds of "lower frequencies" in Ralph Ellison's *Invisible Man*, and the introspective risks of poet Lucille Clifton's "Ten Oxherding Pictures." Consider that after Rutherford Calhoun inadvertently stows away on a ship bound for Africa in *Middle Passage*, he returns to the New Orleans pier changed, no longer a thief after having seen the transatlantic slave trade and survived the disease, starvation, and rebellion on board. He observes:

Looking back at the asceticism of the *Middle Passage*, I saw how the frame of mind I had adopted left me unattached, like the slaves who, not knowing what awaited them in the New World, put a high premium on living from moment to moment, and this, I realized, was why they did not commit suicide. The voyage had irreversibly changed my way of seeing, made of me a cultural mongrel, and transformed the world into a fleeting shadow play I felt no need to possess or dominate, only appreciate in the ever extended present.

To regard the cycle of *samsara* (and its cessation) through the Middle Passage experience, as this quote implies, carries profound cultural resonance for people like myself who are descended from the enslaved Africans that survived the global atrocity. Slavery, as Johnson points out in *Turning the Wheel*, "is, one must say, a frighteningly fertile ground for the growth of a deep appreciation for the First and Second Noble Truths as well as a living illustration of the meaning of impermanence." He also suggests that just as racial difference has been used to build hierarchies of oppression, so do the delusions of our perceived selves keep us from a full awareness of an interdependent reality. All of us, every living being, will confront middle passages in our lives. Will we, too, take to the raft of Dhamma and emerge sea changed?

In my book on the problem of evil in 20th century black American literature, I explore the ways in which black writers engage the classic considerations of God's goodness, justice, and power that are traditionally associated with Christian communities of faith and scripture. Questions of divine justice, I maintain, are at the heart of the post-Emancipation religious reflections by Countee Cullen, Richard Wright, Nella Larsen, James Baldwin, Ernest Gaines, and Toni Morrison. Their characters risk the disapproval of church elders in order to reflect upon black suffering and contemplate the kind of questions that Douglass addresses to the ships at sea: "God, deliver me! Let me be free! Is there any God? Why am I a slave?"

What does it mean, then, to explore what poet Everett Hoagland called "the sea-deep blues of American slavery" through a Buddhist framework? Or to consider modern injustice through a religion that is devoted to obliterating suffering and cherishing others, but that is largely unconcerned with the question of God? What are the consequences of viewing the experiences of African Americans in accordance with the individual and collective dimensions of karmic law or through the precepts of an Eastern religion with its own history and cultural traditions?

One of the ways that Charles Johnson addresses these questions in *Middle Passage* can be seen through Rutherford's realization of himself at sea as a "cultural mongrel" not unlike Douglass's moving multitude of ships. The novel also makes a case for Buddhism as part of our human inheritance through the enslaved Allmuseri, a fictitious African people who embrace a worldview that is very similar to Buddhist monastics (Johnson calls them "a rather Buddhist African tribe" in *Turning the Wheel*). The Allmuseri, with their unlined palms, are healers for whom lying, clinging, or causing harm brings multi-generational consequences. At times, Rutherford seems to romanticize the qualities of the Allmuseri as the "Ur-tribe of humanity," yet the path that he ultimately chooses falls somewhere between the faultless values of their leader Ngonyama and the imperialistic greed of the slave ship captain. The Middle Path.

Such writings open up an important discursive space to consider how Buddha's teachings take shape in black American literary and cultural texts. I am particularly fascinated by the manner in which Buddhist practice intersects with the subversive play of language and form for which writers like Charles Johnson are so well known. Like Rutherford and other African American thinkers, I am also mesmerized by the formless sea, its undertow of suffering as well as its emancipatory potential. After all, it was in the red shirt and tarpaulin hat of a sailor that Frederick Douglass made his final escape as a slave from the Chesapeake Bay. Equipped with his knowledge of ships, another sailor's protection certificate, and the courage of his own convictions, he boarded a train for New York in September 1838 and never looked back. A fitting model, I would say, for those of us who are journeying to the distant shore of enlightenment on our own rafts of Dhamma.

Reference

Charles Johnson. *Middle Passage*. New York: Scribner, 1998. 209+xpp. $12 (paperback).

35

Afterword: Charles Johnson's Quest for a New African-American Narrative and His Literary Genealogy

— Amritjit Singh

> To be free is to be capable of determining, at least to some extent, what one is to be.
>
> —Karsten Harries,
> *The Meaning of Modern Art* (1968), 158

Charles Johnson: Embracing the World, brought together by Dr. Nibir K. Ghosh and Mr. Ethelbert Miller to "celebrate the enduring spirit" of Charles R. Johnson and his artistic output in several mediums and genres, is both timely and appropriate. This gathering of academic and creative writings by and about Johnson, as well as several personal tributes by friends and scholars, will serve as a valuable introduction for South Asian and other readers to an American littérateur who has been building vital bridges of imagination to India, its traditions and philosophies, for nearly half a century. One can only hope that those bonds between Johnson and India will become even stronger when he makes a physical journey to the subcontinent one of these days, as it happened for many but not all African American figures who made such an endeavor in the past 80 years or so. Individuals that come to mind are theologian-scholars Howard W. Thurman (1899-1981) and Benjamin E. Mays (1894-1984), who led African American delegations to meet Mahatma Gandhi in 1935 and 1936 respectively, and their more famous *shishya*, Martin Luther King, Jr., who traveled to India in February 1959 at Jawaharlal Nehru's invitation to study the Gandhian philosophy of non-violence and Satyagraha. In contrast, Jean Toomer, one of Johnson's literary "ancestors," was deeply disillusioned with India at the end of his six-month spiritual journey there in 1939-40. Only time will tell how a similar journey might affect Johnson's own strong and longstanding relationship with India and Eastern religious philosophies.

Nibir and I have been friends and correspondents since the mid-1970s. In Spring 2003, when Nibir decided to spend his Fulbright year at the University of Washington, I became especially aware of Charles Johnson as his Faculty Associate there. Like other students of American and African American Literature, I had been cognizant of Johnson's strong presence on the scene at least since 1990, when his novel *Middle Passage* won the National Book Award, the first African American novel to receive the award since Ralph Ellison's *Invisible Man* (1952). In August 2003, Daniel M. Scott (a Johnson aficionado himself) and I had published *The Collected Writings of Wallace Thurman* and I was thrilled to send through Nibir a dedicated copy of that volume to Professor Johnson.

In a handwritten note to Professor Johnson, I suggested somewhat foolishly a parallel between my own involvements in African American Studies since the early 1970s and Mr. Johnson's deeper and more meditative, life-changing interests in India's religious practices and philosophical precepts since 1962, when the novelist was just 14 years old. As Johnson tells Adam Tolbert, "In the tempestuous mid-to-late 1960s when there was so much violence—political assassinations [JFK, Martin Luther King, Jr., Robert Kennedy, Malcolm X, Medgar Evers, etc.], rioting in the cities, anger and polarization of blacks and whites, old and young—the Buddhadharma provided a place where I could always achieve clarity and peace, and with that as my basis I could always work toward achieving respect, *metta* (loving-kindness), and generosity as a goal in all my social relations with others—in my relations to my parents, teachers, then my own students and colleagues, indeed, in my relations with all sentient beings." In the not as tempestuous mid-1960s in postcolonial India, as a young college student growing up among the refugees of the Partition, I too would hear the metaphorical call of "Buddham Sharanam Gacchami." But surrounded by overpowering sounds and smells of poverty, deprivation, and personal struggle in my dusty hometown of Ambala in Northern India, I sought refuge not in spirituality, but in Nehruvian socialism. But like Charles, young Indians like me were also fascinated by the American Camelot, and we admired Martin Luther King, Jr., even as the latter was inspired by M.K. Gandhi and he viewed India as nothing less than "pilgrimage."

As I look back, my indirect contact with Johnson in 2003 marks the beginning of much that I have learned about and from him. The story of my education in Chuck's wonderful ways should resonate with other narratives by colleagues such as John Whalen-Bridge and Gary Storhoff included in this volume. But if my journey within the magic circle of Charles Johnson has been more gradual than that of others, it is certainly not for want of power in that magic or for any lack of generosity on Chuck's part. In August 2007, Nibir was kind enough to inform Chuck by e-mail about my proposed research visit to Seattle. In response, Chuck was consistently warm, welcoming, solicitous, and flexible. On the phone, he told me with pride about the Faire Gallery/Café run by his daughter, Elisheba, but to suit my convenience, he met me for dinner on August 27 in the University District. At Araya's Vegetarian Restaurant, over richly laid platters of spicy Asian food, Chuck made me feel important, almost like a wise elder, as he listened deferentially to me, an African Americanist in a South Asian body. He was very interested in my current research on South Asian in North America and intrigued to learn that I had been the only doctoral candidate on whose committee Ralph Ellison had served during the latter's NYU years. Chuck talked lovingly and unpretentiously about his family (Joan, Malik, and Elisheba), even as I communicated some of my own unformed thoughts about his work, acknowledging my need to study them more carefully. He told me that he had been studying Sanskrit for many years and I narrated my exciting intellectual adventures as a teenager in the world of Sanskrit that have left an indelible mark on my own sense of language and culture. I felt then and know now that Charles would not give up on his immersion in the East, as T. S. Eliot almost did during his doctoral studies at Harvard. We can celebrate our good fortune that unlike Eliot, Johnson has been willing, even eager, to forget "how to think and feel as an American."[1] At the end of the evening, Chuck gave me an autographed copy of the newly published *Charles Johnson: The Novelist as Philosopher*, which, as Ashraf Rushdy testifies in these pages, remains "a robust and engaging volume" on Johnson's philosophical fiction—exploring in lucid and challenging ways—the specific intersections of European phenomenology, Buddhist philosophy, and American pragmatism.

Since 2007, Chuck and I have managed to keep regularly in touch and I have found his e-mail messages to be informative and thought-provoking, bringing me all kinds of news—including the kind Henry David Thoreau preferred, when he recorded in his journals that "One wise sentence [from the *Vedas*] is worth the State of Massachusetts many times over."[2] Such news included Chuck's taking his formal vows as a Buddhist on November 14, 2007 (on Nehru's birthday) and acquiring the new middle name, "Angyo." From Chuck's messages, I came to learn about such publications as Linda Furgerson Selzer's *Charles Johnson in Context* (2009) and *Philosophy: An Innovative Introduction* (2010); conferences such as the Western Literature Conference in Tacoma, WA, in October 2007 and the AWP in Denver in April 2010 where Ethelbert Miller paid a rousing tribute to Johnson; as well as Chuck's Maxine Cushing Lecture at the University of Washington on November 19, 2010. Over the years, I have received in the mail from Chuck such generous and beautiful gifts, as *Mine Eyes Have Seen: Bearing Witness to the Struggle for Civil Rights*, co-authored by Chuck with the Civil Rights photographer, Bob Adelman, and *I Call Myself an Artist*, edited by Rudolph P. Byrd.

Charles Johnson: Buddhadharma, Language and Narrative

> When we confront phenomena of any kind, we are wise if we assume the position phenomenologist Herbert Spiegelberg called epistemological humility, which is healthy skepticism about what we think we already know.[3]
>
> —Charles Johnson, "The End of the Black American Narrative," 2008

Like most writers who go against the grain, Johnson has attempted to establish the contours of his new thinking on language, literature and philosophy through books, essays and interviews. In fact, *Being and Race: Black Writing since 1970* (1988), a book that offers more than what its subtitle promises, may be viewed as a kind of literary manifesto.[4] Its metonymic opening chapter, although much more detailed in its critique of African American Literature than Richard Wright's "Blueprint for Negro Writing" (1937), is comparable in its aim and its affect to Wright's essay. Mentioning the three bad novels Johnson had written in the naturalistic style of Wright, James Baldwin and John A. Williams and three equally bad ones that he had written under the influence of "Black Aesthetic," *Being and Race* manages to move the discussion of how to record African American historical experience in art beyond Wright's intriguing and powerful notion of "perspective" toward phenomenology and intersubjectivity as the primary modes of creativity, of "Being" in fiction. For Johnson, "Our faith in fiction comes from an ancient belief that language and literary art – all speaking and showing – clarify our experience" (3). As Daniel M. Scott has observed, "By situating this questioning within the sphere of African American experience, [Johnson] radicalizes this faith and makes innovative demands on writing to show and speak the complexities of experience, consciousness and change" ("Interrogating Identity," in *I Call*, 354). It is worth noting that unlike Wright, who was quite dismissive in "Blueprint" of most black American writing before him, Johnson is careful to document how his African American predecessors such as Jean Toomer, Zora Neale Hurston, Wright, Ralph Ellison, Amiri Baraka, and Eldridge Cleaver have contributed – by positive or negative example – to his own development as a writer and thinker.[5]

In "Being and Fiction," the second chapter of *Being and Race*, Johnson declares, citing Maurice Merleau-Ponty, that "being locked in ourselves" is a suicidal choice for a creative writer. For Johnson, as for Keats who defined "negative capability" so memorably, "real fiction" tries to capture "how someone else has suffered, what is in *their* heart, *their* hopes and fears, *their* pain and personal triumphs....Like the great actor who loves people of all kinds, and enjoys being changed by them, the true novelist... is forever obliged to obliterate for the duration of his fiction his own pettiness, to surrender his prejudices in order to seize another's way of seeing, then faithfully present it in the story" (45). As Johnson notes in his Afterword, in literature, as in philosophy, there can be "an endless series of new excavations of experience, but nothing that even remotely resembles a conclusion....Each new story teaches us what a story can be, which underscores for a serious artist the necessity of approaching racial and social phenomena in humble, patient spirit of listening and letting be whatever the world wishes to say to us" (122).

Johnson's evolving sense of his relationship to the past writers and his own understanding of the aesthetic challenges facing black American artists finds an articulation in many of his writings and interviews, including his essay, "The End of the Black American Narrative" that appeared in *American Scholar* in Summer 2008 (http://www.theamericanscholar.org/the-end-of-the-black-american-narrative/). In this essay, Johnson expresses serious concerns about the persistence of "the old black American narrative of pervasive victimization," despite the changing ground realties of race that have transformed African Americans into "a complex and multifaceted people" today. Echoing Zora Neale Hurston's rejection of "the sobbing school of Negrohood" in her well-known essay, "How It Feels to be Colored Me" (1928), Johnson questions "the truth and usefulness of the traditional black

American narrative of victimization," and issues a clarion call for "better stories, new concepts, and new vocabularies and grammar based not on the past but on the dangerous, exciting and unexplored present, with the understanding that each is, at best, a provisional reading of reality....These will be narratives that do not claim to be absolute truth, but instead more humbly present themselves as a very tentative thesis that must be tested in the depths of our own experience." In his AWP Tribute in April 2010, Ethelbert Miller described Johnson's call for new narratives as "language work"—"the crafting of a vision for a better tomorrow... the discovery of the tongue's beauty and the ear's elegance." That "language work" signifies "we live in language," as Johnson had averred in *Being and Race* in rejecting Ron Karenga's argument in favor of black art that is "(1) functional, (2) collective, and (3) committed." For Johnson, "Art is not *useful* in the sense that a commodity is useful.... [Language] works upon us as we upon it – like the presence of another person before us, which in fact it, as a work of consciousness, indirectly is" (23), Johnson's quest for a new aesthetic, like his search for wholeness in life, has taken him more deeply into Buddhadharma over the years as documented in "I Call" and elsewhere. In his essay collection, *Turning the Wheel: Essays on Buddhism and Writing (Scribner*, 2003), Johnson points to the emergence of several philosophically inclined African American writers, some of whom are engaged in one or another form of Buddhist practice. As Qiana Whitted points out, "in all of his fiction, essays, and scholarly writings, Johnson models a way of thinking about Buddhism that posits the philosophical and spiritual complexities of African American narrative as a vehicle for exploring ultimate truths."[6] Such writers include Thulani Davis, Jan Willis, Angel Kyoto Williams, Steven Barnes and Alice Walker, and some of them recognize Jean Toomer, the author of *Cane* (1923), as a literary ancestor of sorts, one whose philosophical and spiritual quests set him apart from his Harlem Renaissance peers.

For Toomer as well as for Johnson (and for the godless Wallace Thurman too), individuals and communities must function from within a cultivated inner strength as they work to free themselves from the visible and invisible shackles of exclusion and otherness, and to overcome the "mind-forg'd manacles" of William Blake's "London." And they must do so through a dedicated and uncompromising pursuit of deeply experienced spirituality, creativity or intellectual achievement. Buddhism opens up one such path, a process if you like, and it has worked well for Johnson and several other artists, black and white. In some ways, Buddhadharma did for the teenaged Johnson in Illinois what books had done for Richard Wright in Mississippi some forty years earlier. Wright without books might have been another Bigger Thomas and Johnson without Buddhadharma would not have found the "clarity and peace" he did in the midst of the angry and violent 1960s. As Johnson notes in his preface to *Turning the Wheel*, "Were it not for the Buddhadharma, I'm convinced that, as a black American and an artist, I would not have been able to successfully negotiate my last half century of life in this country. Or at least not with a high level of creative productivity."

If Johnson as a philosopher has inherited the mantle of European phenomenologists, American pragmatists, and Buddhist thinkers, Johnson the artist is a veritable descendant of many African American writers, including and especially Toomer and Wallace Thurman, who, like Johnson, aimed at catapulting themselves and their compatriots out of debilitating race and class oppression – through the full and fierce cultivation of their creativity, intellectual acumen, and/or spiritual potential. For any individual, even a black American individual, her sense of his or her own worth, what W. E. B. Du Bois called "true self-consciousness" in the opening chapter of *Souls of Black Folk*, must be experienced within herself. Such sense of self-worth and "wholeness" (Toomer's term) must allow an African American individual to withstand and reject the negative effects of that dehumanizing outside gaze, that sense, in Du Bois's memorable phrasing, "of always looking at one's self through the eyes of others, of measuring one's soul by the tape of a world that looks on in amused contempt and pity." More than either Toomer or Thurman, Johnson would acknowledge the valuable contributions of Civil Rights crusaders such as Du Bois and Martin Luther King, Jr., but like Toomer and Thurman, he too would not rely primarily upon the capacity of social and political networks to help a marginalized individual or group to achieve their full human potential.

Jean Toomer: A Literary Ancestor's Spiritual Journey to India

> I came into contact with an entirely new body of ideas. Buddhist philosophy, the Eastern teachings, occultism, theosophy.... These ideas challenged and stimulated me. Despite my literary purpose, I was compelled to know something more about them... and my religious nature, given a cruel blow by Clarence Darrow and naturalism, but not, as I found, destroyed by them—my religious nature which had been sleeping was vigorously aroused.
>
> —Jean Toomer, *The Wayward and the Seeking* (1980), 119

The careers of Jean Toomer and Thurman, the literary progenitors of Charles Johnson evince remarkable parallels to the trajectory of Johnson's life and his creative and critical output. While Toomer gets mentioned sometimes in this context, Thurman is seldom acknowledged as one of his African American "ancestors." In this section, before we establish the relevance of reading Thurman and Johnson together, I sketch Toomer's fascinating and tumultuous journey to India during 1939-40. This chapter in Toomer's life could provide, in its parallels and contrasts, an insight into Johnson's imaginative flights to India over decades through his active engagement with many strands in Eastern religious thought. along with his gradual move toward a full embrace of Buddhism. In connecting Thurman to Johnson in the latter part of this section, I hope to demonstrate the similarities between the two writers' intellectual independence and their unswerving search for a new aesthetic, as well as high artistic and intellectual standards. In considering such connections, we may recognize that while Johnson, like Ralph Ellison, exercises his freedom to choose his "ancestors" from diverse backgrounds, some of his black "relatives" too can qualify as his "ancestors."

Cane was a major presence in the Harlem Renaissance, even though Jean Toomer (1894-1967) himself was not. Toomer was not actively engaged in the literary and aesthetic debates in the 1920s that roused the passions of Du Bois, Alain Locke, Langston Hughes, Hurston, Thurman, and others in distinctive ways.[7] In fact, soon after *Cane* was published in 1923, Toomer had convinced himself that he had already found his desired "intelligible scheme" in Russian mystic George Gurdjieff's philosophy. Despite Locke's attempts to frame and represent him otherwise in *The New Negro* and elsewhere, Toomer made it clear that while he viewed the [Negro] movement as a "splendid thing," it "had no special meaning for me" (Toomer, *Wayward*, 131-32). In his 1932 novel, *Infants of the Spring*, the only book-length satire on the period by a major participant, Thurman's alter-ego, Raymond Taylor, pays Toomer a high tribute indeed: "I know of only one Negro who has the elements of greatness, and that's Jean Toomer. The rest of us are merely journeymen, planting seed for someone else to harvest." In his essay, "The Negro Renaissance: Jean Toomer and the Harlem Writers of the 1920s," Arna Bontemps noted that *Cane* "heralded an awakening of artistic expression by Negroes that brought to light in less than a decade a surprising array of talents." (in *Anger and Beyond*, ed. Herbert Hill, New York: Harper and Row, 1966, p. 27).

So while *Cane* and *Souls of Black Folk* were probably the two most influential and inspiring books for younger Harlem Renaissance writers, Toomer himself had moved away from "race" into his dedicated quest for unity and spiritual growth. His six-month visit to India (July 1939 to January 1940) in search of a guru or a mantra calls for a special comment here in relation to Johnson's deep interests in South Asian religions and philosophies. Could a *direct* contact with India's physical reality—especially the horrific economic conditions that oppressed almost all of the 400 million colonized Indians (the total population of India in 1947, when the British finally left) and which still inflict a similar number (a third of India's population in 2011)—have the high-voltage power to disintegrate the idea of India's spirituality for Toomer, or

Johnson, or any other individual invested in the idea of India's spirituality?

By the mid-1930s, Toomer had begun to feel disenchanted with Gurdjieff, but still felt the powerful need to find a process or precept that would allow him to overcome his sense of fragmentation. As Cynthia Earl Kerman and Richard Eldridge note in *The Lives of Jean Toomer: A Hunger for Wholeness* (LSU Press, 1987), "The year 1937 was one of intense activity.... [and] 1938 seemed almost a blank," and even as Toomer and his second wife, Marjorie Content, were exploring a Quaker community near Philadelphia, Toomer "began to suffer a growing sense of incompleteness, a need for new infusion or a new system of belief" (237). For fourteen years, Toomer had functioned spiritually on the strength of the religious epiphany he had had in 1926, but by April 1938, he was not sure that the "means" he had received "from an Awake Source" in 1926 were truly effective: "Plainly, unless I do awake within the next year, I should again seek him who is awake" (240). He needed the guidance of a wise teacher who would help him to supplant or supplement the Gurdjieffian approach with a method "such as in meditation, applicable in quiet moods" (241).

Despite his own doubts and his wife's anxieties, Toomer had by late 1938 convinced himself that "he had to go to India to find what he was looking for" (242). But Marjorie remained skeptical. Her faith in Toomer's infallibility already shaken, she was concerned too about the physical discomfort, sickness, and language difficulties Jean would likely face in India. In April 1939, "as a kind of rest cure, Jean had gone alone to Bermuda for three weeks, [but] Bermuda proved not enough; Jean insisted on going to India" (242-43). When Marjorie's doting father, Harry Content, agreed to finance the India trip, Toomer wrote him a thank-you letter that justified the trip quite effusively:

> ...I am deeply convinced that going to India is the right thing to do, the only thing to do, and that in a years (sic) time other people will be able to realize that it was the right thing, because they will see in me and in her a new

> vitality, a new energy, a health, a new happiness, an enrichment, and a much greater capacity to be of real service to other human beings (243).

In fact, as Kerman and Eldridge note, Toomer expected India to supply him with "resources necessary to cope with major world problems" (243). It is not clear if Toomer was a victim of hallucination or megalomania or both in cultivating such immense goals. In his correspondence with his father-in-law, Toomer stated, "What I chiefly need is a lot more energy. In other respects I am fairly well-equipped. In India, from ancient times, certain men have known how to teach a man to draw on and use the power that is usually locked away under the surface" (243). In fact, Toomer even expected to "derive a living income" from his future spiritual work, once he had acquired the secret mantra from a guru in India.

Leaving New York by ship on July 19, 1939, Jean and Marjorie had to deal with a cumbersome and annoying journey, passing through Colombo, Ceylon (now Sri Lanka), on their way to Madras (now Chennai), where they were welcomed by Laura Chase, a friend of Marjorie's, at the Theosophical Center in Adyar. Just five days after they arrived in Ceylon in late August, World War II had broken out. The restive Toomer quickly transferred his hopes from Adyar to Maharishi Sri Ramanasramam in his ashram in the village of Arunchalla, just north of the city.[8] When Maharishi Ramana too failed to give Toomer the spiritual "silver bullet," Toomer decided to move North and East to Rabindranath Tagore's Santiniketan (a pleasant visit but no more) and then on to the village of Ghoom, near Darjeeling, where he spent time with a Buddhist monk, Anagarika Govinda, a German who had become a British citizen during the War to avoid harassment.[9] Although Toomer viewed Buddhism as "by all odds the most genuine, most impressive, the most promising Way" that he had encountered in India, he was reluctant to abandon the Gurdjieff way that he had by now practiced for 15 years and instead make the kind of full commitment becoming a Buddhist would require. He was fascinated with M.K. Gandhi, "the man of the India of today, ... the one world figure that India had produced since Buddha," but he decided he was not "moved" enough to meet him (245). After nearly four months in India, he realized "a life of withdrawal from the world" as practiced by many of India's spiritual seekers was not the life for him and that in fact the Gurdjieff work had taken him farther than any system he had encountered in India. By the end of October 1939, Toomer had concluded that Quakerism was "better for Americans than any religion or way of life" he and his wife had seen in India.

Apparently, Toomer's extended exposure to India's largely ascetic modes of spirituality allowed him to appreciate the "catalytic action" potential of Quakers back home. He also began to supplant his quest for "direct means to Being" with the necessity to be made whole: "We must be made whole, I think, before we can truly be ready to enter and abide in Being" (246). In his notebooks, he admits the abject failure of his India mission: "Instead of saying I have entered Being, I can but say I've been around the world. It has cost five thousand dollars to complete my disillusionment" (247). And yet, immediately upon his return in January 1940, Toomer did not hesitate to represent himself as an expert on India in Washington, PA, and give some lectures at the local college. He also proposed to Graham Munson and others the idea of establishing an organization called "The Friends of Being" that would work to eliminate the binarics of body and spirit, "being" and "non-being." In a 1940 play entitled "The Colombo-Madras Mail," Toomer offered an important insight that it would be hard for human beings to find spirituality in the midst of poverty, physical discomfort, greed, and oppression that existed everywhere but were more strongly manifested in India (248). In other words, the pursuit of spirituality, like that of creativity, would require a metaphorical "room of one's own" and some level of economic freedom. As Kerman and Eldridge suggest, Toomer's work, primarily psychological until the India visit, later became mostly religious with roughly the same content. And Toomer, ever the seeker, continued to ponder the "essential concern" of existence, as if in relation to the core Indian belief in reincarnation: "the unending moving of human beings through life after life, through world after world, toward a long-range objective which remains undefined" (251).

Thurman the Predecessor: An "Anti-Race Race Man"

> "[It is] the duty of those who have the will to power in artistic and intellectual fields to shake off psychological shackles, deliberately formulate an egoistic philosophy, develop a cosmopolitan perspective, and soar where they may, blaming only themselves if they fail to reach their goal. Individual salvation may prove a more efficacious emancipating agent for his [the Negro's] generation and for those following than self sacrifice and morbid resentment.
>
> —Wallace Thurman, "Author's Preface," *Aunt Hagar's Children*, 1929, 234

> My position on race... is that it is an illusion, with numerous scientists pointing out that it is a social construct, with more differences within so-called races than between them.... But the point... is that it is a lived-illusion, a delusion that causes enormous suffering.... Any essentialist sense of identity—not just "race"—is an illusion. I always say we are processes, not products. We're verbs, not nouns.
>
> —Charles Johnson, "Monsters and Critics Interview 1," June 2007

Unlike Toomer and Johnson, Wallace Thurman (1902-1934) showed no interest in religion or faith-based spirituality and luxuriated in a world of ideas and images that was unabashedly secular and godless, cosmopolitan and defiantly bohemian. Like Wright, Thurman learned to dislike and mistrust church very early in life, and like Wright again, he successfully thwarted his grandmother's attempts to convert him. Like Toomer, Thurman was a jolly social drinker. Both exhibited strong proclivities to alcoholism, genetic or otherwise. As reflected in his own essays, reviews, and correspondence, as well as in the recognizably autobiographical characters in his two novels, *The Blacker the Berry* (1929) and *Infants of the Spring* (1932), Thurman was a transgressive individual and artist—experimenting freely both with his body (sometimes quite self-destructively) and in his writings in multiple genres, including short fiction, novels, poetry, literary criticism, social and personal essays, plays and screenplays. He had all the makings of a public intellectual à la Edward Said and exercised considerable influence upon his peers during his nine years (1925-34) in Harlem. His social essays, such as "Christmas: Its Origins and Significance" and "In the Name of Purity," sharply question orthodoxies of religious practice, racial binaries, and sexual double standards. His essay, "The Coming Revolution" (in *Aunt Hagar's Children*) is an excellent example of Thurman's skeptical, agnostic, questioning approaches to ideology, religion, and politics: "[G]ladly would I urge the Negro masses to take an active part in the revolution, just to see them, for one moment emerge from their innate sluggishness, massacre their ministers, and perhaps, in the interim, give birth to a few exceptional individuals capable of arising above the mob, Communism, Christianity, and all other such doctrines to become master intellects and creative giants" (*Collected Writings of Wallace Thurman*, 282).

One can only speculate about how much larger Thurman's influence upon later American and African American writers might have been, had he not succumbed to terminal tuberculosis at the young age of 32. Throughout his "short, happy life" that hid significant unresolved sexual and writerly conflicts, Thurman showed a remarkable independence and intensity as a critic, reviewer and theorist. From his days as child and boy in Salt Lake City to his decade of artistic engagement in Harlem, Thurman remained a voracious and eclectic reader. His literary career was characterized by desperation—amounting at times to despair—to achieve the high, near-impossible, artistic standards he had set for himself. In the "maelstrom" of his life and work, "seeking, observing, suffering" in an unmistakably Whitmanic tenor, Thurman attempted to shape the chaos into order in his essays, fiction, and drama. Fed by a desire for literary fame that at times expressed itself in a desperate sense of alienation, Thurman's life was, on the page and in fact, a continual struggle.

Although Thurman has left behind a treasure-trove of valuable critical and theoretical formulations, Thurman's views on matters of race and identity, subjectivity and agency, were always in flux, still evolving. As part of a letter he wrote in 1929 to thank Hughes for feedback on *Aunt Hagar's Children*, a collection of essays, Thurman wrote, "All of my ideas may change overnight. I claim no permanence for them nor infallibility. They are purely expressions of a current mood, guided by certain mental predilections" (*Collected Writings*, xxx). Thurman studied at both the University of Utah and the University of Southern California, but he did not complete a degree at either. So while Thurman was not formally trained in philosophy like Johnson, his insatiable love of reading, his total and joyful immersion in ideas, his sophisticated and pioneering exploration of theoretical and representational issues surrounding writing and aesthetics, as well as his unswerving dedication to literary craft and intellectual achievement would easily qualify Thurman as an unacknowledged literary ancestor of Johnson's. Like Johnson, Thurman was committed to exploring life and creating art that would transcend race. Like Ralph Ellison, both Thurman and Johnson would reject "sociological explanations that deny black individuality, creativity and culture" (Johnson, "Race, Politics and Ralph Ellison," *New York Times*, February 5, 1995; http://www.nytimes.com/books/98/04/05/specials/johnson-intellectual.html?_r=2).

At the same time, in contrast to Toomer, both Thurman and Johnson demonstrate in their multi-pronged, multi-genre work that a quest for "racial transcendence" in life and art is not tantamount to an abandonment of race altogether, or in other words, to "racelessness"—an unfortunate and misleading coinage of Ross Posnock's in *Color and Culture* (Harvard UP, 1998), wherein Posnock rushes to judgment in associating Thurman as a public intellectual with "terminal individualism." Hughes and Thurman anticipate by decades the dual understanding of "race" that Johnson displays: on one hand, Johnson declares "race" to be an illusion, and on the other, he devotes a considerable part of his career writing about "race." This is how Johnson explains this paradox in his extended 2007 "Monsters and Critics" interview: "'[B]lackness' and 'whiteness' are illusions. However my family (predecessors and ancestors) in America have a history important to me, one shaped by the illusion of 'race.' And I've written a great deal about this historical subject .... But the literary scholars who write about my work correctly call me "an anti-race man" .... It is really not an either/or question. One is simply human, and writes about human history, one unavoidable component of which is events based on the illusion of race. One can no more ignore it than one can gender"(http://www.monstersandcritics.com/books/interviews/article_1308738.php/The_M%26C_Interview_1_Charles_Johnson_6_07).

Like Du Bois before him and like Wright afterwards, Thurman views "race" as a social construction, declaring in his best known essay, "Nephews of Uncle Remus" (1927), that "anthropologically the American Negro is really no Negro at all. He retains such an ethnological classification only because there seems to be nothing else to call him. There are probably no pure-blooded Negroes in America." Underscoring the hybridity of the African American experience by noting that "the American Negro has absorbed all of the American white man's culture and cultural appurtenances" (*Collected Writings*, 201-02), Thurman grapples with a variety of racial designations in the void of a classification that can provide a mould for the lived experience of a racialized group and an artistic production striving for "universality." He rejects both particularity and universality, if they are wielded as exclusive terms, but seems to embrace both in their conflictual relation—for example, when he asserts that "no Negro has written about his own people as beautifully or as sympathetically as Du Bose Heyward" (202). And he wants to see both, in this conflictual relation, in the context of an American literature ("The Negro author... can introduce a Negro note into American literature, but in America this can be done by a white writer as well as a black one."). In the striving for artistic universality inflected by "racialized" experience, Thurman seeks liberation from both a sense of inferiority restrictive racial boundaries.

In fact, in "Nephews of Uncle Remus," Thurman outlines the notion of a black aesthetic in positive terms, although he stops short of a programmatic elaboration. This essay is the most explicit statement of Thurman's own positioning within the literary and artistic context. He grapples with the parameters, hitherto stated as paradox, but now brought into a precarious synthesis, of particularist black experience and universalist aesthetic categories. Thus, while Thurman admired the Civil Rights commitments of W. E. B. Du Bois, Walter White, and others, he rejected their notions of art as largely a weapon for propaganda. On more than one occasion in 1926, Du Bois had asserted the need for black writers to abjure artistic freedom in favor of creating portrayals of black life that would effectively challenge and contradict "the net result of American literature [in picturing] the twelve million black Americans as prostitutes, thieves, and fools" ("The Negro in Art," *The Crisis*, February 1926, 165). For Du Bois, then, "all art is propaganda and ever must be, despite the wailing of the purists.... [W]hatever art I have for writing has been used always for propaganda, for gaining the right of black people to love and enjoy.... I do care when propaganda is confined to one side and the other side is stripped and silent" ("The Criteria of Negro Art," *The Crisis*, October 1926, 296). In his essays and reviews and in his work as the editor of both *Fire!!* and *Harlem*, Thurman argued with equal passion the opposite point of view. His method of layering his own argument for unbridled artistic freedom even in the wake of massive Civil Rights challenges, can best be seen at work in his two-page review of Walter White's *Flight* (1926) with the intriguing title, "A Thrush at Eve with an Atavistic Wound." He begins by setting uncompromisingly high standards for all writing, declaring "the writer who has the suitable material and fails to do it justice" as the "more oafish offender" than the writer who "tries to write without first having suitable material." A bit later, Thurman takes by the horns Du Bois' line of thinking by declaring: "All art no doubt is propaganda, but all propaganda is not art. And a novel must, to earn the name, be more than a mere service report, more than a thinly disguised dissertation on racial relationships and racial maladjustment." Again, in "High, Low, Past and Present" (1928), he expresses his fury at Du Bois's negative review of Rudolph Fisher's *The Walls of Jericho*, in the kind of clear and barbed language that Du Bois himself was capable of in his editorials on politics and citizenship. In this review article, Thurman articulates the risks Du Bois's didactic aesthetic criteria pose for African American writing:

> Were [Du Bois] a denizen of "Striver's Row,"scuttling hard up the social ladder, with nothing more important to think about than making money and keeping a high yellow wife bleached out and marcelled, one would laugh at such nonsense and dismiss it from one's mind. But Dr. Du Bois is not this. He is one of the outstanding Negroes of this or any other generation. He has served his race well; so well, in fact, that the artist in him has been stifled in order that the propagandist may thrive. No one will object to this being called noble and necessary sacrifice, but the days for such sacrifices are gone. The time has come now when the Negro artist can be his true self and pander to the stupidities of no one, either white or black
>
> (*Collected Writings*, 219).

In many of Johnson's essays, reviews and interviews, I hear a Thurmanesque clarity and sharpness as he articulates his wide-ranging perspectives as a writer and philosopher.

From the Fishbowl into the Ocean: Johnson's Expanding Vision

> Suffering arises from the belief in a separate, unchanging 'identity' for things. That is the foundation for attachment and craving.
>
> —Charles Johnson, *Turning the Wheel*, 12

When Johnson's career (and he is still mid-career in many ways) is viewed in relation to those of Toomer and Thurman, one is struck by his resilience at the tasks he has set himself as a philosopher, cartoonist, fiction writer, and public intellectual. Surely, as Chuck himself would remind us, meditation, martial arts, and Buddhadharma, as well as his engagement with Eastern and Western thought, have all played a major part in the strength and stamina he has exhibited so far.

Johnson may not have been influenced directly by Thurman or for that matter, Toomer. But as a theorist and practitioner of narrative alert to historical and philosophical antecedents, he has surely been aware of the collective and intense debates on issues of race and representation, aesthetic didacticism and artistic independence that raged within the real and imagined community we know today as the Harlem Renaissance. In contrast, beyond his classic *Cane*, from which he distanced himself in later years, Toomer's search for "wholeness" is probably inspiring more for the process it displayed and clarified than for the fruit it bore in fiction or philosophy. At the same time, Thurman, the *enfant terrible* of the Harlem Renaissance, while he shone like a star much too briefly, managed to articulate with prescient clarity aesthetic precepts that would bolster the thinking of successive generations of artists, African American and others, who must live and work in a society where racial and class boundaries still continue to be patrolled in subtle and complicated ways. For example, to a question such as "Must then a black writer write about white people to establish that he had conquered the provincial in him to embrace the universal?" Thurman would provide a strong and clear response, again in his essay, "Nephews": "[E]very facet of life can be found among Negroes, who being human beings … live, die, hate, love and procreate. They dance and sing, play and fight. And if art is the universal expressed in the particular, there is, if he has the talent, just as much chance for the Negro author to produce great literature by writing of his own people as if were to write of Chinese or Laplanders" (*Collected Writings*, 202).

At one point in his "Monsters and Critics" Interview mentioned above, Johnson suggests that in commenting on contemporary writers, he follows "the step called 'Right Speech' in the [Buddhist] Eightfold Path very seriously.... In other words, we don't need to say publicly everything we know to be true, especially if it will cause more harm than good." Despite this golden principle, some of the polemical flourishes in Johnson's interviews and essays might invite comparison in their impact with similar patches in Faulkner's interviews and lectures from the late1950s. Such rhetorical segments in Johnson's non-fiction have the potential of occasionally distorting or simplifying Johnson's otherwise complex views on the socio-political and economic dimensions of African American life. For example, while he rightly argues in his essay "The End of the Black American Narrative" against the singular model of victimhood for all African American stories, his descriptions of the newly emerging post-Civil Rights black communities that assimilate new immigrants and faiths elide the corrosive consequences of longstanding institutional practices in real estate and banking that still prevent middle-class black families from building wealth and passing on any inheritance to the next generation.

Possibly against this slight risk, much of the best scholarship on Johnson reads his non-fictional writings carefully in conjunction with the short fiction and novels. One such example of this method at work is Ashraf Rushdy's recent essay, "Charles Johnson's Way to Spiritual Literature" (*African American Review*, 43.2, Summer/Fall 2009), which offers an engaging reading of the complex tension between Buddhism and Marxism, between politics and spirituality, in Johnson's short story "Exchange Value" by interweaving ideas from several of Johnson's essays, interviews and novels. Rushdy's essay demonstrates the value of what Johnson's writings individually or collectively often do—help us get out of the "fish bowl" of our own selves into the "ocean" of human inter-subjectivity. Ethelbert Miller, in his AWP tribute, cites a passage from an interview he had done with Johnson two years after the author returned from his first-ever journey to Thailand, a predominantly Buddhist nation. Here is part of what Johnson stated about his experience abroad: "Thailand was extremely important to me because for the first time in my life I was in a country that was 90 per cent Buddhist and that is the exact reverse of here....Ever since I was a kid, I thought there was something a little bit off about America and I could never figure out why people do some of the things they do. But if you step outside this culture, there is a revelation.... It's like we were in a fish bowl and as fish we don't know we're in a fish bowl. But if you take one of us out and put him in the ocean, his vision expands. He looks back, and says to others, you're in a fish bowl and you just don't know it." And we can all implore Chuck as does Mr. Miller, "All I ask of you today, Charles, is that you keep feeding me and everyone else – now and then tap your fingers against the bowl. Remind us again and again, what it means to be human." (Miller, "Tribute to Charles Johnson," AWP, Denver, April 10, 2010).

Notes

1. At Harvard, Eliot was lost in "the mazes of Patanjali's metaphysics," and felt compelled to confront his own realization that in order to overcome the "romantic misunderstanding" of Hindu and Buddhist thought in early 20th-century Europe, his "only hope of really penetrating to the heart of that mystery would lie in forgetting how to think and feel as an American or a European: which, for practical as well as sentimental reasons I did not wish to do" (*After Strange Gods: A Primer of Modern Heresy* (1934, 40-41; Eliot's Page-Borbour Lectures in 1933 at the University of Virginia). To me, it is a stunning admission on Eliot's part that while he could have done something to dispel serious European misconceptions about Indian philosophy, he chose not to do so because he did not want to abandon his Eurocentric ways of thinking and feeling. We can, however, be grateful that Eliot became an influential poet and literary critic. According to Stephen Spender, as late as 1922, just before *The Waste Land* was published, Eliot had seriously considered becoming a Buddhist (Spender, *T. S. Eliot*. New York: Viking, 1976, p. 20).
2. Thoreau, *Journal, Volume 3: 1848-1851*. Edited by Robert Sattelmeyer *et al*. (Princeton: Princeton University Press, 1990), 61. Here is part of what precedes the quoted sentence in the Journal:

"What extracts from the [V]edas I have read fall on me like the light of a higher & purer luminary which describes a loftier curve through a purer stratum—free from particulars—simple—universal —It rises on me like the full moon after the stars have come out wading through some far summer stratum of the sky."

3. Johnson credits Spiegelberg with the introduction of the concept of the "Other," so prevalent in poststructuralist and postcolonial theory. See Connor and Nash, eds., *Charles Johnson: The Novelist as Philosopher*, 146n6.
4. In his essay, "I Call Myself an Artist," Johnson himself describes *Being and Race* as "a phenomenological literary manifesto" (27). "I Call" is a much fuller personal account of the socio-political forces that have shaped Johnson as well as his writerly debts and influences—including his Mom, John Gardner, and Ralph Ellison. See *I Call Myself an Artist: Writings by and about Charles Johnson*. Edited by Rudolph P. Byrd. Bloomington: Indiana UP, 1999.
5. Consider the following notorious statement at the beginning of Section II in "Blueprint": "Generally speaking, Negro writing in the past has been confined to humble novels, poems, and plays, decorous ambassadors who go a-begging to white America. They entered the Court of American Public Opinion dressed in the knee-pants of servility, curtsying to show that the Negro was not inferior, that he was human, and that he had a life comparable to that of other people. These were received as poodle dogs who have learned clever tricks." (*Richard Wright Reader*, ed. Ellen Wright and Michel Fabre. New York: Harper and Row, 1978, 37). See also my essay, "Richard Wright" that discusses Wright in relation to the Harlem Renaissance (noting some striking parallels between Wallace Thurman and Wright) in *Harlem Speaks: A Living History of the Cultural Expression.* Ed. Cary D. Wintz. New York: Sourcebooks, Inc., 2006.
6. Qiana Whitted, "Middle Passages: Charles Johnson and the Raft of Dhamma," *Prapañca: a buddhist journal* (July 2010).
7. According to Rudolph Byrd, Locke, like Waldo Frank, insisted on framing Toomer in racial terms, despite Toomer's vehement protests. See "Jean Toomer and the Writers of the Harlem Renaissance," in Amritjit Singh, et al, eds., *The Harlem Renaissance: Revaluations* (New York: Garland, 1989), 209-218. Byrd cites Toomer's recall of a meeting with Locke during which Toomer made clear that he would prefer not to contribute the kind of race-inflected piece that Locke wanted from Toomer: "But when

Locke's book *The New Negro* came out... there was a story from *Cane,* and there were words about me in the introduction that caused me as much or more misunderstanding [pain?] than Waldo Frank's. [While] Frank helped me at a time when I most needed help... Locke tricked and misused me" (216).

8. For more on Maharishi Ramana, see http://www. sriramana maharshi.org/
9. For images of how World War II prisoners were treated by the British in colonial India, see Anita Desai's novel, *Baumgartner's Bombay* (1988).

The Contributors

Adam Tolbert earned a B.A. in Rhetoric from the University of California, Berkeley, and both the M.A. in English and the M.S. in Education at California State University, East Bay. He has taught comparative cultures at the Academy of Art University in San Francisco, where he is currently a Senior Content Manager and Editor of Online Education.

Dr. Amritjit Singh is Langston Hughes Professor of English at Ohio University, Athens, U.S.A. He has had a long stint as Professor of English at Rhode Island College, Providence, U.S.A. He has authored or edited over a dozen books on American and Indian literatures. He was Fulbright Smith-Mundt Fellow, NYU, during 1968-74 and a Visiting Fulbright Professor at the JFK Institute of North American Studies, Freie University, Berlin, Germany during 2002-03. Past President of *MELUS* (1994-97), he is currently poetry editor of *South Asian Review*. His poems and translations from Punjabi poetry have appeared in *Toronto Review, Re-Markings* and other journals. Currently he is working on a documentary history of South Asians in North America. He received the MELUS Lifetime Achievement Award in 2007.

Dr. Ashraf H.A. Rushdy is Professor of African American Studies and English at Wesleyan University. He is the author of *Neo-Slave Narratives: The Social Logic of A Literary Form* and *Remembering Generations: Slavery and Family in Contemporary African American Literature.*

Aurélie Bayre is currently completing her Ph.D. on Charles Johnson (Interprétation du texte symbolique: politique et esthétique dans l'oeuvre romanesque de Charles R. Johnson) at the University of Reims, France. She has worked on William Golding's first opus (Violence and Tragedy in *Lord of the Flies*) and Toni Morrison's *Beloved* and *Jazz* (L'identité dans Beloved et Jazz de Toni Morrison: constructions et reconstructions). She works in collaboration with poet Ze Jam Afane. Together, they find refreshing inspiration in Charles Johnson's peaceful endurance.

Dr. Charles Johnson is a novelist, essayist, literary critic, short story writer, cartoonist, screenwriter and Professor Emeritus at the University of Washington in Seattle. He is the author of 18 books that include *Turning the Wheel: Essays on Buddhism and Writing* (2003), novels *Middle Passage*, *Dreamer* (1998), *Oxherding Tale* (1982) and *Faith and the Good Thing* (1974) as well as three Story Collections, *The Sorcerer's Apprentice* (1986), *Soulcatcher and Other Stories* (2001) and *Dr. King's Refrigerator and Other Bedtime Stories* (2005). A Ph.D. in philosophy, his work has appeared in numerous publications in America and abroad and has been translated into nine languages. He is a MacArthur Fellow, recipient of an American Academy of Arts and Letters Award for Literature, and winner of the National Book Award for his novel *Middle Passage*. In 2003, The Charles Johnson Society was inaugurated at the American Literature Association.

Chris Thompson is Development and Communications Manager at Humanities Washington.He has worked as a development officer for several Seattle-based nonprofit organizations including Seattle Opera, the Initiative for Global Development, and an online magazine. Previously, he was a Peace Corps Volunteer in Niger, West Africa. He studied journalism at the University of Mississippi.

David Ray is author of several books of poetry, including one about the Holocaust, one about the Iraq Wars, three about India, another about New Zealand, and yet another about Australia. He was one of the founders of American Writers Against the Vietnam War in 1966. He resides in Tucson, Arizona with his wife, the poet and essayist Judy Ray. He lives with gratitude and admiration for India and its cultures, which feed his imagination and Quakerly leanings to better the world through writing and activism.

E. Ethelbert Miller is a literary activist. He is the board chair of the Institute for Policy Studies, a progressive think tank located in Washington, D.C. The author of several collections of poetry—*How We Sleep on the Nights We Don't Make Love, In Search of Color Everywhere, Where are the Love Poems for Dictators?, Whispers, Secrets and Promises, Beyond The Frontier: African-American Poetry for the 21st Century, Season of Hunger* and *Cry of Rain*—he has also written two memoirs, *Fathering Words: The Making of An African American Writer* (2000) and *The 5th Inning* (2009). *Fathering Words* was selected by the D.C. Public Library for its DC We Read, one book, one city program in 2003.

Dr. Gary Storhoff is an Associate Professor of English at UConn, Stamford Campus. He has published widely in journals on American, African-American, and Ethnic literature. He has also published *Understanding Charles Johnson* (U of South Carolina Press, 2004), and has co-edited with John Whalen-Bridge (of the National University of Singapore) a series on Buddhism and American culture. The first volume, *The Emergence of Buddhist American Literature*, was published in 2009 by the State of New York University Press; in 2010, SUNY Press published *American Buddhism as a Way of Life*; and in 2011, SUNY Press will publish the third volume, *Writing as Enlightenment: Buddhist American Literature into the 21st Century*. He is also working on a book provisionally entitled *The Family Crucible: Family Processes in William Faulkner and Toni Morrison.*

Jeffrey M. Davis was born in Seattle, Washington. He is currently pursuing a Ph.D. in English Literature as well as an M.F.A. in Poetry at Penn State University. His research interests include 20th-century American literature, modernism, and modern poetry. He currently teaches English at Penn State and serves as a Research Assistant for the Hemingway Letters Project. He is recipient of the Bunton-Waller Graduate Award from Penn State and the Raleigh-Claire Dickinson Scholarship from Oregon State University, where he received his B.A. in English.

Dr. George Yancy is currently Associate Professor of Philosophy at Duquesne University. He is the author of *Black Bodies, White Gazes: The Continuing Significance of Race.* In 2008, *Black Bodies, White Gazes* received an Honorable Mention from the Gustavus Myers Center for the Study of Bigotry and Human Rights. Yancy has also edited over ten books, three of which won *Choice* Outstanding Academic Title Awards, and has published in a variety of peer review academic journals. Yancy was recently nominated for Duquesne University's Presidential Award for Excellence in Scholarship.

Dr. John B. Parks is a revisionist historian currently editing two manuscripts relating to slavery. One deconstructs the legality of slavery and the other analyzes the legal and political activism of enslaved and free blacks in the British colonies and the United States: Freedom v. Slavery: "The act of stealing Negars is expressly contrary, both to the law of God, and the law of this country" and "so many persons standing up for their freedom:" Caribbean and American Opposition to Enslavement, 1656-1865 respectively. He teaches at Howard University in the Afro-American Studies Department.

Dr. John Whalen-Bridge is Associate Professor of English at the National University of Singapore. He is the author of *Political Fiction and the American Self*, co-editor with Gary Storhoff of *Emergence of Buddhist American Literature* and *American Buddhism as a Way of Life*, and editor of *Norman Mailer's Later Fictions*. With Tan Sor-Hoon he co-edited *Democracy as Culture: Deweyan Pragmatism in a Globalizing World*. He is completing a study of Engaged Buddhism and countercultural writing in postwar America, focusing on Gary Snyder, Charles Johnson and Maxine Hong Kingston.

Dr. Julia A. Galbus is an associate professor of English at the University of Southern Indiana, U.S.A. Her scholarship combines three overlapping areas: American literature, autobiography, and African American literature since the Black Arts Movement. She has published articles about E. Ethelbert Miller, A. Van Jordan, Susan Glaspell and Edith Wharton. She earned her doctorate in American literature at Southern Illinois University at Carbondale. Her dissertation examined five twentieth-century American women writers who critiqued Plato's philosophy through literature.

Dr. Linda Furgerson Selzer is an Associate Professor of English at the Pennsylvania State University-University Park. She is the author of *Charles Johnson in Context* (University of Massachusetts, 2009), and co-Editor of *New Essays on the African American Novel* (Palgrave, 2008). Her work on African American literature and culture has appeared in scholarly collections and in journals such as the *African American Review, Callaloo,MELUS, Massachusetts Review* and *Rhetoric Review*. In 2003 she received the Darwin Turner Award for the year's best essay in *African American Review*. Her present contribution appeared initially in *African American Review* 37 (2003): 105-14.

Dr. Marc C. Conner is Professor of English at Washington and Lee University in Virginia. He took degrees in English and Philosophy at the University of Washington, followed by the Ph.D. degree in English at Princeton University, and has taught at Princeton and at the University of Notre Dame. His books include *The Aesthetics of Toni Morrison: Speaking the Unspeakable*, and *Charles Johnson: The Novelist as Philosopher*, both published by the University Press of Mississippi and *The Poetry of James Joyce Reconsidered*, forthcoming from Florida. In addition, Marc has published dozens of essays and book reviews on American and Irish Modernism.

Dr. Michael Boylan (Ph.D. University of Chicago) is professor of philosophy at Marymount University in Arlington, Virginia. He is the author of over ninety articles and nineteen books in philosophy (one of which he co-authored with Charles Johnson.) He also has three published novels—the latest of which, *The Extinction of Desire*, bears a preface by Charles Johnson. Boylan has two published books of poetry and a children's book. Boylan's latest book is *Morality and Global Justice* (Westview, 2011).

Dr. Nibir K. Ghosh, D.Litt., is Head, Department of English Studies & Research, Agra College, Agra (India). He was Senior Fulbright Fellow 2003-04 at the University of Washington, Seattle, U.S.A. Author of widely acclaimed books, his most recent works include *Shaping Minds: Multicultural Literature* (2010), *W.H. Auden: Therapeutic Fountain* (2010), *Erasing Barricades: Woman in Indian Literature* (2010) and *Perspectives on Legends of American Theatre* (2009). An Associate of Indian Institute of Advanced Study, Shimla, he is the Chief Editor of *Re-Markings* (www.re-markings.com), an international biannual journal of research in English that is in its tenth year of publication.

Dr. Qiana J. Whitted is Associate Professor of English and African American Studies at the University of South Carolina and the author of *A God of Justice?: The Problem of Evil in Twentieth-Century Black Literature.* Her published work has appeared in *African American Review, Southern Literary Journal* and *Callaloo.* This review column first appeared in the online Buddhist journal, *Prapañca.*

Dr. Richard E. Hart is Cyrus H. Holley Professor of Applied Ethics and Philosophy at Bloomfield College in New Jersey, U.S.A. He is the editor/co-editor of four books dealing with environmental ethics, Plato's dialogues, and American philosophy. He has written and spoken extensively on the Nobel prize winning American writer, John Steinbeck. He serves on the editorial boards of the journals, *Metaphilosophy, The Pluralist*, and *The Steinbeck Review*. He regularly teaches courses on literature and philosophy.

Dr. Robert E. Abrams is a Professor of English and American literature at the University of Washington, where he is proud to have remained a colleague and good friend of Charles Johnson for many years. His most noteworthy publication is entitled *Landscape and Ideology in American Renaissance Literature: Topographies of Skepticism,* published by Cambridge University Press in 2003. He was awarded a Simpson Research Fellowship in 2005, and over the years he has published numerous articles on American literature and culture. From time to time, he writes poetry and fiction.

Dr. Sharyn Skeeter is an assistant professor at the University of Bridgeport, U.S.A. Her poetry, articles, and fiction have appeared in literary journals, magazines, and anthologies (including E. Ethelbert Miller's *In Search of Color Everywhere*). She has given readings at arts centers and universities in the United States. She was fiction, poetry, book review editor at *Essence* magazine and editor-in-chief at *Black Elegance*. She has taught journalism, media, and English at universities and colleges, including Emerson College, Gateway Community College, and Fairfield University. Currently, she is working on a novel and a collection of poetry.

Shayla Hawkins lives in Detroit, Michigan and won the 2008 Canute A. Brodhurst Prize in Short Fiction and the 2010 John Edgar Wideman Microstory Contest. Her recent publications include poems in *TORCH: Poetry, Prose, and Short Stories by African American Women*, *Chopin with Cherries*, *St. Somewhere*, *Aunt Chloe* and *Pyrta*, an international online literary journal based in Shillong, a small hill-station town in Meghalaya, India.

Dr. Sunita Rani Ghosh is Associate Professor, Department of Hindi Studies & Research at Agra College, Agra. She was Visiting Scholar at the University of Washington, Seattle, U.S.A., during 2003-04. Her writings have appeared in reputed national and international journals. Her essay "Bani Rahengi Kitaben" is prescribed for undergraduate students in M.P. Government degree colleges. Lessons she has written on Jayshankar Prasad and Jainendra Kumar Jain are prescribed in the syllabus of Vardhman Mahaveer Open University, Kota.

Zachary Watterson grew up in New York City and New Jersey and has been a Fellow at the Jentel Foundation, a Work-Study Scholar at the Bread Loaf Writers' Conference, and a Pushcart Prize nominee. His writing appears in *The Massachusetts Review*, *River Styx*, and the *Glimmer Train* newsletter *Writers Ask*.

The Editors

Dr. Nibir K. Ghosh, D.Litt., is Head, Department of English Studies & Research, Agra College, Agra (India). He was Senior Fulbright Fellow 2003-04 at the University of Washington, Seattle, U.S.A. He is the author of widely acclaimed books: *Beyond Boundaries: Reflections of Indian and U.S. Scholars* (2007), *Multicultural America: Conversations with Contemporary Authors* (2005) and *Calculus of Power: Modern American Political Novel* (1997). His most recent works include *Shaping Minds: Multicultural Literature* (2010), *W.H. Auden: Therapeutic Fountain* (2010), *Erasing Barricades: Woman in Indian Literature* (2010) and *Perspectives on Legends of American Theatre* (2009). He has published a monograph on August Wilson's *The Piano Lesson* and has edited two poetry anthologies—*Poetic Miscellany* and *Spectrum of Poetic Sensibility.* An eminent scholar and critic of American, British and Post-Colonial literatures, he has published over 150 articles and scholarly essays on various political, socio-cultural and feminist issues in prestigious national and international journals. Twenty six scholars have so far been awarded the degree of Ph.D. in English under his supervision. During 1992-96, he was the Executive Member of the Board of Directors for the American Studies Research Centre in Hyderabad. He has given extension lectures and keynote addresses at many university campuses in India and abroad. He has delivered over 60 Radio Talks on wide ranging topics. He has designed lessons on Virginia Woolf, Francis Bacon and Charles Lamb for IGNOU, New Delhi. An Associate of Indian Institute of Advanced Study, Shimla, he is the Chief Editor of *Re-Markings* (www.re-markings.com), an international biannual journal of research in English that is in its tenth year of publication. He has been felicitated for his contribution to teaching, research and cultural activities by numerous organizations in India.

E. Ethelbert Miller is a literary activist. He was born in 1950 and grew-up in the South Bronx. A graduate of Howard University, he was one of the first students to major in African American Studies. Today he is the board chair of the Institute for Policy Studies, a progressive think tank located in Washington, D.C. Mr. Miller is also the director of the African American Resource Center at Howard University, a position he has held since 1974. In 1996, he was awarded an honorary degree of Doctor of Literature from Emory and Henry College. He is the former chair of the Humanities Council of Washington, D.C. He is the author of several collections of poetry—*How We Sleep on the Nights We Don't Make Love, In Search of Color Everywhere, Where are the Love Poems for Dictators?, Whispers, Secrets and Promises, Beyond The Frontier: African-American Poetry for the 21st Century, Season of Hunger and Cry of Rain*—and has also written two memoirs, *Fathering Words: The Making of An African American Writer* (2000) and *The 5th Inning* (2009). *Fathering Words* was selected by the D.C. Public Library for its DC We Read, one book, one city program in 2003. He has taught at UNLV, American University, George Mason University, and Emory and Henry College. For several years he was a core faculty member with the Bennington Writing Seminars.

Charles Johnson: Condensed Biography

Charles Johnson is the author of four novels *Faith and the Good Thing (1974), Oxherding Tale* (1982), *Middle Passage* (1990*),* and *Dreamer (*Scribner, 1998*);* three collection of short stories, *The Sorcerer's Apprentice (*1986*) Soulcatcher and Other Stories* (2001), and *Dr. King's Refrigerator and Other Bedtime Stories* (2005); a work of aesthetics, *Being and Race: Black Writing Since 1970* (1988); two collections of comic art, *Black Humor* (1970) and *Half-Past Nation Time* (1972); *Black Men Speaking* (1997), co-edited with John McCluskey Jr.; *Africans in America: America's Journey through Slavery,* the companion book for PBS' series (Oct., 1998), co-authored with Patricia Smith (The Audio Book for this was selected as one of the best audio books in the History category of the Listen Up Awards in *Publisher's* Weekly); and *King: The Photobiography of Martin Luther King Jr.,* (Viking Studio, 2000), co-authored with Bob Adelman. These works have been translated into eight foreign languages. As a cartoonist and journalist in the early 1970s, he published over 1000 drawings in national publications, a selection of which appears in *Humor Me: An Anthology of Humor by Writers of Color* by John McNally (University of Iowa, 2002). In 1999 Indiana University Press published a collection of his essays on aesthetics, cultural criticism, articles, interviews, speeches, cartoons, out-takes from his novels and book reviews dating back to 1965, entitled, *I Call Myself an Artist: Writings By and About Charles Johnson* (April, 1999) a "Charles Johnson reader," edited by Dr. Rudolph Byrd, with a final section of eight critical articles on his work. *Turning the*

Wheel: Essays on Buddhism and Writing (Scribner) was published in 2003. The University of Washington Press published *Passing the Three Gates: Interviews with Charles Johnson,* edited by Dr. James McWilliams, a collection of interviews dating back to 1978, in 2004. In 2005, Scribner published a new edition of *Oxherding Tale.* In 2007, Johnson co-authored with Bob Adelman *Mine Eyes Have Seen: Bearing Witness to the Struggle for Civil Rights* (Time-Life Books), and in 2008 *Remembering Martin Luther King, Jr: 40 Years Later, His Life and Crusade in Pictures* (Time/Life Books); and his comic art appeared in *The Writer's Brush: Paintings, Drawings and Sculpture by Writers*, edited by Donald Friedman. In 2010, he co-authored with Michael Boylan *Philosophy, An Innovative Introduction: Fiction Narrative, Primary Texts and Responsive Writing* (Westview Press).

Johnson, a Ph.D. in Philosophy, 1998 MacArthur fellow and 2002 recipient of an American Academy of Arts and Letters Award for Literature, received the 1990 National Book Award for *Middle Passage* (he was the first African-American male to win this prize since Ralph Ellison in 1953). *Oxherding Tale* was awarded the 1983 Washington State Govenor's Award for Literature; *Sorcerer's Apprentice* was one of five finalists for the 1987 PEN/Faulkner Award, and *Being and Race* won a 1989 Governor's Award for Literature. His short fiction is included in the *O'Henry Prize Stories (1993), Best American Short Stories (1992), Best American Short Stories of the Eighties,* and he was named in a survey conducted by the University of Southern California to be one of the ten best short story writers in America; and his short fiction and essays are much anthologized. On May 24, 2000 he received the "Lifetime Achievement in the Arts Award" from the Corporate Council for the Arts (former recipients include artists Jacob Lawrence and George Tsutakawa). On July 27, 2001 he received the Pacific Northwest Writers Association's 2001 Achievement Award "for distinguished professional achievement and for enhancing the stature of Northwest literature," and on March 27, 2003 he received one of the first Distinguished Alumni Awards from Evanston Township High School. The spring issue of *Washington Law and Politics*" includes Dr. Johnson in its feature, "The 25 Smartest People in Washington State." In 2003, he was elected to membership in the American Academy of Arts & Sciences; and in 2004 received the Stephen Henderson Award for outstanding contributions to African American literature and culture at the spring conference for the American Literature Association.

He has written over 20 screenplays, among them "Booker" (*Wonderworks,* 1985), which received the international Prix Jeunesse Award, a 1985 Writers Guild Award for "outstanding script in the television category of children's shows," and was released for home-video in 1996 by Bonneville Worldwide Entertainment. That show, along with "Charlie Smith and the Fritter Tree" (*Visions,* PBS, 1978), have been broadcast on the Disney channel. He was one of two writer-producers for "Up and Coming" (KCET, 1981), and earlier created, hosted, and co-produced "Charlie's Pad" (1970), a PBS how-to-draw series that ran nationally for a decade in the U.S. and Canada; and he hosted the 1992 KCTS (Seattle) series "Words with Writers."

He has published 52 reviews in *The New York Times, Los Angeles Times, The Wall Street Journal, The Washington Post* as well as other major newspapers in America and England and published numerous critical articles, among them the introduction for the commemorative edition of Ralph Ellison's *Invisible Man* and the preface for his *Juneteenth.* Dr. Johnson drew a regular feature "LitCrits" for *Quarterly Black Review* and his comic art has appeared in *Literal Latte, Buddha Laughing, The Seattle Times* and *The Seattle Post-Intelligencer.;* he also drew in 1999 a twice-monthly cartoon feature for *Black Issues in Higher Education.* He has served as a fiction judge for the Pulitzer Prize (twice), National Book Award(twice), PEN/Faulkner, Los Angeles Times Book Prize, the Drue Heinz, numerous other fiction prizes and for the Seattle Film Festival, is a nominator for the MacArthur fellowships, serves on the Modern Library editorial board, and is a contributing editor for *Tricycle: The Buddhist Review.* He was the 1999 chair of the fiction judges for the National Book Awards, is a trustee for the Washington Commission for the Humanities and served as a board member for the Seattle Repertory Theater. He has served on the board for the Associated Writing Programs, directed their annual short fiction contest, and was director of the Northwest office for the Fiction Collective. In 1995 his novel *Faith and the Good Thing* was performed as a play by City Lit Theatre and the Chicago Theatre Company, and received two Black Theatre Alliance awards. Recent works include the article "A Sangha By Another Name" in *Tricycle: The Buddhist Review;* the introductory essay for Mark Twain's *What is Man?* (Oxford Twain series); the introduction for Jean Toomer's *Essentials*; an article on Martin Luther King Jr. for *Common Quest,* which has been selected by the U.S. Information Agency for its website; short fiction in Susan Shreve's *Outside the Law* (Beacon, fall 1997); the introductory essay for *Still I Rise,* a cartoon history of black America (Norton, fall 1997); the introductory essay "On the Nature of Tales" for the Book-of-the-Month Club's *A Treasury of North American Folk Tales*; the introduction for Canongate's *Proverbs* in the "Pocket Canon" series published in the UK; the introduction for the two-volume collection of classic slave narratives *I Call Myself a Slave* (Lawrence Hill, 1999); the literary obituary for Eldridge Cleaver published in *The New York Times Magazine* and an article on the Negro National Anthem for *The New York Times'* "Arts and Leisure" section; an essay on meditation and writing for the *Chronicle of Higher Education*; and a critical appreciation of Ralph Ellison in *The Crisis*, the official publication of the NAACP (March/April, 2002). He appeared on Bill Moyers' *Genesis* series (Oct., 1996). And has granted 291 interviews for American and foreign newspapers, scholarly journals, radio, and television, and for Nigeria, South Africa, Singapore, Bombay, and Amman, Jordan via USIA.

Dr. Johnson is one of 12 authors portrayed in a special series of stamps issued in November, 1997 by the Inter-Governmental Philatelic Corporation; these stamps, created to honor the most influential black authors of the 20th century, will be distributed in the former Soviet Union, Asia, Africa, and

South America. He has received both a National Endowment for the Arts grant (1979) and a Guggenheim Fellowship (1986).His novel *Dreamer* was a Book-of-the-Month Club alternate selection and a Quality Paperback Book Club alternate selection.

Dr. Johnson has lectured in nine countries (Eastern Europe, Asia, Spain and Portugal) for the U.S. Information Agency and is a regular speaker at American campuses. He has delivered 349 lectures, readings, and addresses. In 1997 Dr. Jonathan Little's (Alverno College) critical study *Charles Johnson's Spiritual Imagination* was published by the University of Missouri Press. William Nash at Middlebury College published *Charles Johnson's Fiction,* in 2002 (University of Illinois Press). Gary Storhoff's *Understanding Charles Johnson* (University of South Carolina Press) appeared in 2004. In 2005, Dr. Rudolph Byrd published *Charles Johnson's Novels: Making the American Palimpsest* (Indiana University Press). In 2007, *Charles Johnson: The Novelist As Philosophy* was published by University Press of Mississippi, edited by Marc C. Conner and William R. Nash. In April, 2009 Linda Furgerson Selzer published *Charles Johnson in Context* (University of Massachusetts Press). *African-American Review* devoted its winter 1996 issue to Dr. Johnson's work, which has also been the subject of two special sessions of the Modern Language Association (1991 and 1996), and the International Association for Philosophy and Literature (2000 and 2001). The first meeting of the Charles Johnson Literary Society was held on May 24, 2003 at the American Literature Association conference. (May 22-25, 2003).

A former director of the creative writing program at the University of Washington, he holds an endowed chair, the S. Wilson and Grace M. Pollock Professorship for Excellence in English (the first chair in writing at UW), and currently teaches fiction. He served as fiction editor for *the Seattle Review* from 1978-98. In 1995 he received an honorary doctorate in Humane Letters from Southern Illinois University, in 1994 an honorary Doctor of Arts degree from Northwestern, in 1999 an honorary

Doctor of Letters degree from the State University of New York at Stony Brook, and in 2006 a Doctor of Humane Letters degree from Lewis and Clark College. He sponsors the "Marie Clair Davis Award in Creative Writing," given to a secondary student at Evanston Township High School, and the Charles Johnson Student Fiction Award, a national contest, at Southern Illinois University. He is a distinguished member on the Advisory Board of *Re-Markings*, a biannual journal of research in English, edited and published by Nibir K. Ghosh, from Agra, India. Please visit his author's website at www.oxherdingtale.com